Putting the Pieces Together

McMaster Divinity College Press
McMaster New Testament Studies Series, Volume 11

*Christian Mission: Old Testament Foundations and
New Testament Developments* (2010)

Empire in the New Testament (2011)

The Church, Then and Now (2012)

*Rejection: God's Refugees in Biblical and
Contemporary Perspective* (2015)

Rediscovering Worship: Past, Present, and Future (2015)

*The Bible and Social Justice: Old Testament and New Testament
Foundations for the Church's Urgent Call* (2015)

The Letter to the Romans: Exegesis and Application (2018)

Is the Gospel Good News? (2019)

Linguistics and the Bible: Retrospects and Prospects (2019)

The Arts and the Bible (2024)

Putting the Pieces Together

*Formalizing Units and Structures
in the Biblical Languages*

Edited by
STANLEY E. PORTER,
CHRISTOPHER D. LAND,
and JAMES D. DVORAK

☙PICKWICK *Publications* • Eugene, Oregon

PUTTING THE PIECES TOGETHER
Formalizing Units and Structures in the Biblical Languages

McMaster New Testament Studies Series, Volume 11
McMaster Divinity College Press

ISSN 2564-4424(Print)
ISSN 2564-4432(Ebook)

Copyright © 2024 Wipf and Stock Publishers. All rights reserved. Except for brief quotations in critical publications or reviews, no part of this book may be reproduced in any manner without prior written permission from the publisher. Write: Permissions, Wipf and Stock Publishers, 199 W. 8th Ave., Suite 3, Eugene, OR 97401.

McMaster Divinity College Press
1280 Main Street West
Hamilton, ON,
Canada, L8S 4K1

Pickwick Publications
An Imprint of Wipf and Stock Publishers
199 W. 8th Ave., Suite 3
Eugene, OR 97401

www.wipfandstock.com

PAPERBACK ISBN: 979-8-3852-2190-5
HARDCOVER ISBN: 979-8-3852-2191-2
EBOOK ISBN: 979-8-3852-2192-9

Cataloguing-in-Publication data:

Names: Porter, Stanley E., editor. | Land, Christopher D., editor. | Dvorak, James D., editor.

Title: Putting the pieces together / edited by Stanley E. Porter, Christopher D. Land, and James D. Dvorak.

Description: Eugene, OR: Pickwick Publications, 2024. | McMaster New Testament Studies Series 11. | Includes bibliographical references and index.

Identifiers: ISBN 979-8-3852-2190-5 (paperback) | ISBN 979-8-3852-2191-2 (hardcover) | ISBN 979-8-3852-2192-9 (ebook)

Subjects: LCSH: Bible. New Testament--Criticism, interpretation, etc. | Greek language, Biblical--Discourse analysis. | Hebrew language, Biblical--Discourse analysis.

Classification: BS2316 P67 2024 (paperback) | BS2316 (ebook)

VERSION NUMBER 08/08/24

Contents

Lists of Illustrations / vii

Lists of Tables / viii

List of Contributors / ix

Preface / xi

List of Abbreviations / xiii

Putting the Pieces Together: An Introduction to This Volume / xvii
—*Stanley E. Porter, Christopher D. Land, and James D. Dvorak*

1. Linguistic Theory in Hebrew and Greek Language Study / 1
—*Stanley E. Porter*

2. A Systemic Account of Biblical Hebrew Prepositions: Circumstantial Particles from a Monosemic Perspective in Habakkuk / 39
—*David J. Fuller*

3. Chaining and Wrapping: The Quantitative and Qualitative Economies of Greek Syntax / 61
—*Ryder A. Wishart*

4. A Multi-Dimensional Model of the System of Conjunction for the Greek of the New Testament
—*Zachary K. Dawson* / 72

5. "It's Probably Untrue, but It Wouldn't Matter Anyway": Εἰ καί Conditions in the Greek New Testament / 104
—*Mark Proctor*

6. Defining Definers: An Exploration into the Functions of Attributive Adjectives in Koine Greek / 128
—*James D. Dvorak*

7 A Method for Identifying Speech Functions in Koine Greek: Galatians 2:11–21 as a Test Case / 148
   —*David I. Yoon*

8 Information Structure in the Greek of the New Testament / 166
   —*Doosuk Kim*

9 Cohesive Harmony in Acts 15:1–35 / 191
   —*William Craig Price*

10 A Proposal for Systemic Functional Linguistics Register Theory as a Septuagint Commentary Writing Tool / 214
   —*John J. H. Lee*

Modern Authors Index / 237

Ancient Sources Index / 241

Lists of Illustrations

Chapter 2: David J. Fuller
Figure 1. System: Comparison, Location, and Direction / 53

Chapter 4: Zachary K. Dawson
Figure 1. The Initial Systems of Conjunction for Greek / 85
Figure 2. The System of Elaboration Type for Greek / 88
Figure 3. The System of Extension Type for Greek / 92
Figure 4. The System of Expansion Type in Greek / 99
Figure 5. The Overall System of Conjunction for Greek / 100

Chapter 6: James D. Dvorak
Figure 1. Matt 9:37bc / 137

Chapter 7: David I. Yoon
Figure 1. Porter's System Network of Attitude (Mood) for Greek / 153

Chapter 8: Doosuk Kim
Figure 1. The Thematic Unit / 180

Chapter 10: John J. H. Lee
Figure 1. Strata in Human Language / 220
Figure 2. Instantiation and Realization / 221

Lists of Tables

Chapter 6: James D. Dvorak
Table 1. John 4:23b / 135
Table 2. Matt 12:35 (A) / 142
Table 3. Matt 12:35 (B) / 142–43

Chapter 7: David I. Yoon
Table 1. Halliday's Major Speech Functions / 149
Table 2. Porter's Major (Greek) Speech Functions / 154–55
Table 3. Speech Functions for Hellenistic Greek / 158

Chapter 9: William Craig Price
Table 1. Summary of Identity Chains and Token Index Totals / 198
Table 2. Summary of Similarity Chains and Token Index Totals / 201–2
Table 3. Central Token Interaction between Chains / 203–4
Table 4. Summary of Segmentation of Acts 15:1–35 in Sinaiticus and Vaticanus / 206–7

List of Contributors

ZACHARY K. DAWSON is Assistant Professor at Regent University, Virginia Beach, VA, USA

JAMES D. DVORAK is Vice President Academic and Professor of New Testament at McMaster Divinity College, Hamilton, ON, Canada

DAVID J. FULLER is Assistant Professor of Old Testament at Torch Trinity Graduate University, Seoul, South Korea

DOOSUK KIM is Associate Professor of Christian Theology at Kwangshin University, Gwangju, South Korea

CHRISTOPHER D. LAND is Associate Professor of New Testament and Linguistics at McMaster Divinity College, Hamilton, ON, Canada

JOHN J. H. LEE is Managing Editor of McMaster Divinity College Press, Hamilton, ON, Canada

STANLEY E. PORTER is President, Dean, and Professor of New Testament at McMaster Divinity College, Hamilton, ON

WILLIAM CRAIG PRICE is former Professor of New Testament and Greek and Associate Dean of Online Learning at New Orleans Baptist Theological Seminary, New Orleans, LA, USA

MARK PROCTOR is an independent scholar, Cleveland, TN, USA

RYDER A. WISHART is a software developer for Biblica Inc., Palmer Lake, CO, USA

DAVID I. YOON is Research Fellow at McMaster Divinity College, Hamilton, ON, Canada, and Lecturer in Bible at Emmanuel Bible College, Kitchener, ON, Canada

Preface

THE 2018 H. H. Bingham Colloquium in the New Testament at McMaster Divinity College in Hamilton, ON, Canada, held on June 15, was entitled "Putting the Pieces Together: Formalizing Units and Relations in the Biblical Languages." This Colloquium was the twenty-second in a continuing series of Bingham Colloquia held here at MDC, and the second entirely devoted to questions of linguistics in relation to the Bible. This Colloquium was hosted by the Centre for Biblical Linguistics, Translation, and Exegesis at McMaster Divinity College in Hamilton, ON, Canada, which fosters the linguistic exploration of ancient languages and texts, in particular the Greek of the New Testament. By various means, the Centre supports individuals and projects who are applying linguistic methods to the Bible for the purposes of linguistic analysis, translation, and exegesis. It also hosts events, with the goal of encouraging collegial, collaborative dialogue regarding the biblical languages, their translation, and the ways that linguistic methods can contribute to the interpretation of biblical texts.

The Colloquium on June 15 was preceded on June 14 by a workshop devoted to the use of Digital Humanities resources in the study of the Bible. This workshop exemplified how digital tools are making new forms of linguistic research possible and how these tools can be used in practical ways for the study or teaching of biblical languages. Several of the papers at the main Colloquium also took a Digital Humanities approach, exploring the potential of corpus linguistics and exemplifying recent and forthcoming developments related to the OpenText.org project and its annotations of the Greek New Testament. The remaining papers, most of which are contained in this volume, share a concern for the explicit description of either linguistic units or linguistic structures.

Due to the abiding interest in linguistic matters at MDC, we continue to believe that it is important to showcase and promote further such work through our annual Bingham Colloquium, of which this volume is an example. The Bingham Colloquium is named after Dr. Herbert Henry Bingham, who was a noted Baptist leader in ON, Canada. His leadership abilities were recognized by Baptists across Canada and around the world. His qualities included his genuine friendship, dedicated leadership, unswerving Christian faith, tireless devotion to duty, insightful service as a preacher and pastor, and visionary direction for congregation and denomination alike. These qualities endeared him both to his own church members and to believers in other denominations. The Colloquium has been endowed by his daughter as an act of appreciation for her father. We are pleased to be able to continue this tradition.

The first volumes of the Bingham Colloquium were published by Eerdmans Publishing, but since 2010 all the volumes in this series have been published by McMaster Divinity College Press, in conjunction with Wipf & Stock Publishers of Eugene, OR, in the McMaster New Testament Series. We appreciate this active and continuing publishing relationship and encouraged interested readers to examine previous Colloquium volumes and their wide range of topics pertinent to the life of the church.

I finally would like to thank the individual contributors for their efforts in the preparation and presentation of papers that make a significant contribution to linguistics and the Bible. We were pleased to welcome several outside scholars to present their scholarship as part of the Colloquium, and we look forward to welcoming them and others back at some time in the future. I am particularly gratified that several of our former students have had their work accepted for publication in this volume. I would especially like to thank my New Testament colleagues, Christopher Land and Francis Pang, for organizing the conference out of which this volume has emerged, and James Dvorak for his help in editing this volume for publication. He was helpfully aided by his Graduate Assistant, Yoshihiro Takahashi, as well as John J. H. Lee of McMaster Divinity College Press. We would like to thank the staff and student helpers and volunteers at McMaster Divinity College, all of whom were integral in creating a pleasant environment and a supportive atmosphere for the Colloquium.

Stanley E. Porter
McMaster Divinity College
Hamilton, ON, Canada

List of Abbreviations

AB	Anchor Bible
AcTSup	Acta Theologica Supplementum
AnOr	Analecta Orientalia
BAGL	*Biblical and Ancient Greek Linguistics*
BBET	Beiträge zur biblischen Exegese und Theologie
BDAG	Walter Bauer, Frederick W. Danker, W. F. Arndt, and F. W. Gingrich. *Greek English Lexicon of the New Testament and Other Early Christian Literature*. 3rd ed. Chicago: University of Chicago Press, 2000.
Bib	*Biblica*
BINS	Biblical Interpretation Series
BLG	Biblical Languages: Greek
BLH	Biblical Language: Hebrew
BT	*Bible Translator*
BZAW	Beihefte zur Zeitschrift für die alttestamentliche Wissenschaft
CBET	Contributions to Biblical Exegesis and Theology
ConBNT	Coniectanea Biblica: New Testament Series
CTL	Cambridge Textbooks in Linguistics
FAT	Forschungen zum Alten Testament
FGS	Functional Grammar Series
FN	*Filología Neotestamentaria*
GBS	Guides to Biblical Scholarship

HS	Hebrew Studies
HSM	Harvard Semitic Monographs
HSS	Harvard Semitic Studies
JBL	Journal of. Biblical Literature
JBLMS	Journal of Biblical Literature Monograph Series
JGRChJ	Journal of Greco-Roman Christianity and Judaism
JL	Journal of Linguistics
JLIABG	Journal for the Linguistics Institute of Ancient and Biblical Greek
JNSL	Journal of Northwest Semitic Languages
JQR	The Jewish Quarterly Review
JPS	Jewish Publication Society
JSNTSup	Journal for the Study of the New Testament Supplement Series
JSOTSup	Journal for the Study of the Old Testament Supplement Series
LBS	Linguistic Biblical Studies
LENT	Linguistic Exegesis of the New Testament
LNTS	The Library of New Testament Studies
LSAWS	Linguistic Studies in Ancient West Semitic
Neot	Neotestamentica
NIGTC	New International Greek Testament Commentary
NTM	New Testament Monographs
NTTS	New Testament Tools and Studies
OG	Old Greek
SBG	Studies in Biblical Greek
SBLDS	Society of Biblical Literature Dissertation Series
SCS	Septuagint and Cognate Studies
SNTG	Studies in New Testament Greek
SNTSMS	Society for New Testament Studies Monograph Series

SSN	Studia Semitica Neerlandica
START	*Selected Technical Articles Related to Translation*
SubBi	Subsidia Biblica
UF	*Ugarit-Forschungen*
WBC	Word Biblical Commentary
WTJ	*Westminster Theological Journal*

Putting the Pieces Together

An Introduction to This Volume

Stanley E. Porter, Christopher D. Land, and James D. Dvorak

This volume will strike some readers as a technical, perhaps even overly technical, volume in Greek and Hebrew linguistics—and it is such a technical volume, although arguably not overly technical. There are many different ways in which the Greek and Hebrew languages have been studied over the years. There is no attempt here—nor a need—to defend traditional means of teaching and studying ancient languages, including the Greek of the New Testament and the Hebrew of the Old Testament. Such means may have been helpful at one time (although this is highly debatable), but one of the features of such study has been that they employed what might now best be styled as pre-linguistic approaches to language. They focused upon individual elements of the language, often in isolation, and the smallest of these elements, such as words, were unduly focused upon. In ways sometimes reflected in both elementary grammars and even in supposedly more advanced works, such as commentaries, the results have left the impression that learning ancient language is much like learning mathematics—the simple committing to memory of some basic additive principles. The product of such a slide-rule approach to language has often been mechanistic and atomistic language learning and study, much to the detriment of language understanding. There is little wonder that there have been various types of rebellion, at least in some circles, to such approaches to learning and using ancient Hebrew and Greek. The major tenets of linguistics have often been either unknown or certainly neglected or overlooked in such language study. As a result, synchronic notions such as language as system, the importance of difference to establish meaning, the need to push to higher ranks or strata of language, and, above all, the role of function and meaning have often been absent. This volume attempts to address some of these issues by providing new insights into how such important linguistic notions play an important role in our understanding of Greek and Hebrew, and thereby provide a basis for not just language learning but language description.

One of the ways in which the detriment of pre-linguistic approaches to language has been manifested is in attempting to find ways to stave off the wholesale rejection of such study of languages, which study is often tacitly characterized as unhelpful or unenlightening. Many educational institutions today struggle to create interest in study of ancient Hebrew and Greek, which is no wonder when the learning of such languages is not connected with understanding of the language and hence of the texts of the Bible. There have also been attempts to revive interest in the study of the biblical languages through various means. One of these is to provide rudimentary courses in the tools associated with language study. In such courses, students are introduced to such basic works as lexicons and basic grammars, along with some supporting tools such as online resources, as a means of bridging the gap between language and exegesis. Understanding of the language as language, rather than a technical puzzle, is clearly lacking. On the other hand, there has also been growing interest in alternative approaches to the teaching of biblical languages. Many voices are calling for greater emphasis on internalization, rapid sight reading, and even conversational speaking. Since fewer and fewer people seem eager to learn the biblical languages, any attempt to inspire and foster the ability to read and understand the biblical languages can only be applauded. It is important to enable more people to read the languages more effectively. At the same time, however, there remains an important place for explicit linguistic formalizations. One does not need to be able to explain the language of a text in order to read and understand it, but one *does* need to be able to do this in order to explain (or advocate for) one's understanding. Despite the risks of oversimplifying and overgeneralizing, therefore, it is important that scholars persist in developing clearly articulated claims about the biblical languages that can support the important work of biblical exegesis. Such work is best carried out with humility and in community, because—as in any field of research that seeks to develop hypotheses in order to explain data—scholars of biblical Hebrew and Greek need to have their ideas discussed, debated, tested, critiqued, and refined. This volume attempts to be part of an ongoing effort to encourage explicit linguistic formalization to encourage further exploration of the biblical languages.

In the lead chapter of this volume, Stanley E. Porter addresses the question of how linguistic theory is fundamental to the interpretation of the Hebrew Bible and the Greek New Testament, and how knowledge of such theory advances the study of the Bible in its various derived enterprises, regardless of whether practitioners of such enterprises are conscious of this fact. Porter begins his chapter with examining various linguistic theories, especially those that subsume a number of syntactical theories, as the entry point into the wider linguistic enterprise. He then examines whether and to what extent such theories are utilized in Hebrew or New Testament Greek studies. Porter concludes his chapter with observations about some of the reasons for the state of the current discussion with particular reference to New Testament Greek.

In the only chapter focused solely on Hebrew, David J. Fuller seeks to develop a Hebrew-based account of circumstantials, beginning with prepositions as the most common realization. He takes an explicitly systemic and monosemic approach, understanding Hebrew prepositions as being systemically organized according to a network of oppositional choices. Using the book of Habakkuk as a test case, he surveys the prepositions in Habakkuk through the lens of Michael Halliday's categories of meaning, notes the different forms used for each category of meaning, inductively attempts to ascertain intrinsic shades of meaning for the different forms, and, finally, posits a network of oppositions by which Hebrew prepositions can be systemically organized.

The next three chapters all pertain to the use of syntactic markers in New Testament Greek. In his contribution, Ryder A. Wishart explores the potential of Greek in relation to the broad phenomenon of marking syntactic relations. Beginning with the traditional distinction between coordinating and subordinating conjunction, Wishart argues that this traditional distinction exemplifies two different kinds of syntactic structure, which he refers to as chaining and wrapping. Chaining he describes as quantitative in nature, involving strings of functionally equivalent units; wrapping he describes as qualitative in nature, with wrappers serving to change the functional potential of units. Wishart contends that, together, chaining and wrapping allow for the quantitative and qualitative augmentation of Greek syntactic units of all ranks of discourse.

Zachary K. Dawson considers the ways in which the system of conjunction has been modeled within the field of Systemic Functional Linguistics (SFL), where the task has been taken up to identify all the possible ways that segments of text of various lengths (e.g., words, word-groups, clauses, and clause-complexes) can be connected to each other. Comparatively, Dawson shows that the study of Greek conjunction is well behind the curve, with relatively little work having been done in New Testament Greek scholarship that considers Greek conjunction in light of logico-semantic relations as modeled in SFL or the generally accepted division between external and internal conjunction. Then, to push development of this area forward, Dawson models the system of conjunction for Greek, focusing on how logico-semantic relations become realized at the stratum of lexico-grammar in Greek and how these realizations can be construed as experiential, textual, and interpersonal relations.

Mark Proctor examines the structure and interpretive significance of εἰ καί conditions, surveying all the twenty-two instances in the Greek New Testament. He argues that the adverbial καί in this construction serves to signal that neither the condition's fulfillment nor unfulfillment nullifies the apodosis. While the protasis of an εἰ καί condition usually presents a contrary-to-fact notion, this logical relationship is not always the case. In every case, however, Proctor insists that the New Testament writers make use of the εἰ καί structure, at least in part, to indicate they would concede the truth of the protasis only with reluctance. Thus, whereas a second-class conditional denies the truth of its apodosis (and also its protasis by extension), an εἰ καί conditional statement instead affirms its apodosis while also casting doubt on the protasis. This understanding contrasts with the opinion that εἰ καί conditional statements can be concessive. To exemplify the differences, Proctor examines the NRSV and identifies several problematic concessive translations, suggesting alternative translations in accordance with his view of the underlying conditional construction.

James D. Dvorak sets out to describe adjectives in attributive structures to a greater degree of delicacy, making use of Halliday's experiential categories—namely, Deictic, Numerative, Epithet, Classifier, and Thing—in order to explore different types of definers. In addition to

Putting the Pieces Together: An Introduction to This Volume xxi

considering structural matters, Dvorak also attends to the potential roles these elements can play in relation to the social purposes of a discourse as social interaction. To accomplish this, he situates definers within a broader perspective by bringing to bear other SFL-influenced models, including Critical Discourse Analysis and social-scientific criticism. The result is a richer understanding of types of definers and the ways they can contribute meaning to texts.

The next several chapters focus upon the various functions of language, especially as this concept is used in SFL. In chapter 7, David I. Yoon outlines resources for evaluating interpersonal meaning in the Greek of the New Testament by reviewing recent developments in the linguistic study of the New Testament, with particular reference to advances in the modeling of speech functions. These advances concern the role that grammatical mood plays in the process of enacting various kinds of negotiations at the level of the clause. Yoon also attempts to differentiate between speech functions at both semantic and contextual levels. He then applies these categories to the analysis of Gal 2:11–21, the so-called Antioch Incident, in which a variety of clause types and speech functions can be observed functioning to negotiation interpersonal meanings, including Paul's own recollections, as well as the enacting of persuasive and instructive moves in the discourse.

Then, in the first of three chapters on the textual function of language, Doosuk Kim discusses the history of various approaches to the notion of information structure in modern linguistics. Tracing its roots to the Prague School of linguistics and its subsequent development in SFL in particular, Kim explores how SFL's model of information structure as theorized for English can be adopted or adapted for the Greek of the New Testament. He finds that several adaptations need to be made and so proceeds to construct a model for the Greek of the New Testament that accounts for the categories of theme, rheme, given, and new as they can be applied to understand the particularities of Greek as a non-configurational and epigraphic language.

In chapter 9, Craig Price addresses the textual functions of cohesion and coherence in Acts 15 taking as significant that Acts 15 occupies the physical center of the book of Acts and that it serves as a pivotal chapter in Luke's narrative whereby major participants and social groups come together in a clash over opposing ideological views. To sort through the combination of narrative, speeches, and even an embedded letter in Acts

15, Price employs Ruqaiya Hasan's functional model for cohesive harmony analysis, which helps to measure the level of cohesion and assess the coherence of the episode. By analyzing identity and similarity chains, Price maps the cohesion-making patterns in the text and then uses these patterns to examine the paragraph breaks in Codex Alexandrinus and Codex Vaticanus, which, in turns, helps enter into dialogue with early examples of text segmentation as additional indicators of the cohesive harmony of Acts 15:1–35.

In chapter 10, the final chapter of this volume, John J. H. Lee moves the discussion to the contextual stratum in SFL and the notion of register. The concept of register has become a very productive topic in recent linguistic discussion of the Greek of the New Testament, being used to create descriptions and comparisons of typical patterns of language within various sections and books. However, in this chapter, Lee, drawing upon previous register studies, explores its possible role in Septuagint studies. Contemporary Septuagint studies are divided in their approaches, with some focused upon the close relationship of the Hebrew and Greek texts and others exploring more wholistic and literary approaches. Lee contends that register analysis adds a new dimension to Septuagint study by providing a means of describing Septuagint texts as Greek texts in relation to their situational contexts, and thereby providing greater linguistic insight into their function and use, the kinds of insights that would benefit commentaries.

This volume does not pretend to provide more than it does, but it need not apologize for what it does provide—linguistically explorative studies of important topics within contemporary Greek and Hebrew studies. The kinds of topics treated here, often and usually at the forefront of discussion, attempt to advance beyond rudimentary observations all too often found in contemporary observations upon the Greek or Hebrew language and offer insights that challenge further study as we attempt to take a close examination at and reassemble the pieces of the language into the systems that we know as ancient Greek or Hebrew.

1

Linguistic Theory in Hebrew and Greek Language Study

STANLEY E. PORTER

INTRODUCTION

THE TITLE OF THE conference from which this volume emerged is "Putting the Pieces Together: Formalizing Units and Relations in the Biblical Languages." There is much implied in this title that merits further examination, much more in fact than one essay such as this can deliver. However, the conference title itself, and now the volume that has emerged, suggest a particular perspective on linguistic description, especially of what we might usually call syntax, that merits further explication at the outset, so as to help us to understand the nature of the linguistic enterprise, or at least the enterprise as it is conceived by the originators of the conference, even if not all of the contributors (although many if not most of the contributors probably accede to the major tenets that I will describe below). The purpose of this paper is to attempt to address the question of how linguistic theory is fundamental to the interpretation of Hebrew and Greek texts and how knowledge of such theory advances the study of the Bible in its several various derived enterprises, regardless of whether practitioners of such enterprises explicitly or even ostensibly realize this fact. In this paper, I will begin by examining various linguistic theories, especially those that subsume several syntactical theories, as an entrance point into the linguistic enterprise. I will then examine how such theories are or are not utilized in Hebrew or New Testament Greek studies. I will then examine some of the reasons for the state of the current discussion, focusing upon New Testament Greek.

ENTERING THE LINGUISTIC ENTERPRISE BY MEANS OF LINGUISTIC THEORIES

I suppose it is appropriate in a discussion of linguistics to begin by invoking a binary opposition. It is a commonplace within linguistics to distinguish between two major approaches to linguistic theory, which has been variously described but which is essentially a distinction between Noam Chomsky and the others, that is, those who do not follow Chomsky. This is referred to in various ways and has in a helpful way been developed by Robert Van Valin and Randy LaPolla as a difference between the "syntactocentric" and the "communication-and-cognition" perspectives.[1] Van Valin and LaPolla discuss a range of linguistic theories that subsume various syntactic theories, and this provides the point of initial discussion for this paper.

The syntactocentric perspective is attributed to Chomsky and his many followers and is characterized—whether in its earliest phrase-structure grammar or transformational grammar or later Government and Binding Theory/Principles and Parameters or minimalist program (with recursion as the minimal feature of language)[2]—by its being an "autonomous cognitive faculty"[3] that results in human internal grammar that follows linguistic universals. Such linguistics investigates not language use (performance) but the speaker's competence, and especially the psychological dimensions of language such as its acquisition, even if one is not concerned with psychological processes themselves. According to Van Valin and LaPolla, this approach to linguistics pro-

---

1. The following is dependent upon Van Valin and LaPolla, *Syntax*, 8–15, but with reference to other works interposed as appropriate. I do not include speech-act theory, for which there are works in both Greek and Hebrew, because here I am concentrating on syntactical/semantic theories as per Van Valin and LaPolla, rather than pragmatic theories that are more a philosophy of language than linguistic (apart from mentioning Relevance Theory below).

2. Chomsky, *Syntactic Structures*; *Aspects*; *Lectures*; *Minimalist Program*, among many other works.

3. Croft and Cruse, *Cognitive Linguistics*, 1.

vides an analysis of grammar but not of language, if language is defined as what humans actually produce. It has spawned a number of further theories, according to Van Valin and LaPolla, such as Generalized Phrase Structure Grammar, Relational Grammar, and Categorial Grammar.

The communication-and-cognition perspective, according to Van Valin and LaPolla, essentially includes everything else, unified around the view that linguistics focuses upon the use of language either for communicative purposes or as a reflection of cognitive processing in relation to other cognitive systems, with grammar or syntax as relatively less significant to these greater concerns.[4] As Van Valin and LaPolla admit, the linguistic theories that this perspective subsumes are numerous and diverse. They include Functional Grammar or grammars in their various types (including Continental, St. Petersburg, and West Coast or Oregon forms), Role and Reference Grammar, Systemic Functional Grammar (SFG), Tagmemics, Lexical-Functional Grammar, Head-Driven Phrase Structure Grammar, Construction Grammar, Autolexical Syntax, Word Grammar, Meaning-text theory, Cognitive Grammar, Prague School Dependency Grammar, and French functionalism, to list only what must be an incomplete list (and it is, as one can also think of Stratificational Grammar or Columbia School Linguistics, both Functionalist models), along with a number of what they call independent linguists.[5] Whereas Chomsky dominates the first group, there is no single dominant figure in the second group, only a relatively unified yet widespread rejection of the syntactocentric perspective. However, Van Valin and LaPolla also admit that there is a continuum from communicative on the one hand and cognitive theories on the other end of the continuum of communication-and-cognition perspectives. On the communicative side is Michael Halliday's SFG, which they characterize as "perhaps the most radical discourse-pragmatic view, a 'top-down' analytic model which starts with discourse and works 'down' to lower levels of grammatical structure."[6] On the cognitive side is Ronald Langacker's Cognitive

---

4. See also Butler, *Structure and Function*.

5. Van Valin and LaPolla (*Syntax*, 12) list as independent linguists Michael Silverstein, Ray Jackendoff, Ellen Prince, Talmy Givón, Susumu Kuno, Leonard Talmy, Sandra Thompson, and Anna Wierzbicka. Not all might fit as conveniently as others, and one might also think of others to place in this category. I would have thought that most of these were classifiable, some of them even in the syntactocentric and others in the communication-and-cognition perspective. However, see below on these categories.

6. Van Valin and LaPolla, *Syntax*, 12.

Grammar, which is reducible to three major components, semantics, phonology, and symbolic representation.[7] Van Valin and LaPolla place the other theories in the middle of the continuum, singling out Role and Reference Grammar (Van Valin and LaPolla's own theory) and Simon Dik's (Continental) Functional Grammar for exemplary reference within this medial position.

This categorization may, however, require further refinement or refinements. For example, if we utilize Van Valin and LaPolla's division, Construction Grammar, with its descriptive and non-transformational properties is closer to Langacker's Cognitive Grammar than it is to the theories listed as standing in the middle with some of their functional tendencies. Further, Tagmemics has some features in common with Role and Reference Grammar, such as a rank scale or levels of representation, but it has arguably more in common with SFG, with not only a rank scale but what SFG would call levels or strata (a non-formal rank scale, in essence), a top-down approach, and a comprehensive and encompassing theory of context as well as structures. Being more aggressively critical, one might question entirely the divide along the lines of Chomsky and his universal grammar against all the rest, and instead place Chomsky and his major developers, whether positively or negatively, so long as they pursue a psychological or cognitive dimension, on the one side, with the other perspectives lumped together on the other. The result here would be that Chomsky is joined by (from the choices of Van Valin and LaPolla) Lexical-Functional Grammar, Head-Driven Phrase Structure Grammar, Construction Grammar, probably Autolexical Syntax, and, most noteworthily perhaps, Cognitive Grammar,[8] forming a group that might be characterized as syntacto-cognitive-centric. This would leave, on the resulting cline, Role and Reference Grammar on the one extreme (closest to the syntacto-cognitive-centric models) with movement toward Word Grammar, various dependency grammars (Mel'cuk and Prague), Functional Grammars (Continental, Russian, US, and French), Tagmemics, and then SFG on the other, forming a relatively smaller and more focused yet still diverse group of functional theories.[9] For that

---

7. Van Valin and LaPolla, *Syntax*, 13; cf. Langacker, *Cognitive Grammar*, 5.

8. The development of Cognitive Grammar is often attributed to such former Chomskyans as Ronald Langacker and George Lakoff.

9. I have been helped in my re-categorizations by Droste and Joseph, eds., *Linguistic Theory*; and ten Hacken, *Chomskyan Linguistics*.

reason, if one were to explore these categorizations in more detail, one would no doubt wish to refine significantly this continuum as one places various theories along the several clines.

There are numerous lumpings and splittings in this categorization of theories by Van Valin and LaPolla. Nevertheless, as unsatisfactory as such a brief survey may be in its particular details, it has the virtue of providing a brief overview of the field of linguistic theory, especially in relation to theories of syntax (since all of the theories that they mention have syntactical theories of one sort or another within them). It is adequate enough at this point to set the stage for a discussion of linguistic study of Hebrew and the Greek of the New Testament, and more importantly questions about what exactly we are doing in such linguistic descriptions.

LINGUISTICS AND ANCIENT HEBREW AND NEW TESTAMENT GREEK LANGUAGE STUDIES

At this stage in my argument, I wish to examine more closely how various linguistic models have been utilized in ancient Hebrew and New Testament Greek language studies. This is a large undertaking, one that I realize I am not as adequately equipped for as I might be (I am not a Hebraist). Nevertheless, as a linguist, I will attempt to categorize a large but far from inclusive number of works within each language into their appropriate categories, with some words of commentary and critique especially following the discussion of Greek.[10]

Hebrew Language Studies

The field of ancient Hebrew language studies has a much longer and more developed history than does the study of New Testament Greek, although it is still not nearly as diverse as the characterization of linguistics provided by Van Valin and LaPolla. The history of the study of ancient Hebrew is not as well-known as that of other languages but can be divided into two major periods, the Eastern Jewish and the Western non-Jewish study.[11] Eastern Jewish study of Hebrew goes back to at least the

---

10. I generally avoid discussing Hebrew and Greek grammars, except as necessary to make a linguistic point, and confine myself for the most part to referring to monograph-length treatments.

11. My encapsulation is influenced by Waltke and O'Connor, *Introduction to Biblical Hebrew Syntax*, 31–43; who follow Tene and Barr, "Hebrew Linguistic Literature"; cf.

tenth century, patterned after the study of Arabic and undertaken for the sake of the study of the Hebrew Bible and other Jewish literature. Once the centers of Judaism shifted from the East to the West, in the late medieval period, study of the Hebrew language shifted to models developed in the West for Latin, so that by the sixteenth century the major Hebrew scholars were primarily non-Jewish, with some noteworthy exceptions (such as Baruch Spinoza), as study moved into the Enlightenment period. If one were to trace the course of the development of linguistics (apart from the study of Hebrew), one might well identify the rationalist period of the eighteenth and early nineteenth century, the comparative period of the nineteenth and very early twentieth century, and the modern linguistic period of the twentieth century beginning with Saussure. Modern study of ancient Hebrew can also be divided into three major periods coinciding with developments in Western intellectual thought as well as linguistics. The first is the rationalist period, when there was a tendency to see Hebrew in terms of categories of Western languages, extending from the eighteenth into the early nineteenth centuries. For example, at this stage many grammarians equated tense-form with absolute time.[12] The second period is the comparative philological period, coinciding with the rise of comparative philology in the wider study of languages, from the early eighteenth century until almost the middle of the twentieth century. Aspectual theories such as those by Heinrich Ewald and later S. R. Driver were first influenced by Arabic and then by discoveries of a number of other Northwest Semitic languages, then later by Akkadian and finally Ugaritic.[13] The major grammar that reflects this period was by Wilhelm Gesenius, going through numerous editions.[14] Later in that period, from the mid-nineteenth to the mid-twentieth centuries, study of Indo-European languages and developmental theories of Hebrew had a sizable influence, in some ways resulting in a move away from aspectual and back to temporal and modal theories of the Hebrew verbal system. In around 1940, the modern linguistic period of Hebrew study began, continuing to the present.

---

van der Merwe et al., *Biblical Hebrew Reference Grammar*, 6–12.

12. For examples, see Cook, *Time*, 83–86, who cites grammarians such as Elias Levita, N. W. Schroeder, and Philip Gell.

13. See Cook, *Time*, 86–120.

14. See Kautzsch, *Gesenius' Hebrew Grammar*, 17–22, for its own history of Hebrew study.

I note from this brief survey several trends within Hebrew language study. The first is that Hebrew language study is, in many ways, at least as old, if not older, than study of most other languages, because, at least in its early days before its demotion during the late medieval period, it was seen as essential for understanding the Hebrew Bible. At this stage, study of Hebrew, even if done by Jewish scholars, was comparative, as Arabic was often used as the basis for Hebrew description, based upon the Arabic intellectual tradition that preceded study of Hebrew. The second observation is that, once study of Hebrew moved to the West, the Western linguistic categories came to influence and then dominate the study of Hebrew, especially the influence of the comparative-historical method and developmental models. Although views of ancient Hebrew were more inclined to draw upon the metalanguage of other linguistic descriptions while appreciating the characteristics of Hebrew (e.g., in the work of Ewald), in later times Hebrew came to be described as simply one more of the languages within an emerging comparative-historical developmental typology, subject to the same categories of discussion. A third observation is that, despite the modern linguistic period of ancient Hebrew study beginning in the 1940s and coming fully to bear in the 1970s and subsequently, there is still much persistent work that utilizes earlier models, either rationalist or comparative-historical, so that much of the contemporary teaching and even study of ancient Hebrew might well be classified as following the patterns not of modern linguistic study but of traditional grammar (which will be explicated in more detail below when I discuss Greek, where the ongoing influence of traditional grammar is even stronger). The result is some grammars, especially beginning ones, continuing to utilize a metalanguage dependent upon easy equations of tense-form and time, lists of classifications of usage, and other features. The fourth observation, however, is that, nevertheless, the study of ancient Hebrew in relation to the Bible was in several ways far in advance of study of the Greek of the New Testament, as will be demonstrated below.

The linguistic study of ancient Hebrew is not as diverse as the categories suggested by Van Valin and LaPolla, but their categories are useful for characterization of Hebrew language studies.[15] I will not focus upon

---

15. Helpful in this discussion are van der Merwe, "Short Survey"; van der Merwe, "Overview of Hebrew Narrative Syntax"; van der Merwe, "Overview of Recent Developments"; and van der Merwe, "Some Recent Trends," although not all the ap-

work that primarily addresses questions of translation, even though there is some linguistic work that continues to be done in this area, and I will focus upon book-length rather than journal article treatments of the topic. I have identified six major organizational categories of Hebrew linguistic discussion. These include structuralism, syntactocentric perspectives, Tagmemics, Functional Grammar, Systemic Functional Linguistics (SFL), and Cognitive Linguistics. Some of the earliest linguistic work within ancient Hebrew studies was inspired by fundamental ideas within structuralism, first promoted in the early years of the twentieth century by Ferdinand de Saussure and the Prague School of linguistics. Structuralism as it is found in Hebrew studies draws upon such categories as emphasis, opposition, and syntax, semantics, and pragmatics as a coordinated system, and hence much of the early research was done by Continental European scholars, although the trend has continued among a broader range of scholars, with an increasing use of distributional studies playing a significant role in their findings. This structuralist work includes the publications of Takamitsu Muraoka on emphasis in Hebrew using a very general notion of emphasis,[16] Frithiof Rundgren on Hebrew aspect using the structuralism of Saussure and various theories of opposition from the Prague School,[17] Péter Kustár on Hebrew aspect,[18] and Jacob Hoftijzer on the function and use of imperfect verb forms.[19]

This tendency to draw upon a relatively eclectic form of structuralist-inspired linguistics has continued in more recent Hebrew linguistic study as well.[20] Several good examples are the early work of Walter Gross on pendent or verbless constructions in ancient Hebrew followed by his

---

proaches mentioned below are mentioned or given adequate treatment in his surveys or classified in the same way. See also the similarities and differences in the overviews offered in van Wolde, *Narrative Syntax*, and Dallaire et al., eds., *Where Shall Wisdom Be Found?* although Dallaire et al. have some linguistically anomalous discussions (e.g., Peter Bekins on the "definite" article [21–36]; Brian Bompiani on prepositions [37–64]).

16. Muraoka, *Emphatic Words*, which is a revision of his 1969 Hebrew University dissertation. Cf. van der Merwe, "Short Survey," 169.

17. Rundgren, *Das althebräische Verbum*, esp. 25–56. Cf. also his student Eskhult, *Studies*, 9–11, 18.

18. Kustár, *Aspekt*, esp. 3 and 56–62.

19. Hoftijzer, *Function and Use*, 1–2, with emphasis on structuralism.

20. I recognize that some of the works placed in this category might arguably also or even better belong in the category of Functional Grammar discussed below.

later work in the semantics and pragmatics vein,[21] Ernst Jenni's study of the Hebrew preposition,[22] Yoshinobu Endo using basic Saussurian descriptive structuralism to examine the Hebrew verb in the Joseph story,[23] Tal Goldfajn on establishing the temporal basis of the verbal forms using narrative,[24] Ziony Zevit on anterior constructions in Hebrew using very basic structuralist categories,[25] the early work of Cynthia Miller (now Miller-Naudé) on the representation of speech in Hebrew narrative, where she relies heavily upon distinctions between syntax, metapragmatics, and discourse pragmatics,[26] Adina Moshavi on the use of pragmatics (focus or topicalization), including markedness and word-order typology, in the study of the Hebrew finite clause,[27] Nicholas Lunn on variation in word order on the basis of pragmatics,[28] Miller's former doctoral student John Cook on the Hebrew verbal system, where he tries to mediate between what he calls formalist/structuralist and functionalist/substantialist frameworks (he might also be placed below under discussion of functionalism),[29] Scott Callahan employing typological study of modality and the Hebrew infinitive absolute,[30] and Jan Joosten on the Hebrew verbal system using an explicitly Saussurian structuralism emphasizing langue/parole, paradigmatic/syntagmatic opposition, and semantics, all outlined in just short of two pages.[31] Although successive scholars have continued to develop ideas within this basic structuralist framework, the influence of the work of these scholars has been more inspirational than theoretically directive, with few subsequent scholars specifically drawing upon the earlier frameworks proposed. Similarly,

---

21. Gross, *Pendenskonstruktion*; *Satzteilfolge*; *Doppelt besetztes Vorfeld*. Gross also has some functional tendencies based on the work of the functionalist Simon Dik and the Hebrew functionalism of Wolfgang Richter (see below). He is followed by Michel, *Theologie*, on coordination in ancient Hebrew.

22. Jenni, *Die hebräischen Präpositionen*, 1:13–16.

23. Endo, *Verbal System*.

24. Goldfajn, *Word Order*.

25. Zevit, *Anterior Construction*.

26. Miller, *Representation*, 14–39, although the approach is very eclectic.

27. Moshavi, *Word Order*, 1–17.

28. Lunn, *Word-Order Variation*, esp. 9.

29. Cook, *Time*, 176–91, esp. 190.

30. Callahan, *Modality*; see esp. 5, where he consciously distances himself from any more specific method.

31. Joosten, *Verbal System*, esp. 9–10.

there have been some Hebrew linguists influenced by the German scholar Harald Weinrich,[32] such as Alviero Niccacci,[33] but this work has not been influential in establishing continued research in what is more a philosophy of time than a linguistic framework. One can say that much of this structuralist linguistic examination of Hebrew is recognizably linguistic in that it draws upon the categories of thought developed by Saussure and the Prague School linguists and other structuralists. However, these various elements are often interpreted and conceptualized only very basically or suggestively (as in the work of Muraoka). This leaves many of these works standing on their own, positing categories that do not necessarily fit within the kinds of developed frameworks that are usually found within non-biblical linguistics and that Van Valin and LaPolla describe.

If we turn to the basic linguistic bifurcation of Van Valin and LaPolla, we examine first the syntactocentric perspective of Chomsky. Chomskyan linguistics was the single most significant force in linguistic thought during the last fifty or so years of the twentieth century, especially in North America, so it is not surprising that there has been some Chomskyan work in Hebrew linguistics. However, the surprise is how little Chomskyan work has been done in monograph form, even if there is more in the journal literature.[34] One such monograph that also uses computer technology to search databases is Janet Dyk's study of the participle in Hebrew using X-bar theory from government and binding theory,[35] and a variety of moderately Chomskyan works by Robert Holmstedt. In three volumes, as well as many articles, Holmstedt consistently writes within the syntactocentric perspective of Chomsky. Holmstedt's first major work, his doctoral dissertation at the University of Wisconsin-Madison (under Miller) on the relative clause in Biblical Hebrew, was revised and finally published in 2016, in which he draws explicitly upon not only the Chomskyan minimalist program, but Chomsky's fundamental belief in a universal grammar.[36] This work has

---

32. Weinrich, *Tempus*.

33. Niccacci, *Syntax*, 19–22, whose work is oriented toward the level of discourse (text linguistics).

34. Besides the work of Holmstedt, cited in his works noted above, see van der Merwe, "Some Recent Trends," 15nn48–55.

35. Dyk, *Participles*, esp. 41–45.

36. Holmstedt, "Relative Clause," 149–72, with application to Hebrew in 172–96 (he

provided the basis of Holmstedt's later work, in particular grammatical handbooks on Ruth and especially Esther,[37] in which in the latter, he explicitly draws upon the minimalist principles and parameters (government and binding) textbook of Andrew Cairnie,[38] but also incorporates into the discussion other structuralist work, such as that of Cook on Hebrew verb structure (with whom he has also written an elementary Hebrew grammar).[39] Whereas Holmstedt's monograph reflects the Chomskyan program, as do many if not most of his journal articles, the Chomskyan framework presented in the handbooks on Ruth and Esther is very basic, with many readers probably missing the significance of his attention to constituency, syntactic roles, and valency, which is very much concentrated upon phrase structure and syntactic and semantic roles, without reference to many of the other categories often found in such Chomskyan discussions.

If we shift to the communication-and-cognition perspective of Van Valin and LaPolla, we find that there has been much more linguistic research on the ancient Hebrew language. The first major influence by a recognizable school of linguistics, apart from the general structuralists categorized together and discussed above, was Tagmemics, developed by Kenneth Pike and later by Robert Longacre. No doubt due to Pike being a Christian (along with Longacre), he had a direct influence upon many biblical scholars. One of the earliest to explore linguistics in ancient Hebrew studies was the Australian scholar Francis Andersen. Andersen wrote two important early works, *The Hebrew Verbless Clause in the Pentateuch* and, in particular, *The Sentence in Biblical Hebrew*, both of which have had a significant impact upon Hebrew language study. Andersen's *Hebrew Verbless Clause* claims to be what he calls "holistic" in approach, although it directly utilizes the syntagmeme from Tagmemics as the unit of analysis, and has prompted continuing discus-

---

also, however, discusses pragmatics in a chapter); Holmstedt, *Relative Clause*.

37. Holmstedt, *Ruth*, 3–9; Holmstedt and Screnock, *Esther*, esp. 2–7. I would not normally draw on such handbooks, except as they are important within the history of biblical linguistic thought. I find it odd that Chomsky is not, however, listed in the author index of the volume on Ruth, nor in the bibliography of Esther (Esther has no modern author index).

38. Cairnie, *Syntax*.

39. Cook and Holmstedt, *Beginning Biblical Hebrew*, although a mix of linguistic frameworks seems to be drawn upon.

sion of the topic.[40] His exposition of Tagmemics in relation to Hebrew in *The Sentence in Biblical Hebrew* is a thorough and detailed theoretical exposition of this linguistic perspective, to the point that some, even those linguistically sympathetic to the approach, have criticized its abundance of theory and apparatus over clear exposition.[41] Longacre, himself primarily a linguist as opposed to a biblical scholar, also made a contribution to the study of Hebrew (as well as Greek; see below), writing a tagmemic analysis of the Joseph story patterned after the discourse theory that he developed in his discourse grammar based upon his own version of Tagmemics.[42] There have been several others who have used Tagmemics in their research into Hebrew linguistics. These include David Dawson's approach to text-linguistics, using what he fashions as a much more straightforward and accessible form of especially Longacre's Tagmemics but with attention to such foundational concepts as empiricism, patterning, closure, choice, notional and surface structure, particle, wave, and field, and, of course, tagmemes and syntagmemes, all recognizably familiar to those who use Tagmemics,[43] and Roy Heller's arguable return to tagmemic complexity in his examination of clause function in narrative according to what he calls discourse constellations.[44] Tagmemics has not continued to generate much further work, even though it is a rigorous and comprehensive functional model. This may be because of the waning influence of Pike, and along with him of Longacre, its two greatest proponents in biblical studies, but it may also be because its complex apparatus demands much of its practitioners (it attempts to be a unified theory of knowledge, no small task). In any case, the notion of a stratal functional system that connects text to context is one that, nevertheless, has had enduring value in Hebrew and other language study.

At this point, I return to what might best be called various forms of Functional Grammar, whose various types I compile here in a single discussion due to a number of similarities.[45] There are several treatments

---

40. Andersen, *Hebrew Verbless Clause*, 25–27. Cf. Miller, *Hebrew Verbless Clause*.

41. Andersen, *Sentence*, 8–9. For criticism of theory over comprehensibility, see Dawson, *Text-Linguistics*, 51.

42. Longacre, *Joseph*; cf. Longacre, *Grammar of Discourse*.

43. Dawson, *Text-Linguistics*, 7, 70–122.

44. Heller, *Narrative Structure*.

45. As noted above, one might argue that more of the structuralist treatments above

of Hebrew that broadly draw upon general principles of Functional Grammar, by which is meant that they are concerned with describing how various features of Hebrew function within the language and hence within text to present and organize its information. For biblical scholars, one of the most important works that provides background to their functionalist work is by Knud Lambrecht,[46] although they draw on a variety of the significant features of various functional theories. Wolfgang Richter draws upon the major principles of structuralism, along with recognition of the importance of function, in arguably the first Hebrew grammar written using principles of modern linguistics.[47] Other general functionalist studies include works such as Eep Talstra and his text-linguistic study of 2 Kgs 3,[48] followed in his approach by his student François den Exter Blokland on principles of defining text-segmentation through syntactical analysis.[49] Geoffrey Khan examines Semitic syntax in Arabic, Biblical Hebrew, Aramaic (Biblical and Syriac), Akkadian, and Amharic (Ethiopian), in a study that combines traditional comparative-historical concerns with a rigorous but highly eclectic functionalist linguistic perspective.[50] E. J. Revell, who draws relatively lightly on pragmatics and sociolinguistics, examines participants and what he calls expressive usage (emphasis).[51] Andreas Disse examines the notion of information structure in ancient Hebrew, utilizing a corpus-based approach to several books of the Hebrew Bible.[52] Jean-Marc Heimerdinger's study of topic, focus, and foreground in Hebrew narratives draws upon major categories of thought within functionalism, in his case in opposition to Tagmemics. Lénart de Regt examines participant reference and its rhetorical significance within a functionalist perspective.[53] Katsuomi

---

belong in this category, although it might also be argued that some of the studies here are more structuralist than functionalist. Cf. van der Merwe, "Some Recent Trends," 17–19.

46. Lambrecht, *Information Structure*.

47. Richter, *Grundlagen*, 1:9–35; cf. Richter, *Untersuchungen*. See van der Merwe, "Short Survey," 171–72.

48. Talstra, *2 Kön. 3*, based upon Wolfgang Dressler.

49. den Exter Blokland, *In Search of Text Syntax*, esp. 11–17.

50. Khan, *Studies*, esp. xxxii–xxxix, where he draws upon a wide range of functionalist theories, and more, in performing a type of discourse analysis.

51. Revell, *Designation*, 15–20. Cf. Dempster, Review of *Designation*.

52. Disse, *Informationsstruktur*.

53. de Regt, *Participants*, especially the work of Talmy Givón.

Shimasaki writes on how word order and information structure function to create focus in ancient Hebrew.[54] Finally, Hélène Dallaire utilizes a functionalist approach to comparative grammar, with attention to social interaction, in her work on the syntax of volitives in Hebrew and Amarna Canaanite prose.[55] Functionalists drawing specifically upon the Continental Functional Grammar of Simon Dik,[56] whose work is recognized as the basis of one of the major functional models, include Michael Rosenbaum in his study of variation in word order within Hebrew, especially Isa 40–55, and N. Winther-Nielsen, who develops under the influence of Robert Longacre a functional discourse grammar of Joshua using rhetorical structure theory, a method for describing the organization of texts.[57] In some ways, this discussion of functionalism should precede Tagmemics, because it is broader in scope in the way that it has been applied to Hebrew. However, due to its more robust and continuing development and utilization, I have placed it after Tagmemics to represent its current status as a well-used, even if variably applied, framework.

A much more recent development within Hebrew studies, and arguably a suitable and perhaps even more refined functional model, has been the use of Systemic Functional Linguistics. SFL, or SFG as it is sometimes called, has already been mentioned and characterized by Van Valin and LaPolla as the most radical of the top-down discourse-pragmatic models. SFL is characterized by dissolving the boundary between langue and parole, emphasizing paradigmatic choice over syntagmatic structure, and seeing meaning as comprising several complex semiotic systems. Whereas it has been much more popular in New Testament Greek studies (see below), SFL has been recently introduced to Hebrew language study. The first apparent work to make widespread use of SFL in a book-length treatment of Hebrew linguistics was the handbook on Gen 1–11 by Barry Bandstra.[58] In the introduction to his handbook, he lays out a very clear approach to SFL, utilizing the three metafunctions

---

54. Shimasaki, *Focus Structure*, 30–33.

55. Dallaire, *Syntax of Volitives*, 1–35, with reference to many different linguistic orientations.

56. Dik, *Theory*, especially part 1 on the clause.

57. Rosenbaum, *Word-Order Variation*; Winther-Nielsen, *Functional Discourse Grammar*, 1, 10–20. Cf. Mann and Thompson, "Rhetorical Structure Theory."

58. Bandstra, *Genesis 1–11*. Again, I only draw upon such a handbook because of the significant place it plays within the history of Hebrew linguistic thought. Bandstra began his linguistic work in Tagmemics. See van der Merwe, "Short Survey," 170n69.

in relation to mood (interpersonal), transitivity (experiential), and textuality (textual). Although he has not been directly influential on their use of SFL, several others have taken up the challenge of this linguistic perspective on Hebrew.[59] In the same year, a lengthy comparative study of the Hebrew verb (*qatal/yiqtol*) was published by Silviu Tatu, in which tense sequence was examined in Hebrew and Ugaritic poetry.[60] Colin Toffelmire has produced a discourse and register analysis of the prophet Joel, in which he explores the SFL categories of field, tenor, and mode, including cohesion, as a means of characterizing the context of situation, especially in relation to the new form criticism.[61] Mary Conway draws upon a particular facet of SFL, appraisal theory, in her study of the book of Judges in order to examine the ideology of the book.[62] Appraisal theory adds a further dimension to the tools of SFL by introducing more formalized means of evaluation within texts, and she applies this to how characters are presented within Judges. David Fuller provides a discourse analysis of the book of Habakkuk by linguistically comparing the organizational units within the first several chapters.[63] There are several problematic factors to consider in using SFL to study Hebrew, problems increasingly realized by those who have applied it. All the SFL proponents above have noted that one cannot simply take the categories of SFL, which were developed for English, and use them to describe Hebrew. Bandstra reconceptualizes the metafunctions, Conway introduces appropriate means of appraisal other than simply lexis, and Fuller addresses questions of syntactical configuration. This necessary reconceptualization constitutes one of the promises and challenges of SFL in Hebrew linguistics.

The last category of discussion is arguably the most fervent within recent Hebrew linguistic study, those who work within the cognitive lin-

---

59. One cannot help but notice that, apart from the first, the next three works were all PhD dissertations at McMaster Divinity College, under the primary supervision of Mark J. Boda and secondary supervision of Stanley E. Porter (see below).

60. Tatu, *Qatal//Yiqtol (Yiqtol//Qatal) Verbal Sequence*. Tatu provides an introduction to SFL (see esp. 75–152). Racher, "Interpersonal Sketch," responds to both Bandstra and Tatu on the interpersonal metafunction, one of few major articles pursuing SFL in Hebrew linguistics.

61. Toffelmire, *Discourse and Register Analysis*, 1, 17–46, who notes its recent use in Hebrew studies.

62. Conway, *Judging the Judges*.

63. Fuller, *Discourse Analysis*.

guistic perspective. Cognitive Linguistics is differentiated by Van Valin and LaPolla from the syntactocentric perspective of Chomsky primarily based upon his universal grammar. However, because of its origins and its mentalism, Cognitive Linguistics is arguably to be associated and categorized with Chomskyanism, with its typological orientation and cognitive commitment (see discussion below). However, for the sake of discussion, I will treat Cognitive Linguistics here, as the final perspective regarding Hebrew. Some scholars within biblical studies wish to associate cognitive and functionalist categories as forming what are characterized as Cognitive-Functional frameworks, influenced by the work of Robert Dooley and Stephen Levinsohn, and more of these are discussed under Greek linguistics below.[64] There are two major types of work to discuss under Cognitive Linguistics. The first type is exemplified by those who have drawn upon various theories of conceptual metaphor, whether that includes mental space theory, conceptual blending, or other developments, mostly based upon the work of George Lakoff and Mark Johnson.[65] There is an increasing number of studies pursuing the use of cognitive metaphor. These include Carl Martin Follingstad, who draws upon mental space theory to understand deictic viewpoint in analysis of the Hebrew particle *ki*, Sarah Dille on the mixing of biblical metaphors in a cognitive metaphor context with reference to Lakoff and Johnson's "metaphoric coherence" in Deutero-Isaiah,[66] Albert Kamp on a cognitive linguistic approach to Jonah including conceptual space,[67] Philip King on metaphor, images, and schemas,[68] and Job Jindo on biblical metaphor within the poetic prophecy of Jer 1–24.[69] More general cognitive treatments include a variety of approaches that deal with cognition and how cognition is related to language and text, and so involve such things as cognitive processing. Several studies have recently appeared that utilize Cognitive Linguistics in study of Hebrew. These include Elizabeth Hayes on what she characterizes as the "pragmatics

---

64. Dooley and Levinsohn, *Analyzing Discourse*.

65. Lakoff and Johnson, *Metaphors*.

66. Follingstad, *Deictic Viewpoint*; Dille, *Mixing Metaphors*, 1–20, citing Lakoff and Johnson, *Metaphors*.

67. Kamp, *Inner Worlds*.

68. King, *Surrounded by Bitterness*.

69. Jindo, *Biblical Metaphor Reconsidered*, 25–53.

of perception and cognition" in Jeremiah,[70] Ellen van Wolde on the general nature of cognition and how it applies to interpretation of the Hebrew biblical text,[71] Pierre Van Hecke, who integrates what he calls a functional and cognitive approach to Job 12–14, bringing together these two perspectives in a way that biblical scholars increasingly seem to be doing,[72] Wendy Widder on the semantic field or domain of words for "teach" in Hebrew,[73] and Elizabeth Robar on the verb and the paragraph from a cognitive perspective.[74] Cognitive studies of Hebrew, like cognitive studies in non-biblical linguistics, tend to deal with larger and more abstract categories, as they examine cognitive processing of texts.

The above study has offered an overview of some of the major studies in Hebrew linguistics, especially during the so-called modern linguistic period. This period for Hebrew linguistic study began in the middle of the last century and has increasingly come to focus upon functional and cognitive linguistic perspectives.

New Testament Greek Language Studies

The field of New Testament Greek language studies is not nearly as diverse as the characterization provided by Van Valin and LaPolla of linguistics in general. In fact, one might well argue that the field of Greek linguistics for New Testament studies is relatively underdeveloped by comparison, in some ways even when compared with Hebrew studies. There are several reasons for this. The first is that the field of linguistics is a primary discipline, and it has developed accordingly over the course of the last one-hundred plus years, from its emergence out of the comparative language studies of the nineteenth century by means of the influence of the developing structuralist agenda of Saussure and the Prague School of linguistics. Unlike Hebrew, New Testament Greek linguistics by comparison is a secondary discipline, by which I mean that its primary orientation is not linguistic but linguistic theories are imported from the outside as a means of enhancing description and interpretation. The second is that the historical and chronological relationship just mentioned

---

70. Hayes, *Pragmatics of Perception*, 1–44.
71. van Wolde, *Reframing Biblical Studies*.
72. Van Hecke, *From Linguistics to Hermeneutics*, 21–37.
73. Widder, *"To Teach" in Ancient Israel*.
74. Robar, *Verb*, 1–2.

in relationship to the history of New Testament scholarship to a large extent dictates a particular relationship of the linguistics of the Greek New Testament to linguistics as a general discipline, even with its wide diversity. Many of the major interpretive categories of New Testament study originated before synchronic linguistics had fully developed, and so it has found itself always attempting to establish its legitimacy within the wider field of New Testament interpretation. The third is that traditional grammar has maintained a preternatural grip upon the field of New Testament Greek studies. There is room for abundant speculation on the reasons for this near stranglehold—such as the inherent conservatism of the field of biblical studies, earlier advancements in traditional grammar that became entrenched within the field as a historical discipline, and the production of major reference works that continue to leverage traditional grammar—but regardless of its cause it has had a stultifying effect upon linguistic advancement.

As noted above, non-biblical language study can be divided into the rationalist period of the eighteenth and early nineteenth century, the comparative period of the nineteenth and very early twentieth century, and the modern linguistic period of the twentieth century beginning with Saussure. By contrast, and in comparison with the sketch of Hebrew grammatical study noted above, one might chronicle the development of New Testament Greek language study as the rationalist period up to the late nineteenth century, the comparative period from the late nineteenth century well into the mid twentieth century, and the modern linguistic period from 1961 to the present, although admittedly with a strong continuation of the influence of thought from the earlier periods, both the rationalist and the comparative. At this point in discussion of New Testament Greek, there are two major competing traditions regarding the study of Greek. One tradition continues to emphasize what might best be called forms of traditional grammar, and the other promotes some types of linguistically influenced analysis. Traditional grammar tends to be influenced by the rationalist more than the comparative approach, although comparative linguistics still often enters the discussion, especially when evaluative comments are made about New Testament Greek in relation to other broad or narrow varieties. One of the major trends in some of this work is the acknowledgment of the importance of linguistics and perhaps even the making of an eclectic appeal to some of its descriptive categories, while essentially continuing to function within the traditional grammatical paradigm. The traditional grammatical approach is represented by such characteristics as an emphasis upon written over spoken language and literary over documentary language, the use of traditional categories often derived from the study of Latin, an emphasis upon a regularized form of the language, the use of translation as the medium of study, the imposition of standards of logic upon natural languages, the study of language in light of (or for the sake of) other subjects, and, perhaps most importantly, the isolationist and often historical (diachronic) as opposed to systematic and synchronic examination of language.[75]

Within the framework suggested by Van Valin and LaPolla, we can note that there has been New Testament Greek linguistic research that has fallen into both the syntactocentric and the communication-and-cognition sides of their opposition. In New Testament studies, as in Hebrew study, although even to a much lesser degree, the syntactocentric or Chomskyan approach to linguistics has been relatively insignificant.[76] This includes publications by Reinhard Wonneberger, Daryl D. Schmidt, J. P. Louw, and Micheal Palmer. Wonneberger probably did the most to generate interest in Chomskyan linguistics, although his lasting effect has been minimal. He wrote a major monograph on syntax and exegesis, in which he utilized a form of Chomsky's standard theory to create thirty-seven rules for the syntax of New Testament Greek, as well as publishing a number of articles on generative grammar.[77] The last one so far as I can determine reflects Wonneberger's later concerns with electronic data processing, in which he attempts to unite data processing and generative grammar in Greek syntax.[78] Daryl Schmidt wrote a brief monograph on complementation using Chomsky's extended standard theory including both transformational and lexicalist hypotheses to nominalizations.[79] In this work, Schmidt notes that his work is part of a larger research project on a transformational-generative grammar of Hellenistic Greek—to my knowledge a project that never went beyond

---

75. Porter, "Studying Ancient Languages," 164–66.

76. I do not discuss elementary grammars, some of which have claimed to be linguistically informed.

77. Wonneberger, *Syntax und Exegese*; "Beitrag"; and "Generative Stylistics."

78. Wonneberger, "Greek Syntax."

79. Schmidt, *Hellenistic Greek Grammar*.

local photocopies.[80] Louw utilizes what appears to be his own form of constituent structure analysis that is similar to Chomsky's phrase structure grammar, with the explicit admission that *meaning* is a prerequisite of analysis.[81] Palmer had a predecessor in the work of Robert Funk,[82] who was influenced by American structuralism, in particular the constituent analysis of Leonard Bloomfield as interpreted by Henry Gleason. Palmer drew upon slightly later developments in Chomsky, including not only his lexicalist hypothesis but intermediate levels of syntactic structure, which resulted in x-bar theory, to provide a formalist description of phrase structure in Greek.[83] Since these studies, very little significant work has been done using Chomsky and Chomskyan engendered linguistic theories in description of the Greek of the New Testament. One might well ask why this has been the case. In one sense, the kinds of formalist descriptions that are found in these treatments are well-suited to the limitations of knowledge of an ancient language, in which we have access to the morphosyntactic elements in a more immediate way than we do the semantics. I do not wish to go into a lengthy discussion of such possible reasons, but I will make some tentative suggestions. One reason may be that semantics (however this term is defined and extended to include or encompass pragmatics) is always at play in linguistic description, even if the analysis does not readily concede this. How one identifies syntagmatic units and their constituents and their relationships is often as much semantic as it is syntactic (an argument for dependency over constituency). Another reason is that the functions of language are at least as important as the structures of language, even if they are related to each other (in admittedly varying ways). Theories that do not address the functions of language have less inherent attraction than those that ask questions of function, even if the functions are realized by formal structures. A third reason is that there was perhaps a feeling of insignificance as to what had been accomplished by the previous studies. In other words, there may have been the question of *so what* that could not be answered, whether that was because the semantic or functional or some other questions were not being answered. In any case, there

---

80. Schmidt, *Hellenistic Greek Grammar*, ix, 41.
81. Louw, *Semantics*, 67–89.
82. Funk, *Beginning-Intermediate Grammar*. Cf. McGaughy, "Robert W. Funk."
83. Palmer, *Levels*; cf. Palmer, "How Do We Know."

has been relatively little significant work in the syntactocentric theories applied to New Testament Greek since the work of Palmer.

By contrast, there has been a relative abundance of work within the communication-and-cognition perspective that has spanned the continuum, even if it has been concentrated upon certain types of linguistic theories.[84] I begin with those who are on the cognitive end of the cline and move to the functionalist end. As above, I will concentrate upon monograph-length or similar works. The major examples to note across the spectrum include cognitive linguistic work of various sorts though not all of them grammatical and virtually none of them syntactic, the Construction Grammar/Case Frame Analysis of Paul Danove, the eclecticism of Stephen Levinsohn, and especially a wide range of work in SFL by a variety of scholars.[85] Before I discuss these approaches, I do note that, as in Hebrew language study, there are some works that utilize very rudimentary structuralist linguistic approaches, often eclectic in nature. These include Birger Olsson on the structure and meaning of John's Gospel,[86] Bruce Johanson on 1 Thessalonians,[87] and Kuo-Wei Peng on Romans 12:1—15:1.[88] However, these studies are relatively fewer than the other more explicit models that are being used.

I begin with the cognitive end of the cline. Several scholars have worked within the field of Cognitive Linguistics as a developing area of cognitive science. One of the dominant models has been conceptual metaphor theory, with some of its developments including conceptual

---

84. I will limit my discussion to those who work within New Testament studies, and not address those who work within the field of Translation Studies, such as those primarily associated with SIL (Summer Institute of Linguistics) and related organizations.

85. I focus upon monographs, and do not attempt to describe the journal or chapter literature in any significant way. Role and Reference Grammar has garnered a small amount of recent support, as evidenced in an essay on Greek prohibitions by Michael Aubrey ("Greek Prohibitions"). Role and Reference Grammar is described by Aubrey as a Cognitive Linguistic framework that is a "cousin" of Construction Grammar and positioned between European and West Coast functionalism. He models RRG as being stratal, including nuclear predicate, core predication, and clausal proposition, with a semantic-syntax interface, and the predicate and its argument forming the basic semantic component. It is noteworthy that RRG has no structures beyond the clause and does not include a significant discussion of context—even though Aubrey draws upon context as the decisive factor in his linguistic descriptions.

86. Olsson, *Structure and Meaning*.

87. Johanson, *To All the Brethren*.

88. Peng, *Hate the Evil*.

blending theory, an attempt to expand the range of metaphor by blending various metaphors together into larger conceptual constructs, all within conceptual integration theory.[89] Conceptual metaphor theory contends that all of language is based upon mapping conceptual spheres upon each other, especially more remote upon more familiar, such as the body, etc. This area within Cognitive Linguistics is not directly considered by Van Valin and LaPolla. There have been significant works in conceptual metaphor theory within New Testament studies. These include works by Bonnie Howe on 1 Peter, Beth Stovell on John's Gospel (although she also uses other theories of metaphor, such as SFL), Jennifer McNeel on 1 Thessalonians, Frederick Tappenden on resurrection in Paul, William Robinson on Romans in particular, Erin Heim on Pauline metaphors for adoption, and Gregory Lanier on the use of metaphors in Luke's Christology, among others.[90] Whatever value there may be in these works, what is clear is that they are not really theories of linguistics so much as theories of cognition, arguably very different categories both definitionally and phenomenologically.[91] Related to this area is Relevance Theory, a theory that also does not appear in Van Valin and LaPolla, perhaps because of their focus upon syntax. Relevance theory is a cognitive theory that rejects code theories of language to argue for what is called a "principle of relevance," that is, that "[h]uman cognitive processes . . . are geared to achieving the greatest possible cognitive effect for the smallest possible processing effort."[92] Ernest-August Gutt has applied Relevance Theory to translation,[93] and it has been applied to New Testament studies by Stephen Pattemore, Joseph Fantin, Margaret Sim, and Nelson Morales. Pattemore applies Relevance Theory to the book of Revelation

---

89. The notion of space is fundamental to conceptual integration theory, in which various concepts occupy space and are brought into relation with each other.

90. Howe, *Because You Bear This Name*; Stovell, *Mapping Metaphorical Discourse*; McNeel, *Paul as Infant and Nursing Mother*; Tappenden, *Resurrection*; Robinson, *Metaphor*; Heim, *Adoption*; Lanier, *Old Testament Conceptual Metaphors*, 15–34. Cf. Green and Howe, eds., *Cognitive Linguistic Explorations*.

91. I note that the linguist mentioned above, Anna Wierzbicka, has written on the New Testament, in *What Did Jesus Mean?* This study combines elements of linguistics, psychology, and cognition. Wierzbicka is known for her theory of semantic privatives that cross cultural boundaries.

92. Sperber and Wilson, *Relevance*, vii.

93. Gutt, *Translation and Relevance*.

in both of his volumes.[94] Fantin treats the Greek imperative in one and applies Relevance Theory to the confession "Jesus is Lord" in the other.[95] Sim examines the use of the Greek particles ἵνα and ὅτι in one volume and on a range of topics, especially conditional constructions in the other.[96] Morales uses Relevance Theory to examine how James uses the Old Testament.[97] In one of his two works, Fantin combines Relevance Theory with Neuro-Cognitive Stratificational Linguistics (NCSL), a direct and not-too-different descendant of Stratificational Grammar.[98] As Fantin himself admits, however, it is highly questionable whether Relevance Theory is even a theory of linguistics (being arguably more a theory of communication), and NCSL, despite its stratal view of language and emphasis upon language as comprising systems of relationships into a network, is an attempt to model the way that the brain functions.[99] Cognitive Linguistics holds to two fundamental assumptions—the generalization commitment, with its categorization based upon family resemblances, polysemy, and metaphor (see above), and the cognitive commitment, with its language profiling[100]—that only approximate to grammar, through symbolic relationships (according to Langacker, who attempts such a linkage). Most of the studies above, when they deal with grammar, are studies in pragmatics, not studies in grammar.

Construction grammar, developed primarily by Charles Fillmore and Paul Kay of Stanford University, has been virtually uniquely utilized in New Testament Greek study by Paul Danove in what he calls Case Frame Analysis. I note that Simon Wong also used a very early form of Case Theory first proposed by Fillmore,[101] but this has not led to any subsequent work as it has in the Case Frame Analysis of Danove. In fact, in virtually every monograph that Danove has written, Construction Grammar or Case Frame analysis has played a role, and he continues to

---

94. Pattemore, *Souls under the Altar*; Pattemore, *People of God*.
95. Fantin, *Lord of the Entire World*; Fantin, *Greek Imperative Mood*.
96. Sim, *Marking Thought*; Sim, *Relevant Way to Read*.
97. Morales, *Poor and Rich*.
98. This is based upon the work of Lamb, *Outline*, with some minimal developments. His more recent work is *Pathways*.
99. Fantin, *Greek Imperative Mood*, 333, 334.
100. Evans and Green, *Cognitive Linguistics*, 28–44.
101. Wong, *Classification*.

utilize it in his publications.[102] Case Frame analysis is a descriptive and non-transformational theory that is concerned to describe predicators, that is, words that "license" other phrasal elements called arguments and adjuncts. A Valence Description is the fundamental descriptive mechanism for describing the predicator, displaying such analysis in terms of three strata: syntactic function (e.g., verbal subject, complement, etc.), semantic function (based upon twenty-one thematic roles), and lexical information (realizations by various phrases, such as noun, verb, etc.). The surprise is that more New Testament scholars have not taken up Case Frame analysis, as its descriptive displays are based upon New Testament usage. However, the reasons are probably related to the fact that there are several features of the analysis that are not readily apparent. The predicator is the unit of analysis, but the relationships among the levels of predicators are not made obvious. Predicator is usually associated with the notion of verb, but for Case Frame analysis a predicator is any word that licenses other phrasal elements, and thus there is the potential for embedding and recursion that is not adequately theorized. There is also difficulty with the notion of function, as it is used of both syntax and semantics, and the strata are aligned. More complex syntax is provided by the C function, but that seems to take the Case Frame analysis beyond its comfortable boundaries. Despite his enthusiasm for the approach, Danove appears to be the single major figure utilizing this approach in any kind of ongoing fashion.

The approach of Stephen Levinsohn, followed in most if not all significant respects by Steven Runge, has come to be characterized as cognitive-functional in nature.[103] This labeling probably reflects the fact that Levinsohn explicitly labels his approach as eclectic, and apparently has elements from much of the spectrum of functionalists to cognitivists (although not all these elements are equally easy to see). By this he means exactly what one might imagine—that he draws upon various linguistic theories in his descriptions—to the point where he admittedly draws opposite conclusions from these theories as do others. One of those he specifically mentions is Talmy Givón (listed in a footnote above as one

---

102. Danove, *End of Mark's Story*; *Linguistics and Exegesis*; *Rhetoric*; *Grammatical and Exegetical Study*; and *New Testament Verbs*, among others. I use *New Testament Verbs*, 1–21, for the description provided.

103. Levinsohn, *Discourse Features*, vii–ix; Runge, *Discourse Grammar*, 5–16. As surprising as it may seem, the entire framework is laid out in these few pages by Levinsohn, not much better developed in Runge.

of the individual linguists of significance), who is associated with West Coast Functionalism. He also specifically mentions that his approach is functional in that it attempts to describe the uses of linguistic structures and it is structural in that it describes linguistic structures. In relation to functionalism, Levinsohn notes that he ascribes to the principle that "choice implies meaning," indicating that when authors exercise choice they are also expressing a difference in meaning.[104] Runge, Levinsohn's closest follower, takes a similar approach. He states that his approach is cross-linguistic, stating that he is interested in "how languages tend to operate rather than just focusing on Greek," a tendency seen in much recent discussion of typology, and that his approach is function-based.[105] He then defines this function-based approach as presupposing that "choice implies meaning," that there is a difference between semantic meaning and pragmatic effect, that the system of choice implies default versus marked members often based upon quantity, and, adding a feature not found in Levinsohn, that prominence and contrast capture a fundamental pragmatic implication. The major problem with such an approach—which does not really merit being called an approach—is that it is not a linguistic theory at all but is founded upon a relatively small set of generalizations and assertions without foundation or exemplification. Levinsohn treats a limited number of discourse features, all oriented to information structure. These include constituent order, sentence conjunctions, patterns of reference, backgrounding and highlighting, reporting of conversation, and boundary features. Runge is in fact even more limited in the features of his discourse grammar. After treating conjunction in a chapter in his foundations, he treats forward-pointing devices, information structuring devices, and thematic highlighting devices. One notices that all the elements treated in both of these works are concerned with information structure or the textural dimension. The

---

104. I note that this wording appears to be based upon but is reformulated from the wording "meaning implies choice" by Bazell, *Linguistic Form*, 81, endorsed by numerous linguists (cf. Halliday, IFG1, xiv, in which he states that SFL "is a theory of meaning as choice"). The difference might be that this reflects a bottom-up approach by Levinsohn, in which the language potential is found in forms realized in meanings, whereas the other reflects a top-down approach in which meanings are realized in systemic choices. Both might be true, but they reflect a theoretical difference in linguistic models.

105. Runge, *Discourse Grammar*, xviii. He also states that his approach is not language specific but shows "how humans are wired to process language" (5), using the terminology of Cognitive Linguistics.

linguistic descriptions that Levinsohn as well as Runge provides often result in judgments being made that imply a cognitive framework, for which there is nothing explicit in their approach that lays the foundation for such analysis. This bottom-up approach seems to be fairly wooden in design, although the wide range of exegetical descriptions offered suggests that there are a number of unstated (and perhaps unrecognized or unassimilated) assumptions also at play.

The final linguistic theory is forms of SFL, which has been hugely productive in New Testament Greek study. SFL is defined by Van Valin and LaPolla as the most radical discourse-pragmatic theory (I am not sure how many SFL proponents would describe it this way, but Van Valin and LaPolla are not systemicists). There are a variety of definitions of SFL available, but one of the best summaries of the broad tenets of the theory is found in Margaret Berry's introduction, which I draw upon but supplement here. There are seven important relatively widely accepted notions. The first is that SFL places a high emphasis upon the sociological or communicative aspects of language. A second is that SFL sees language as a form of linguistic behavior rather than a form of knowledge of a language, thus viewing Saussure's langue as the language potential that is realized in parole. The third is that SFL utilizes different matrices for describing language, including clines, ranks, strata, and levels, often reflecting degrees of delicacy. The fourth is that SFL utilizes the notion of text as a semantic unit whose instances are used to verify the various linguistic hypotheses, often through corpus linguistic means (the linking of the two has existed for some time, as seen in Halliday's probabilistic grammar). The fifth is that SFL recognizes the varying features of different languages and differentiates varieties of language according to situational use (the powerful notion of register). The sixth is that SFL emphasizes the function of language in terms of three metafunctions that bisect the levels from context to expression. Seventh and finally, SFL recognizes two axes of system and structure, while emphasizing the system network as the primary means of modeling language.[106] Since SFL was introduced in 1985 to New Testament studies,[107] there have been

---

106. Berry, *Introduction*, 1:22–32; cf. Butler, *Structure and Function*, 1:43–48, whose definition, even after nearly thirty years, is surprisingly similar (emphasizing communication, function, semantics and pragmatics as central, and context, along with raising questions about cognition and typology). Cf. Halliday, IFG1, xiii–xvi, which does not include linguistic systems, though they were added in subsequent editions.

107. See Gotteri and Porter, "Ambiguity."

several significant monographs that draw directly upon it. These include major monographs by Stanley Porter,[108] Jeffrey Reed, Gustavo Martín-Asensio, Stephanie Black, Ray Van Neste, Cynthia Westfall, Matthew Brook O'Donnell, Ivan Kwong, Jae-Hyun Lee, Beth Stovell, Gregory Fewster, Wally Cirafesi, Ronald Peters, Christopher Land, and Bryan Dyer, among others who have published shorter works or who have drawn upon SFL in significant ways. Porter utilized system networks to describe the Greek verbal system in his first book, and followed that with a volume on linguistic analysis of the Greek New Testament with a number of chapters on SFL and a linguistic commentary on the book of Romans using register discourse analysis.[109] Reed provided a summary of Hallidayan SFL organized by metafunction and drew them into discussion of the debate over literary integrity in Philippians.[110] Martín-Asensio examined transitivity in Acts as a means of indicating foregrounding.[111] Black treated conjunctions in Matthew, supplemented by Relevance Theory.[112] Van Neste examined the cohesion of the Pastoral epistles.[113] Westfall utilized a form of SFL discourse analysis to examine the form and meaning of Hebrews.[114] O'Donnell utilized various elements of SFL as a part of his study of corpus linguistics.[115] Kwong examined word order patterns in Luke's Gospel as a means of foregrounding.[116] Lee provided a discourse analysis of Rom 1–8, supplemented by some elements from Robert Longacre's Tagmemics.[117] Stovell discussed metaphor in John's Gospel, in conjunction with conceptual metaphor theory.[118] Fewster drew upon grammatical metaphor as a means of treating creation language in Romans 8.[119] Cirafesi re-visited verbal aspect theory

---

108. I note that Porter in some journal/chapter literature has explored some other linguistic theories, such as several that draw upon Prague School linguistics.

109. Porter, *Verbal Aspect*; *Linguistic Analysis*; and *Letter to the Romans*.

110. Reed, *Discourse Analysis*.

111. Martín-Asensio, *Transitivity-Based Foregrounding*.

112. Black, *Sentence Conjunctions*.

113. Van Neste, *Cohesion and Structure*.

114. Westfall, *Discourse Analysis*.

115. O'Donnell, *Corpus Linguistics*.

116. Kwong, *Word Order*.

117. Lee, *Paul's Gospel*.

118. Stovell, *Mapping Metaphorical Discourse*.

119. Fewster, *Creation Language*.

in Synoptic parallel passages.[120] Peters examined the Greek article in relation to relative pronouns.[121] Land utilized SFL's notions of text and context to examine the integrity of 2 Corinthians.[122] Finally, Dyer drew upon notions of context of situation to explore the situation of Hebrews.[123] There are also other works that could be included within such a list. The several factors that they have in common are their incredible diversity and variety, yet all written within various elements of the SFL framework. Some of them are very broad in presenting a full and robust model of SFL (such as Reed), while others are much more focused in their examination of individual elements (e.g., verbal structure, conjunction, the article). Some treat SFL as a linguistic theory of syntax or semantics, while others conceive of it as a form of discourse analysis (e.g., Westfall, Porter in Romans).[124] Some studies have drawn upon the productive notion of register, a linguistic category to which SFL has given a particular definition, while others hint at ways to examine literature. There have also been studies that have utilized SFL along with other linguistic approaches in an attempt to address questions for which SFL has not seemed to have adequate theoretical potential or power (e.g., Black on conjunctions or Stovell on metaphor).

There may be some other linguistic theories that have made their way into New Testament studies—and no doubt there are within the journals and other secondary literature—but these seem to be the major ones that are operative at this time.

IMPLICATIONS REGARDING LINGUISTIC THEORY IN NEW TESTAMENT STUDY

In light of this discussion, one might well ask what the implications are regarding linguistic theory in Hebrew and New Testament Greek language study. There are several observations that one might make on the basis of the evidence above.[125]

---

120. Cirafesi, *Verbal Aspect*.
121. Peters, *Greek Article*.
122. Land, *Integrity of 2 Corinthians*.
123. Dyer, *Suffering*.
124. The encouragement to treat SFL as a form of discourse analysis is found in IFG1, ix, where Halliday notes that the volume grew out of a small set of lectures for a course in "functional grammar and discourse analysis."
125. Butler (*Structure and Function*) provides a comparison of SFL, Functionalism

The first is that there are many linguistic theories that apparently have not been explored in either Hebrew or New Testament studies. The list provided by Van Valin and LaPolla includes a number even within the communication-and-cognition category. It is possible that some of these theories—if they continue to prove to be robust—might be explored in the future, as we see in some recent work on Role and Reference Grammar. However, there has also been exploration of other earlier models, such as Case Grammar or even Chomskyan linguistics, that has resulted in very little work, even if there had been initial enthusiasm. The question to ask is why it is that some theories seem to attract more attention than others. There seems to be no clear correlation between theoretical complexity and adaptability, as SFL is as complex as any theory—at least so far as its nomenclature is concerned—and this has not prevented it from garnering numerous adapters.

The second observation is that the number of linguistic models that have been adopted in Hebrew or New Testament Greek study is relatively limited. The two major recent ones are various cognitive linguistic models, including conceptual metaphor theory and Relevance Theory and possibly even Role and Reference Grammar, and SFL, alongside some more general structural and functional work, especially in Hebrew study. There appears to be a growing number of explorations of conceptual metaphor within both Hebrew and New Testament Greek studies (note that SBL has published a good number of them), with some of these explorations examining a particular metaphor while others explore the notion of metaphor more broadly. This increased interest is consistent with a more widespread growth in interest in Cognitive Linguistics within the field of linguistics itself and cognitive science as a discipline. Cognitive Linguistics appears to be one of the fastest growing fields of linguistics, especially with its linkage to the wider field of cognitive science and a host of related disciplines on which it is having a major influence. The other model is SFL, although those who are using SFL are often associated with McMaster Divinity College either directly or by influence. This is perplexing, until one realizes that SFL as a linguistic theory has been far more widely utilized, especially in the field of education, in various cultures where there is not a high emphasis upon biblical studies (e.g., Australia, China, etc.), whereas the cognitive sciences are thriving in North America where there still remains vibrant

---

(both Continental and West Coast), and RRG.

study of the New Testament within the church and a more ostensively Christian culture.

The third observation is that the cognitive-functional school represented by Levinsohn seems to lack theoretical or even practical or applied robustness. The theory-developing proponents are relatively limited, and their work, at least as it is evidenced above, is highly conformative. There is some continuing publication of journal and chapter literature that explores various individual studies within this framework, but such studies are rarely the kinds of significant studies that are found in monographs. The two major works that have been published by Levinsohn and Runge are both styled as discourse oriented. Levinsohn's is addressed to informational structure and Runge's to discourse grammar. However, as noted above, the contents of the volumes indicate that the scope of their exploration is relatively limited, being confined to what SFL would label as the textual metafunction, and even that is a fairly narrow construal of the term that excludes some of the major important categories within the metafunction, such as cohesive harmony.

The fourth observation is to examine what it is that SFL provides that has allowed it to develop as robustly as it has. There appear to be several considerations. The first is that the linguistic approach itself is wide and diverse, and it provides plenty of scope for a variety of explorations, as has already been exemplified. A second is that the theory itself is subject to diversity of conception that lends itself to continuing development. For example, SFL is currently divided into at least three major camps, with some smaller ones. These are the Halliday school, the Sydney school, and the Cardiff Grammar. All three of these approaches would generally agree with the description offered above (which is why I offered such a general one) even if they would disagree over such things as the nature and number of the strata (Sydney) or the number of metafunctions (Cardiff) or the ways to draw system networks (formal or functional or both). These areas themselves offer room for further refinement. A third consideration is that SFL attempts to model language through a variety of helpful heuristic means. Several of these have been mentioned above, including system networks, strata that differentiate semantics from the lexicogrammar (note that it is not called syntax, to avoid the syntax versus semantics opposition and to create a pattern of realization and activation between strata), the concept of register, to name just a few. There are even instances of theoretical dispute where SFL is amendable to a variety of positive proposals. For example, SFL purports to be a constituency grammar but its use of constituency has many characteristics of dependency and is compatible with a dependency framework as well. A fourth consideration is that SFL embraces at least in part the Sapir-Whorf hypothesis on linguistic determinism—that one's language affects how one structures the world—and, at least in theory (though clearly not in practice in many instances, where linguistic modeling is highly dependent upon English alone), recognizes the differences among and particularities of various languages, to the point that one must model each language individually, even if one adopts generalized categories such as the metafunctions. For example, one might believe that the metafunctions constitute a type of semantic universal, and so attempt to describe one's chosen language in terms of the metafunctions at the different strata. However, one might well find that the lexicogrammatical features realized for a given metafunction might arguably be different from one language to another (just as there have been differences of this sort even for English within SFL) or that one might even need to posit additional metafunctions depending upon the modeling of that language. A fifth and final consideration is that the contextual dimension of language—noted above as its social or communicative dimension—is more explicitly modeled in SFL than in many other linguistic approaches, some of which do not even consider context. This provides a particularly powerful means of linking text to context, and register and its components are often the means of doing this. The notion of register as a type of language use and register analysis as a means of drawing upon the resources of register study for description of texts, provide a means of extending linguistic analysis well beyond the lexicogrammar and even the semantic stratum so as to place language within its situational context. In New Testament studies, all these features are to be welcomed as tasks to be performed in more robust ways and by more robust methods.

CONCLUSION

This paper has attempted to form a bridge between some linguistic approaches and developments within Hebrew and New Testament Greek studies. I have attempted to place such work within the wider field of linguistic theory to show both the limitations and possibilities for further research. The evidence indicates that there are a variety of ways that one might approach the study of Hebrew or the Greek New Testament. On the one hand, there are many possibilities open to further exploration. On the other, not all theories appear to be equal as some have clearly been more profitable and productive than others. Whereas we wish to encourage the development and use of a variety of linguistic theories, we must also attend to those that offer the most potential for further continuing and productive textual study.

BIBLIOGRAPHY

Andersen, Francis I. *The Hebrew Verbless Clause in the Pentateuch*. JBLMS 14. Nashville: Abingdon, 1970.

———. *The Sentence in Biblical Hebrew*. Janua Linguarum Series Practica 231. The Hague: Mouton, 1974.

Aubrey, Michael. "Greek Prohibitions." In *The Greek Verb Revisited: A Fresh Approach for Biblical Exegesis*, edited by Steven E. Runge and Christopher J. Fresch, 486–538. Bellingham, WA: Lexham, 2016.

Bandstra, Barry. *Genesis 1-11: A Handbook on the Hebrew Text*. Waco, TX: Baylor University Press, 2008.

Bazell, Charles E. *Linguistic Form*. Istanbul: Istanbul Press, 1953.

Berry, Margaret. *Introduction to Systemic Linguistics*. 2 vols. London: Batsford, 1975–1977.

Black, Stephanie L. *Sentence Conjunctions in the Gospel of Matthew: καί, δέ, τότε, γάρ, οὖν and Asyndeton in Narrative Discourse*. JSNTSup 216. SNTG 9. London: Sheffield Academic, 2002.

Butler, Christopher S. *Structure and Function: A Guide to Three Major Structural-Functional Theories*. 2 vols. Amsterdam: Benjamins, 2003.

Cairnie, Andrew. *Syntax: A Generative Introduction*. 2nd ed. Malden, MA: Blackwell, 2006.

Callahan, Scott N. *Modality and the Biblical Hebrew Infinitive Absolute*. Wiesbaden: Harrassowitz, 2010.

Chomsky, Noam. *Aspects of the Theory of Syntax*. Cambridge, MA: MIT Press, 1965.

———. *Lectures on Government and Binding*. Dordrecht: Foris, 1981.

———. *The Minimalist Program*. Cambridge, MA: MIT Press, 1995.

———. *Syntactic Structures*. The Hague: Mouton, 1957.

Cirafesi, Wally V. *Verbal Aspect in Synoptic Parallels: On the Method and Meaning of Divergent Tense-Form Usage in the Synoptic Passion Narratives*. LBS 7. Leiden: Brill, 2013.

Conway, Mary L. *Judging the Judges: A Narrative Appraisal Analysis*. LSAWS 15. University Park, PA: Eisenbrauns, 2020.

Cook, John A. *Time and the Biblical Hebrew Verb: The Expression of Tense, Aspect, and Modality in Biblical Hebrew*. LSAWS 7. Winona Lake, IN: Eisenbrauns, 2012.

Cook, John A., and Robert D. Holmstedt. *Beginning Biblical Hebrew: A Grammar and Illustrated Reader*. Grand Rapids: Baker Academic, 2013.

Croft, William, and D. Alan Cruse. *Cognitive Linguistics*. CTL. Cambridge: Cambridge University Press, 2004.

Dallaire, Hélène M. *The Syntax of Volitives in Biblical Hebrew and Amarna Canaanite Prose*. LSAWS 9. Winona Lake, IN: Eisenbrauns, 2014.
Dallaire, Hélène M., et al., eds. *Where Shall Wisdom Be Found? A Grammatical Tribute to Professor Stephen A. Kaufman*. Winona Lake, IN: Eisenbrauns, 2017.
Danove, Paul L. *The End of Mark's Story: A Methodological Study*. BINS 3. Leiden: Brill, 1993.
———. *Grammatical and Exegetical Study of New Testament Verbs of Transference: A Case Frame Guide to Interpretation and Translation*. LNTS 329. London: T. & T. Clark, 2009.
———. *Linguistics and Exegesis in the Gospel of Mark: Applications of a Case Frame Analysis and Lexicon*. JSNTSup 218. Sheffield: Sheffield Academic, 2001.
———. *New Testament Verbs of Communication: A Case Frame and Exegetical Study*. LNTS 520. London: Bloomsbury, 2015.
———. *The Rhetoric of Characterization of God, Jesus, and Jesus' Disciples in the Gospel of Mark*. JSNTSup 290. London: T&T Clark, 2005.
Dawson, David Allan. *Text-Linguistics and Biblical Hebrew*. JSOTSup 177. Sheffield: JSOT, 1994.
Dempster, Stephen G. Review of *The Designation of the Individual*, by E. J. Revell. *Journal of Hebrew Scriptures* 6 (2006). No pages.
Dik, Simon C. *The Theory of Functional Grammar: Part 1. The Structure of the Clause*, edited by Kees Hengeveld. 2nd and rev. ed. FGS 20. Berlin: de Gruyter, 1997.
Dille, Sarah J. *Mixing Metaphors: God as Mother and Father in Deutero-Isaiah*. JSOTSup 398. London: Continuum, 2004.
Disse, Andreas. *Informationsstruktur im Biblischen Hebräisch: Sprachwissenschaftliche Grundlagen und exegetische Konsequenzen einer Korpusuntersuchung zu den Büchern Deuteronomium, Richter und 2 Könige*. St. Ortillien: EOS Verlag, 1998.
Dooley, Robert A., and Stephen H. Levinsohn. *Analyzing Discourse: A Manual of Basic Concepts*. Dallas: SIL International, 2001.
Droste, Flip G., and John E. Joseph, eds. *Linguistic Theory and Grammatical Description*. Amsterdam: Benjamins, 1991.
Dyer, Bryan R. *Suffering in the Face of Death: The Epistle to the Hebrews and its Context of Situation*. LNTS 568. London: Bloomsbury, 2017.
Dyk, Janet W. *Participles in Context: A Computer-Assisted Study of Old Testament Hebrew*. Amsterdam: VU University Press, 1994.
Endo, Yoshinobu. *The Verbal System of Classical Hebrew in the Joseph Story: An Approach from Discourse Analysis*. Assen: Van Gorcum, 1996.
Eskhult, Mats. *Studies in Verbal Aspect and Narrative Technique in Biblical Hebrew Prose*. Stockholm: Almqvist & Wiksell, 1990.
Evans, Vyvyan, and Melanie Green. *Cognitive Linguistics: An Introduction*. Edinburgh: University of Edinburgh Press, 2006.
Exter Blokland, A. François den. *In Search of Text Syntax: Towards a Syntactic Text-Segmentation Model for Biblical Hebrew*. Amsterdam: VU Uitgeverij, 1995.
Fantin, Joseph D. *The Greek Imperative Mood in the New Testament: A Cognitive and Communicative Approach*. SBG 12. New York: Peter Lang, 2010.
———. *The Lord of the Entire World: Lord Jesus, a Challenge to Lord Caesar?* NTM 31. Sheffield: Sheffield Phoenix, 2011.
Fewster, Gregory P. *Creation Language in Romans 8: A Study in Monosemy*. LBS 8. Leiden: Brill, 2013.

Follingstad, Carl Martin. *Deictic Viewpoint in Biblical Hebrew Text: A Syntactic and Paradigmatic Analysis of the Particle Ki*. Dallas: SIL International, 2001.

Fuller, David J. *A Discourse Analysis of Habakkuk: The Earth Will Be Filled with the Knowledge of the Glory of YHWH*. SSN 72. Leiden: Brill, 2019.

Funk, Robert W. *A Beginning-Intermediate Grammar of Hellenistic Greek*. 3rd ed. 1973. Reprint, Sonoma, CA: Polebridge, 2013.

Goldfajn, Tal. *Word Order and Time in Biblical Hebrew Narrative*. Oxford: Clarendon, 1998.

Gotteri, Nigel J. C., and Stanley E. Porter. "Ambiguity, Vagueness and the Working Systemic Linguist." *Sheffield Working Papers in Language and Linguistics* 2 (1985) 105–18.

Green, Joel B., and Bonnie Howe, eds. *Cognitive Linguistic Explorations in Biblical Studies*. Berlin: de Gruyter, 2014.

Gross, Walter. *Die Pendenskonstruktion im Biblischen Hebräisch*. Studien zum althebräischen Satz I. Münchener Universitätsschriften AT 27. St. Ottilien: EOS Verlag, 1987.

———. *Die Satzteilfolge im Verbalsatz alttestamentlicher Prosa: Untersucht an den Büchern Dtn, Ri und 2Kön*. FAT 17. Tübingen: Mohr Siebeck, 1996.

———. *Doppelt besetztes Vorfeld: Syntaktische, pragmatische und übersetzungstechnische Studien zum althebräischen Verbalsatz*. Berlin: de Gruyter, 2001.

Gutt, Ernst-August. *Translation and Relevance: Cognition and Context*. Manchester: St. Jerome, 2010.

Hacken, Pius ten. *Chomskyan Linguistics and its Competitors*. London: Equinox, 2007.

Halliday, M. A. K. *An Introduction to Functional Grammar*. London: Arnold, 1985. (IFG1)

Hayes, Elizabeth R. *The Pragmatics of Perception and Cognition in MT Jeremiah 1:1–6:30: A Cognitive Linguistics Approach*. BZAW 380. Berlin: de Gruyter, 2008.

Heim, Erin M. *Adoption in Galatians and Romans: Contemporary Metaphor Theories and the Pauline HUIOTHESIA Metaphors*. Leiden: Brill, 2017.

Heller, Roy L. *Narrative Structure and Discourse Constellations: An Analysis of Clause Function in Biblical Hebrew Prose*. HSS 55. Winona Lake, IN: Eisenbrauns, 2004.

Hoftijzer, Jacob A. *The Function and Use of the Imperfect Forms with Nun-paragogicum in Classical Hebrew*. SSN 21. Assen: Van Gorcum, 1973.

Holmstedt, Robert D. *The Relative Clause in Biblical Hebrew*. University Park: Pennsylvania State University Press, 2016.

———. "The Relative Clause in Biblical Hebrew: A Linguistic Analysis." PhD diss., University of Wisconsin–Madison, 2002.

———. *Ruth: A Handbook on the Hebrew Text*. Waco, TX: Baylor University Press, 2010.

Holmstedt, Robert D., and John Screnock. *Esther: A Handbook on the Hebrew Text*. Waco, TX: Baylor University Press, 2015.

Howe, Bonnie. *Because You Bear This Name: Conceptual Metaphor and the Moral Meaning of 1 Peter*. BINS 81. Leiden: Brill, 2008.

Jenni, Ernst. *Die hebräischen Präpositionen*. 3 vols. Stuttgart: Kohlhammer, 1992–1999.

Jindo, Job Y. *Biblical Metaphor Reconsidered: A Cognitive Approach to Poetic Prophecy in Jeremiah 1–24*. HSM 64. Cambridge, MA: Harvard University Press, 2010.

Johanson, Bruce C. *To All the Brethren: A Text-Linguistic and Rhetorical Approach to I Thessalonians*. ConBNT 16. Stockholm: Almqvist & Wiksell, 1987.

Joosten, Jan. *The Verbal System of Biblical Hebrew: A New Synthesis Elaborated on the Basis of Classical Prose*. Jerusalem: Simor, 2012.
Kamp, Albert. *Inner Worlds: A Cognitive Linguistic Approach to the Book of Jonah*. Translated by David Orton. Leiden: Brill, 2004.
Kautzsch, E. *Gesenius' Hebrew Grammar*, edited by A. E. Cowley. 2nd ed. Oxford: Clarendon, 1910.
Khan, Geoffrey. *Studies in Semitic Syntax*. London Oriental Series 38. Oxford: Oxford University Press, 1988.
King, Phil. *Surrounded by Bitterness: Images, Schemas and Metaphors for Conceptualizing Distress in Classical Hebrew*. Eugene, OR: Wipf and Stock, 2012.
Kustár, Péter. *Aspekt im Hebräischen*. Basel: Reinhardt, 1972.
Kwong, Ivan Shin Chung. *The Word Order of the Gospel of Luke*. LNTS 298. London: T. & T. Clark, 2006.
Lakoff, George, and Mark Johnson. *Metaphors We Live by*. Chicago: University of Chicago Press, 1980.
Lamb, Sydney. *Outline of Stratificational Grammar*. Washington, DC: Georgetown University Press, 1966.
———. *Pathways of the Brain: The Neurocognitive Basis of Language*. Amsterdam: Benjamins, 1999.
Lambrecht, Knud. *Information Structure and Sentence Form: Topic, Focus, and the Mental Representations of Discourse Referents*. New York: Cambridge University Press, 1994.
Land, Christopher D. *The Integrity of 2 Corinthians and Paul's Aggravating Absence*. NTM 36. Sheffield: Sheffield Phoenix, 2015.
Langacker, Ronald W. *Cognitive Grammar*. Oxford: Oxford University Press, 2008.
Lanier, Gregory R. *Old Testament Conceptual Metaphors and the Christology of Luke's Gospels*. London: T. & T. Clark, 2018.
Lee, Jae Hyun. *Paul's Gospel in Romans: A Discourse Analysis of Rom 1:16—8:39*. LBS 3. Leiden: Brill, 2010.
Levinsohn, Stephen H. *Discourse Features of New Testament Greek: A Coursebook on the Information Structure of New Testament Greek*. 2nd ed. Dallas: SIL International, 2000.
Longacre, Robert E. *The Grammar of Discourse*. New York: Plenum, 1983. 2nd ed., 1996.
———. *Joseph: A Story of Divine Providence: A Text Theoretical and Textlinguistic Analysis of Genesis 37 and 39-48*. Winona Lake, IN: Eisenbrauns, 1989. 2nd ed., 2003.
Louw, J. P. *Semantics of New Testament Greek*. Philadelphia: Fortress, 1982.
Lunn, Nicholas. *Word-Order Variation in Biblical Hebrew Poetry: Differentiating Pragmatics and Poetics*. Paternoster Biblical Manuscripts. Milton Keynes: Paternoster, 2006.
Mann, William C., and Sandra A. Thompson. "Rhetorical Structure Theory: Towards a Functional Theory of Text Organization." *Text* 8 (1988) 243–81.
Martín-Asensio, Gustavo. *Transitivity-Based Foregrounding in the Acts of the Apostles: A Functional-Grammatical Approach to the Lukan Perspective*. JSNTSup 202. Sheffield: Sheffield Academic, 2000.
McGaughy, Lane C. "Robert W. Funk and the Evolution of New Testament Greek Grammar." In *Evaluating the Legacy of Robert W. Funk: Reforming the Scholarly Model*, edited by Andrew D. Scrimgeour, 27–34. Atlanta: SBL, 2018.

McNeel, Jennifer. *Paul as Infant and Nursing Mother: Metaphor, Rhetoric, and Identity in 1 Thessalonians 2:5-8*. Atlanta: SBL, 2014.

Merwe, C. H. J. van der. "An Overview of Hebrew Narrative Syntax." In *Narrative Syntax and the Hebrew Bible: Papers of the Tilburg Conference 1996*, edited by Ellen van Wolde, 1–20. Leiden: Brill, 1997.

———. "An Overview of Recent Developments in the Description of Biblical Hebrew Relevant to Bible Translation." AcTSup 2 (2002) 228–45.

———. "A Short Survey of Major Contributions to the Grammatical Description of Old Hebrew since 1800 AD." *JNSL* 13 (1987) 161–90.

———. "Some Recent Trends in Biblical Hebrew Linguistics: A Few Pointers towards a More Comprehensive Model of Language Use." *HS* 44 (2003) 7–24.

Merwe, C. H. J. van der, et al. *A Biblical Hebrew Reference Grammar*. 2nd ed. London: Bloomsbury, 2017.

Michel, Andreas. *Theologie aus der Peripherie: Die gespaltene Koordination im Biblischen Hebräisch*. BZAW 257. Berlin: de Gruyter, 1997.

Miller, Cynthia L. *The Representation of Speech in Biblical Hebrew Narrative: A Linguistic Analysis*. HSM 55. Atlanta: Scholars, 1996. 2nd ed., Winona Lake, IN: Eisenbrauns, 2003.

Miller, Cynthia L., ed. *The Hebrew Verbless Clause in Biblical Hebrew: Linguistic Approaches*. LSAWS 1. Winona Lake, IN: Eisenbrauns, 1999.

Morales, Nelson. R. *Poor and Rich in James: A Relevance Theory Approach to James's Use of the Old Testament*. University Park, PA: Eisenbrauns, 2018.

Moshavi, Adina. *Word Order in the Biblical Hebrew Finite Clause*. LSAWS 4. Winona Lake, IN: Eisenbrauns, 2010.

Muraoka, Takamitsu. *Emphatic Words and Structures in Biblical Hebrew*. Jerusalem: Magnes, 1985.

Niccacci, Alviero. *The Syntax of the Verb in Classical Hebrew Prose*. Translated by Wilfred G. E. Watson. JSOTSup 86. Sheffield: JSOT, 1990.

O'Donnell, Matthew Brook. *Corpus Linguistics and the Greek of the New Testament*. NTM 6. Sheffield: Sheffield Phoenix, 2005.

Olsson, Birger. *Structure and Meaning in the Fourth Gospel: A Text-Linguistic Analysis of John 2:1–11 and 4:1–42*. ConBNT 6. Lund: Gleerup, 1974.

Palmer, Micheal W. "How Do We Know a Phrase Is a Phrase? A Plea for Procedural Clarity in the Application of Linguistics to Biblical Greek." In *Biblical Greek Language and Linguistics: Open Questions in Current Research*, edited by Stanley E. Porter and D. A. Carson, 152–86. JSNTSup 80. Sheffield: JSOT, 1993.

———. *Levels of Constituent Structure in New Testament Greek*. SBG 4. New York: Peter Lang, 1995.

Pattemore, Stephen. *The People of God in the Apocalypse: Discourse, Structure and Exegesis*. SNTSMS 128. Cambridge: Cambridge University Press, 2004.

———. *Souls under the Altar: Relevance Theory and the Discourse Structure of Revelation*. New York: UBS, 2003.

Peng, Kuo-Wei. *Hate the Evil, Hold Fast to the Good: Structuring Romans 12:1—15:1*. LNTS 300. London: T. & T. Clark, 2006.

Peters, Ronald D. *The Greek Article: A Functional Grammar of ὁ-items in the Greek New Testament with Special Emphasis on the Greek Article*. LBS 9. Leiden: Brill, 2014.

Porter, Stanley E. *The Letter to the Romans: A Linguistic and Literary Commentary*. NTM 37. Sheffield: Sheffield Phoenix, 2016.

———. *Linguistic Analysis of the Greek New Testament: Studies in Tools, Methods, and Practice*. Grand Rapids: Baker Academic, 2016.

———. "Studying Ancient Languages from a Modern Linguistic Perspective: Essential Terms and Terminology." *FN* 2 (1989) 147–72.

———. *Verbal Aspect in the Greek of the New Testament, with Reference to Tense and Mood*. SBG 1. New York: Peter Lang, 1989.

Racher, Eric T. "An Interpersonal Sketch of the Biblical Hebrew Clause." *Functional Linguistics* 4 (2017) 1–41.

Reed, Jeffrey T. *A Discourse Analysis of Philippians: Method and Rhetoric in the Debate over Literary Integrity*. JSNTSup 100. Sheffield: Sheffield Academic, 1997.

Regt, L. J. de. *Participants in Old Testament Texts and the Translator: Reference Devices and Their Rhetorical Impact*. SSN 39. Assen: Van Gorcum, 1999.

Revell, E. J. *The Designation of the Individual: Expressive Usage in Biblical Narrative*. CBET 14. Kampen: Kok Pharos, 1996.

Richter, Wolfgang. *Grundlagen einer althebräischen Grammatik*. 3 vols. Münchener Universitätsschriften Arbeiten zu Text und Sprache im Alten Testament 8, 10, 13. St. Ottilien: EOS Verlag, 1978–1980.

———. *Untersuchungen zur Valenz althebräischer Verben*. 2 vols. St. Ottilien: EOS Verlag, 1985–1986.

Robar, Elizabeth. *The Verb and the Paragraph in Biblical Hebrew: A Cognitive-Linguistic Approach*. Studies in Semitic Language and Linguistics 78. Leiden: Brill, 2015.

Robinson, William E. W. *Metaphor, Morality, and the Spirit in Romans 8:1–17*. Atlanta: SBL, 2016.

Rosenbaum, Michael. *Word-Order Variation in Isaiah 40–55: A Functional Perspective*. SSN 35. Assen: Van Gorcum 1997.

Rundgren, Frithiof. *Das althebräische Verbum: Abriss der Aspektlehre*. Stockholm: Almqvist & Wicksell, 1961.

Runge, Steven E. *Discourse Grammar of the Greek New Testament: A Practical Introduction for Teaching and Exegesis*. Peabody, MA: Hendrickson, 2010.

Schmidt, Daryl Dean. *Hellenistic Greek Grammar and Noam Chomsky*. SBLDS 62. Chico, CA: Scholars, 1981.

Shimasaki, Katsuomi. *Focus Structure in Biblical Hebrew: A Study of Word Order and Information Structure*. Bethesda, MD: CDL, 2002.

Sim, Margaret G. *Marking Thought and Talk in New Testament Greek: New Light from Linguistics on the Particles ἵνα and ὅτι*. Eugene, OR: Pickwick, 2010.

———. *A Relevant Way to Read: A New Approach to Exegesis and Communication*. Eugene, OR: Pickwick, 2016.

Sperber, Dan, and Deirdre Wilson. *Relevance: Communication and Cognition*. 2nd ed. Oxford: Blackwell, 1995.

Stovell, Beth M. *Mapping Metaphorical Discourse in the Fourth Gospel: John's Eternal King*. LBS 5. Leiden: Brill, 2012.

Talstra, Eep. *2 Kön. 3: Etüden zur Textgrammatik*. Amsterdam: Free University Press, 1983.

Tappenden, Frederick S. *Resurrection in Paul: Cognition, Metaphor, and Transformation*. Atlanta: SBL, 2016.

Tatu, Silviu. *The Qatal//Yiqtol (Yiqtol//Qatal) Verbal Sequence in Semitic Couplets: A Case Study in Systemic Functional Grammar with Applications on the Hebrew Psalter and Ugaritic Poetry*. Piscataway, NJ: Gorgias, 2008.

Tene, David, and James Barr. "Hebrew Linguistic Literature." In *Encyclopedia Judaica*, edited by Cecil Roth, 16:1352–1401. 26 vols. Jerusalem: Keter, 1971.

Toffelmire, Colin M. *A Discourse and Register Analysis of the Prophetic Book of Joel*. SSN 66. Leiden: Brill, 2016.

Van Hecke, Pierre. *From Linguistics to Hermeneutics: A Functional and Cognitive Approach to Job 12–14*. SSN 25. Leiden: Brill, 2011.

Van Neste, Ray. *Cohesion and Structure in the Pastoral Epistles*. JSNTSup 280. London: T. & T. Clark, 2004.

Van Valin, Robert D., Jr., and Randy J. Lapolla. *Syntax: Structure, Meaning and Function*. CTL. Cambridge: Cambridge University Press, 1997.

Waltke, Bruce K., and M. O'Connor. *An Introduction to Biblical Hebrew Syntax*. Winona Lake, IN: Eisenbrauns, 1990.

Weinrich, Harald. *Tempus: Besprochene und erzählte Welt*. 2nd ed. Stuttgart: Kohlhammer, 1971.

Westfall, Cynthia Long. *A Discourse Analysis of the Letter to the Hebrews: The Relationship between Form and Meaning*. LNTS 297. London: T. & T. Clark, 2005.

Widder, Wendy. *"To Teach" in Ancient Israel: A Cognitive Linguistic Study of a Biblical Hebrew Lexical Set*. BZAW 456. Berlin: de Gruyter, 2014.

Wierzbicka, Anna. *What Did Jesus Mean? Explaining the Sermon on the Mount and the Parables in Simple and Universal Human Concepts*. Oxford: Oxford University Press, 2001.

Winther-Nielsen, N. *A Functional Discourse Grammar of Joshua: A Computer-Assisted Rhetorical Structure Analysis*. Stockholm: Almqvist & Wiksell, 1995.

Wolde, Ellen van. *Reframing Biblical Studies: When Language and Text Meet Culture, Cognition, and Context*. Winona Lake, IN: Eisenbrauns, 2009.

Wolde, Ellen van, ed. *Narrative Syntax and the Hebrew Bible: Papers of the Tilburg Conference 1996*. Leiden: Brill, 1997.

Wong, Simon S. M. *A Classification of Semantic Case-Relations in the Pauline Epistles*. SBG 9. New York: Peter Lang, 1997.

Wonneberger, Reinhard. "Der Beitrag der generativen Syntax zur Exegese: Ein Beispiel (2.Kor 5,2f) und neun Thesen." *Bijdragen* 36 (1975) 312–17.

———. "Generative Stylistics: An Algorithmic Approach to Stylistic and Source Data Retrieval Problems based on Generative Syntax." In *Bedeutung, Sprechakte und Texte: Akten des 13*, edited by Marc Velde and Willy Vandeweghe, 389–99. Linguistischen Kolloquiums 2. Tübingen: Niemeyer, 1979.

———. "Greek Syntax: A New Approach." *Literary and Linguistic Computing* 2 (1986) 71–79.

———. *Syntax und Exegese: Eine generative Theorie der griechischen Syntax und ihr Beitrag zur Auslegung des Neuen Testaments, dargestellt an 2. Korinther 5.2 und Römer 3.21–26*. BBET 13. Frankfurt am Main: Peter Lang, 1979.

Zevit, Ziony. *The Anterior Construction in Classical Hebrew*. Atlanta: Scholars, 1998.

2

A Systemic Account of Biblical Hebrew Prepositions
Circumstantial Particles from a Monosemic Perspective in Habakkuk

DAVID J. FULLER

INTRODUCTION

MY NOW PUBLISHED DOCTORAL dissertation sought to perform a reasonably rigorous discourse analysis of the book of Habakkuk.[1] Even though my corpus was only three chapters, I found myself having to be increasingly selective in the data I examined due to the sheer mass of information that presented itself whenever I attempted to comprehensively survey any given linguistic category. One of the key concepts from Functional Grammar that I simply had to omit entirely from my analysis was the circumstantial part of the clause within the ideational metafunction. While circumstantials (usually realized by an adverbial group or prepositional phrase) are clearly more marginal to the core meaning of the clause than are the subject and predicate, they nonetheless provide important details about what is taking place.

Aside from the pressing need to focus only on core data points, one of the other reasons I left circumstantials out of my dissertation is that

1. Fuller, "Enigmatic Enemies"; *Discourse Analysis of Habakkuk*.

their information is difficult to make use of at the discourse level. While substantial precedent exists demonstrating the value and applicability of the statistical tabulation of clausal subjects and process types (for example) throughout various parts of a discourse, it is less obvious how to make use of circumstantials at the discourse level, given that by their nature the type of meaning they contribute is more or less tied to the predicate of an individual clause. It is not surprising, then, that relatively little has been done on circumstantials proper in previous examples of linguistic discourse analysis in biblical studies. In Jeffrey Reed's 1997 monograph on Philippians, he simply lists percentages for the type of circumstantials found throughout the letter and makes some brief remarks on how Paul uses each category, an exercise that occupies a mere three pages.[2] A different approach with similarly minimal results is found in Toffelmire's monograph on Joel, in which he simply lists recurring circumstantials in his description of participant sets and draws from them occasionally in his descriptions of the ideational arena.[3]

In a previous paper,[4] I experimented with three different ways of organizing and drawing conclusions from circumstantials at the discourse level: (1) grouping circumstantials by clausal subject; (2) grouping circumstantials of the same category of usage (such as location or cause); and (3) comparing the use of circumstantials in one pericope of a discourse to another. After applying these lenses in a preliminary way to Habakkuk, I tentatively concluded that grouping circumstantials by clausal subject had the most to offer, as it allowed for the discovery of some insights regarding the characterization of different participants throughout the book. However, as I began to examine the specific resources from the Hebrew language used to realize these circumstantials, I realized that I had been putting the cart before the horse: ideally, I should be beginning with categories of meaning based on the Hebrew forms themselves, rather than just imposing Halliday's categories of meaning, as helpful as they are.

Therefore, this essay undertakes some necessary groundwork by working out some of the questions involved in formulating a Hebrew-based account of circumstantials, using Habakkuk as a test case. When I surveyed the complete picture of the linguistic resources used to realize

2. Reed, *Discourse Analysis*, 343–46.
3. See, e.g., Toffelmire, *Discourse and Register Analysis*, 105–6.
4. Fuller, "Clausal Circumstantials."

circumstantials in Habakkuk, I found that aside from certain adverbs, and the occasional noun or participle, the most common devices used were prepositions. This being the case, it is sensible to isolate this usage of prepositions to better understand their precise contribution of meaning to the surrounding context. As anyone with any level of familiarity with Biblical Hebrew knows, Hebrew prepositions are translated in notoriously diverse ways in English. This difficulty of multiple types of potential *meanings* for each preposition presents itself as one of the initial challenges for such a project. Above and beyond each preposition in isolation, a systemic-functional approach would also want to view the entirety of Hebrew prepositions as a group, understanding them in terms of a network of oppositional choices.

Therefore, the present study will proceed as follows. After an overview of the current state of research on prepositions within Hebrew grammar, it will introduce some foundational assumptions: monosemy and systemic organization. The body of the analysis will (1) survey the usage of certain prepositions in Habakkuk (specifically בְּ, כְּ, לְ, מִן, אֶל, and עַל) through the lens of Halliday's categories of meaning, (2) note the different forms used for each category of meaning, (3) inductively attempt to ascertain intrinsic shades of meaning for the different forms, and (4) develop a network of oppositions that organize the forms.

LITERATURE REVIEW

Traditional Philology

Within Hebrew Bible scholarship, two contrasting schools of thought can be identified regarding the treatment of prepositions: traditional-philological and synchronic. While the present study obviously follows the latter, it is nonetheless worthwhile to survey traditional approaches (with an eye towards the six prepositions in focus here), as they still represent a means of grappling with the data in all its bulk and difficulty.

The traditional-philological school of thought encompasses (and can draw from) several streams of inquiry, including both medieval Jewish grammars and modern comparative Semitics. A recurring conclusion of work performed within this idiom is that the various prefixed prepositions are largely overlapping in meaning and can often be substituted for one another for reasons other than intrinsic meaning.

An appropriate place to start is with Sarna's 1959 article titled "The Interchange of the Prepositions *Beth* and *Min* in Biblical Hebrew."[5] He begins with the observation that, because the equivalents of the -בְּ preposition in Akkadian, Ugaritic, Aramaic, and Old South Arabic can mean "from" as well as "in," Hebrew likely exhibits this feature as well. He provides three types of examples: (1) the two prepositions being used in the same sense with an identical verb;[6] (2) two places where the Masoretic *qere* reading replaces the *kethib*'s בְּ with a מִן (Josh 3:16; 2 Kgs 23:33); and (3) parallel passages in Samuel–Kings, Chronicles, and Psalms where two synoptic clauses exhibit different prepositions, but with the same meaning.[7] He closes with three contested passages in Job where a בְּ only makes sense when rendered as "from."[8]

In 1970, William Chomsky took this a step further and posited that בְּ, מִן, and also לְ are often "interchangeable."[9] While he mostly supported this using lists of verses compiled by medieval grammarians,[10] he also cites Cyrus Gordon's work on the Ugaritic prepositions.[11] While this evidence is helpful, his conclusion may leave some enterprising exegetes bewildered when he recommends simply replacing a troublesome preposition with one that seems to fit better in difficult cases.

Dahood's short note on בְּ in Isa 1:22 in 1978 added a further level of difficulty.[12] Dahood concludes on comparative-historical grounds that "wine weakened with water" (סָבְאֵךְ מָהוּל בַּמָּיִם) could not possibly be correct as a curse formula due to the prevalence of this practice. Consequently, he adopts a comparative function for the preposition

---

5. Sarna, "Interchange."

6. Sarna, "Interchange," 312. See Lev 7:17 (וְהַנּוֹתָר בַּבָּשָׂר) and 8:32 (וְהַנּוֹתָר מִבְּשַׂר), both rendered by JPS as "But/and that which remaineth of the flesh . . ."

7. Sarna, "Interchange," 312. Compare 1 Chr 14:3 (וַיִּקַּח דָּוִיד עוֹד נָשִׁים בִּירוּשָׁלָֽםִ) "And David took more wives at Jerusalem" (JPS) with 2 Sam 5:13 (וַיִּקַּח דָּוִד עוֹד פִּלַגְשִׁים וְנָשִׁים מִירוּשָׁלַםִ) "And David took him more concubines and wives out of Jerusalem" (JPS). Sarna's position could be challenged here, as the Chronicler could well have decided to utilize the בְּ to mitigate the potentially pejorative implications of the מִן that he was taking women *away from* Jerusalem.

8. Sarna, "Interchange," 313–16. He covers Job 4:21; 5:21; and 20:20.

9. Chomsky, "Ambiguity," 86–89 (86).

10. Chomsky, "Ambiguity," 88. As an example of this kind of evidence, he points to Kimḥi, who thought that the בְּ in Ps 33:1 (רַנְּנוּ צַדִּיקִים בַּיהוָה) "Rejoice in the Lord, O ye righteous" (JPS) was a replacement for the לְ that was "actually" intended by the author.

11. Gordon, *Ugaritic Grammar*.

12. Dahood, "'Weaker than Water.'"

(which he translates as "wine weaker than water") and surmises that the writer chose not to use the more obvious מִן in order to evade having several occurrences of מִן in succession (as a result of prefixing the preposition to מַיִם "water").

In the same year, Futato issued a word of caution to the entire enterprise by reviewing Pardee's then recent (1975) study on Ugaritic prepositions and considering its significance for Hebrew.[13] Following James Barr, Pardee had taken stock afresh of Ugaritic prepositions by using the category of position rather than direction and arguing for semantic overlap rather than interchangeability, the result being a view of prepositions in which each one had a clear and distinct, albeit generalized meaning.[14] Futato applied Pardee's guiding principles to Dahood's list of claimed examples for places in the Psalter where the בְּ means "from,"[15] and concluded that significantly fewer uses of בְּ than what Dahood claimed require the rendering "from."[16]

The conversation again advanced significantly in 1994 with an article by Althann in the *Journal of Northwest Semitic Languages*.[17] Again reviewing the evidence of overlap between בְּ and מִן, Althann suggests, following the later diachronic development of Phoenician, that Hebrew did not originally have the מִן preposition, and so בְּ performed its functions until it was eventually introduced. He then reviews Pardee's position on Ugaritic prepositions (see above) and suggests that the fundamental debate is about whether each preposition has a single fundamental sense. Finally, he appraises the then-available portions of Ernst Jenni's multivolume German work on Hebrew prepositions and expresses disagreement with his synchronic approach.[18] His conclusion asserts that

13. Futato, "Preposition."

14. Pardee, "Preposition." Therefore, in Ugaritic, "*b* means position within the confines of; *l* means position at, pertaining to or belonging to; *'m* means along with and position within; *'l* means 'above' or position at or near the top" (Futato, "Preposition," 71).

15. Futato does not provide page numbers, but simply notes that all his examples came from Dahood, *Psalms III*.

16. Futato, "Preposition," 76. A typical example is Ps 60:8 (אֱלֹהִים דִּבֶּר בְּקָדְשׁוֹ), which Dahood rendered as "God spoke from his sanctuary" (cf. JPS "God spoke in his holiness"). Futato simply reiterates his point that, since the core meaning of בְּ is "confines within which," בְּ having range of usage that encompasses both "from" and "at" is not surprising, but that in this case the former rendering is clearly more contextually appropriate than the latter.

17. Althann, "Approaches."

18. Jenni, *Die hebräischen Präpositionen*.

due to the relatively small amount of available Biblical Hebrew, comparison with other cognate languages is necessary for proper understanding.

This traditional position exemplified above was reiterated by Haber in the journal *Maarav* in 2009,[19] in an article that draws from both medieval grammars and comparative Semitics to argue for both the late addition of מִן and consonantal interchange. Significantly, Haber notes (as will be documented below), that virtually all modern Biblical Hebrew grammars eschew this line of research entirely.

A final significant work on prepositions from a traditional perspective is the 2014 University of Chicago dissertation of Hardy, which examines the diachronic development of Hebrew prepositions with grammaticalization theory, drawing from not only cognate languages but also cross-linguistic typology.[20] Because he only deals with complex prepositions with roots traceable to other words, his conclusions cannot be brought into conversation with the focus area of the present study.[21]

Synchronic Approaches

Some reference works are relatively unhelpful for clarifying the relationships among Hebrew prepositions. Most of the lexica simply list numerous categories of meaning, as do some of the reference grammars, such as Arnold and Choi.[22] The short treatment of Gesenius is more interested in diachronic and morphological notes than meaning.[23] Joüon and Muraoka represent a movement towards a synchronic approach. They write, "Most prepositions originally had a *local*—whether spatial or temporal—meaning; then they were used to express logical relationships,"[24] then proceed to provide succinct explanations for each of the major monoconsonantal prepositions. The only notable conclu-

---

19. Haber, "Significance."
20. Hardy, "Diachronic Development."
21. Also comparable is the festschrift contribution of Bompiani, "Prepositions," who reiterates much of the same diachronic and comparative-Semitic perspective covered above and provides a short overview of the major uses of seventeen of the most common Biblical Hebrew prepositions. Aside from the resources already surveyed here, he makes notable use of Blau, *Phonology and Morphology*, and Jenni, "Preposition."
22. Arnold and Choi, *Guide*, 95–126.
23. Kautzsch, *Gesenius' Hebrew Grammar*, 297–300.
24. Joüon and Muraoka, *Grammar*, 456.

sion they provide is that אֶל means "toward" (or "motion *towards*")[25] and לְ means "to," the latter being less precise than the former as it can involve "neither direction nor motion."[26]

The next significant discussion of prepositions is in Waltke and O'Connor, who begin by listing three different ways of looking at prepositions: (1) nominal: "prepositions are taken as nouns in the adverbial accusative, governing nouns in the genitive";[27] (2) as particles, some of which have complex morphology; and (3) the semantic perspective, which they illustrate with the question, "What is the meaning of the relation between the noun that the preposition governs and the clause in which the prepositional phrase occurs?"[28] Adopting the semantic perspective, Waltke and O'Connor exposit their own framework by first pointing to Pardee's work on Ugaritic prepositions, namely, that the meaning of a usage of a preposition "is always governed by the verb (or predicate) of the clause and, more broadly, by the perspective from which an action is viewed."[29] They then state,

> Most prepositions have a spatial sense, which it is convenient to take as basic. From this notion other senses, referring to temporal and logical relations, can be seen as having developed. The role of the spatial sense should be qualified: usage, not etymology, decides meaning. The prepositions have distinctive meanings; although their semantic fields overlap, no two exhibit complete interchangeability. Nonetheless, because of the overlapping meanings, it is possible that sometimes the choice among essentially similar verb-preposition combinations was chiefly stylistic ... However, to a large degree the meaning of the preposition is consistent and capturable, even with the variations due to the meanings of the verbs used with it.[30]

Nonetheless, in the following section where they describe the meanings of the different prepositions, they tend towards providing a significant number of varying categories for each preposition.

25. Joüon and Muraoka, *Grammar*, 456.
26. Joüon and Muraoka, *Grammar*, 458.
27. Waltke and O'Connor, *Introduction*, 188.
28. Waltke and O'Connor, *Introduction*, 190.
29. Waltke and O'Connor, *Introduction*, 191.
30. Waltke and O'Connor, *Introduction*, 192.

The most consistently synchronic approach amongst the grammars is embodied by van der Merwe et al. Following the multivolume work of Jenni (noted above), they essentially make three points about Biblical Hebrew prepositions as a whole: (1) most prepositions have a fundamentally spatial meaning; (2) the prepositions express varying degrees of specificity; and (3) additionally, "some semantic functions that are attributed to prepositions are largely due to the verbs that govern those prepositions. This feature of some prepositions has not been dealt with systematically."[31] They helpfully provide succinct explanations of the most basic senses of the major prepositions:[32] בְּ "indicates localization ... temporal frame ... realizes an action";[33] לְ "indicates very general relationship between two entities that can at best be described as 'x as far as y is concerned'";[34] מִן "indicates spatial positioning: source ... basic spatial function is movement away from x";[35] and אֶל "localizes the goal of a movement or process."[36]

Two other relevant works that take a synchronic perspective are both by Lyle, who works within cognitive semantics. In his 2012 Stellenbosch MA thesis, he studies עִם and אֵת (both often glossed as "with") in order to discover their core senses as well as range of derivative meanings, concluding that in terms of their core senses they are "near-synonyms."[37] In a 2014 *Hebrew Studies* article, he details—but does not apply—a new methodology for understanding the semantic range of Hebrew prepositions, based on Cognitive Linguistics and grammaticalization.[38] While some of the data points in these methods are diachronic, the type of answers such a study would seek are far closer to the synchronic studies surveyed above than to that of the older philological approaches. Porter has made this point regarding both English and Greek grammar and has also noted that this search for a "foundational" sense predates Cognitive Linguistics itself.[39]

---

31. van der Merwe et al., *Biblical Hebrew Reference Grammar*, 276–77.
32. van der Merwe et al., *Biblical Hebrew Reference Grammar*, 277–93.
33. van der Merwe et al., *Biblical Hebrew Reference Grammar*, 280–81.
34. van der Merwe et al., *Biblical Hebrew Reference Grammar*, 284.
35. van der Merwe et al., *Biblical Hebrew Reference Grammar*, 287.
36. van der Merwe et al., *Biblical Hebrew Reference Grammar*, 277.
37. Lyle, "Cognitive Semantic Assessment."
38. Lyle, "New Methodology."
39. Porter, "Greek Prepositions," 33–35.

METHODOLOGY

My own study of prepositions will employ two operative guiding principles: monosemy and the systemic nature of language. A helpful definition of monosemy is provided by Fewster, who states, "the meaning that is associated with a lexeme is general and abstracted, relying on co-textual and contextual features to provide further semantic and functional specification and constraint. This is, therefore, a minimalist program, which posits that any meaning added by the co-text is not part of a lexeme's semantic content."[40] Systemic description was developed by Halliday in a number of essays in the 1950s and 1960s. A "system" proper is "a representation of relations on the paradigmatic axis, a set of features contrastive in a given environment."[41] If the selection of a given feature leads to another system, or set of choices, the network is said to increase in "delicacy" as one progresses through successive choices. Thus, Halliday states, "For any set of systems associated with a given environment it is possible to construct a *system network* in which each system, other than those simultaneous at the point of origin, is hierarchically ordered with respect to at least one other system."[42]

A final heuristic tool that needs to be introduced is Halliday's own set of categories for circumstantials from his *Introduction to Functional Grammar* (IFG1). This rubric is a top-down set of meanings that he devised to represent functions accomplished more or less universally across languages. While this device may seem initially foreign to the bottom-up, morphological primacy of this study, it nonetheless will function as a useful grid to assign categories of usage (based on the larger context of a clause), within which the specific functions of individual prepositions can be studied, and ideally, their own unique "core" meanings brought into sharper focus.

For the purposes of this study, the simple iterations of the system of circumstantials found in the first edition of *Introduction to Functional Grammar* are most appropriate. Halliday provides six categories (some of which include subcategories) of use for circumstantials, along with helpful examples:

---

40. Fewster, *Creation Language*, 47–48.
41. Halliday, "Some Notes," 110.
42. Halliday, "Deep Grammar," 111.

1. *Extent* and *Location*: This category covers spatial and temporal modifiers ("work in the kitchen" or "get up at six o'clock").
2. *Manner*: This includes the means by which something takes place ("she beat the pig with a stick"), the quality of a variable of the process ("it was snowing heavily"), and comparison ("it was like an earthquake").
3. *Cause*: This includes the reason a process happened, the purpose for which it took place, and the entity on whose behalf it happened ("she did it for him").
4. *Accompaniment*: ("Fred came with Tom").
5. *Matter*: ("I worry about her health").
6. *Role*: ("I come here as a friend").[43]

While this study uses the categories from the first edition of Halliday's Functional Grammar, it is relevant to note that a much more developed system appears in the fourth edition, titled *Halliday's Introduction to Functional Grammar* (IFG4). In this edition, circumstantials comprise a system of their own, starting with the initial choices of enhancing, extending, elaborating, and projection. Most of the traditional categories (extent, location, manner, cause, contingency) fit under the heading of enhancing, while extending leads to accompaniment, elaborating leads to role, and projection leads to matter and angle.[44]

With these parameters in place, it is now appropriate to proceed with the four-fold procedure of analysis outlined in the introduction.

ANALYSIS

When the circumstantials in Habakkuk are viewed in their entirety (see appendix), a range of Hebrew resources are used to actualize them, but the most frequently used devices are six monosyllabic prepositions. (For the sake of convenience, the usage of prepositions with an infinitive construct has been eschewed here.)

The Uses of Individual Prepositions

Some of the prepositions are used with a surprising range of meanings. To start with ל, in descending order of usage, the meaning categories

---

43. The remainder of this paragraph draws from Halliday, IFG1, 137–44.
44. Halliday, IFG4, 313–14.

are *cause: behalf* (5x); *location: spatial* (5x); *cause: purpose* (3x); *extent: spatial* (1x); *cause: reason* (2x); *extent: temporal* (2x); and *matter* (1x). Similarly diverse is בְּ, which is used to realize *location: spatial* (9x); *manner: means* (4x); *manner: quality* (3x); *cause: purpose* (2x); *location: temporal* (3x); *cause: reason* (1x); *extent: temporal* (?) (1x); *cause: behalf* (3x); and *matter* (2x). Slightly more focused is מִן, which realizes *location: spatial* (9x); *cause: reason* (2x); *manner: comparison* (1x). The remaining prepositions have usages that are much more stable: עַל is used for *location: spatial* (7x); *cause: behalf* (1x); אֶל is used for *cause: behalf* (2x); *role* (1x); and finally, כְּ is used for *manner: comparison* (7x). With this data in mind, we can see that some of the prepositions (namely לְ and בְּ) are used in more diverse ways than others.

Prepositions Grouped by Categories of Meaning

Another helpful lens for making sense of the data comes from using the meaning-categories to group the prepositions themselves. When we do this, we find that *cause: behalf* is realized by בְּ/עַל/אֶל/לְ; *cause: reason* is realized by לְ/בְּ/מִן; *cause: purpose* is realized by לְ/בְּ; *location: spatial* is realized by מִן/בְּ/עַל/לְ; *extent: temporal* is realized by לְ/בְּ; *matter* is realized by לְ/בְּ; and *manner: comparison* is realized by כְּ/מִן. Just as with the prepositions themselves above, it is clear that some of the meaning-categories have a broader range of linguistic resources used to realize them than others. For the remaining four meaning-categories occurring in this corpus, only one preposition each realizes them. These are *extent: spatial* (לְ); *location: temporal* (בְּ); *role* (אֶל); *manner: means* and *manner: quality* (בְּ).

Towards Core Meanings through Meaning-Categories

While space does not permit an exhaustive analysis of every usage, it is appropriate to begin with some of the most diversely used resources and categories as a starting place to attempt to determine any possible minimal core meaning contributed by the forms themselves.[45]

To start with a simple example, *cause: purpose* is realized by both לְ and בְּ. The usage of לְ in this capacity is quite straightforward: in 1:12c

---

45. While *extent: temporal* was listed above as being realized with multiple prepositions, these category assignments are tentative enough that further analysis would be unproductive. The categories that are only realized with one preposition are not covered in this section for obvious reasons.

and 1:12d, YHWH appoints the Babylonians to execute judgment, and in 3:13a YHWH goes out for the salvation of his people. The use of בְּ is a bit more difficult; see the pair of clauses in 2:13b and 2:13c. The NASB (followed closely by the JPS) renders these as "peoples toil for fire, and nations grow weary for nothing." So, is the בְּ doing something here that is different than the previous occurrences of לְ? Consultation of the ancient versions may reveal that there is no obligation to render this בְּ with a sense of purpose: for "peoples toil for fire" the OG uses the preposition ἐν, rendered by the NETS as "enough peoples have expired in fire." So, a simple function of locating may be more appropriate here than purpose.

A clearer example may be found in the case of the category of *cause: reason*, which uses לְ, בְּ, and מִן. The preposition מִן is used in the parallel statements in 2:8 and 2:17, "because of human bloodshed." The preposition בְּ is used in 1:16, "through them [i.e., his nets] his portion is rich." Finally, the preposition לְ is used in 3:16, "at the sound my lips quivered." While textual variants prevent the OG from being of use in the case of 3:16, for the מִן in 2:8, 17 there is διά with an accusative (NETS "on account of"), and for the בְּ in 1:16 there is ἐν (NETS "by them"). This would seem to indicate that מִן is working from a root cause that has had consequences, while בְּ again is pinpointing a location of a key object. For its part, לְ seems to be identifying a direction of influence.

Another brief example is the category of *matter*. A pair of בְּ prepositions are used in 3:18a–18b ("I exalt in YHWH/I will rejoice in the God of my salvation"), and לְ is used in 2:3.5 ("wait for it [the vision]"). The occurrences of בְּ are rendered in the OG with ἐν and ἐπί with the dative, respectively, while לְ is simply represented by an accusative intensive pronoun. Here a fundamental static/dynamic contrast between בְּ and לְ seems to be at work. The בְּ locates the place of the prophet's worship, while the לְ is expressing a stretch towards something.

A more densely populated circumstantial category is that of *cause: behalf*. Here there are five usages of לְ: "princes are a joke to him" (1:10b); "he sacrifices to his net/he makes offerings to his dragnet" (1:16a–16b); "you will become plunder to them" (2:7c); and "you have devised a shameful thing for your house" (2:10a). There are three occurrences of בְּ, in 3:8a–8c, all variants of "did YHWH rage against the rivers." There are two occurrences of אֶל: "He gathers for himself all nations/and collects as his own all peoples" (2:5e–2:5f). Finally, there is an עַל: "the nations take up a taunt-song against him" (2:6a). Again, לְ seems to carry a general sense of direction, while אֶל is more specific. Compare the לְ in 1:16a ("he sacrifices to his net") with the אֶל in 2:5e ("he gathers for himself all nations"). The former in the OG is simply rendered with dative nouns, while the latter uses the accusative with ἐπί and πρός (again a suggestion of specificity). The occurrences of בְּ in 3:8 are all rendered with ἐν in the OG (NETS "with"), while the עַל in 2:6 has κατά with the genitive (NETS "against"). While the English gloss of "against" is doubtless appropriate in both these cases, the עַל seems to be more specific than the בְּ, which here seems to just be conveying a kind of general orientation.

A short note on *manner: comparison* is appropriate. Seven of its eight occurrences in Habakkuk use כְּ and clearly express equivalence. Two such examples are 1:8e ("they fly like an eagle") and 1:14a ("you make men like the fish of the sea"). However, the one occurrence that uses מִן expresses a comparison in which the two items are very different: 2:16a ("you are filled with disgrace rather than honor").

For a final example of preposition usage based on a particular circumstantial category, we will examine *location: spatial*, which is quite common in Habakkuk. Within this category, we find nine uses of בְּ, seven uses of עַל, six uses of מִן, and four uses of לְ. Regarding the uses of בְּ, they seem to express location in a fairly generic sense: "look among the nations" (1:5a); "he gathers them in his dragnet" (1:15c); "his life is not right within him" (2:4b); "there is no breath inside it" (2:19d); "YHWH is in his holy temple" (2:20a); "YHWH treaded on the sea" (3:15a); "decay enters into my bones" (3:16d); "there is no fruit on the vines" (3:17b); "there is no herd in the stalls" (3:17f). The עַל-preposition is somewhat more specific, almost always conveying a "location upon" spatial relationship, or movement from a greater to lesser power in a metaphorical sense: "I will take my stand on my watchpost/I will station myself on the tower" (2:1a–1b); "make it plain on tablets" (2:2d); "the cup of the Lord's hand will come on you" (2:16d); "disgrace will be on your glory" (2:16e); "on my high places he makes me walk" (3:19c).

In occurrences of מִן for *location: spatial*, the preposition consistently indicates some sort of source, or remote point from which something comes: "from him his justice and authority will go out" (1:7b); "his horsemen come from afar" (1:8d); "stone will call out from the wall" (2:11a); "God came from Teman" (3:3a). And finally, the four occurrences of לְ are as follows: "rays are from his hand to him" (ambiguous) (3:4b); "plague goes out from his feet" (3:5b); "to the light your arrows went//your spear went to the great lightning" (3:11b–11c). The uses of לְ clearly have a sense of direction.

Towards "Core" Meanings of Biblical Hebrew Prepositions

Now that we have performed a basic survey of the contrasting tendencies of the different prepositions when operating in similar categories of meaning, it is appropriate to draw some conclusions about the prepositions themselves. The preposition כְּ consistently expresses a comparison of equivalence, so it can be left alone. The only overlap in meaning is מִן, which can also express comparison, but of things that are different. For its part, מִן can also express *location* (a remote origin point) and *cause* (a separate factor leading to something). This leads to the conclusion that מִן conveys some basic idea of "separation from a different entity." The preposition עַל, whether expressing *location* or *cause*, always involves some kind of relative "location upon" spatial positioning. The preposition אֶל, whether conveying *cause: behalf* ("he gathers for himself all nations") or *matter* ("you cannot look on wickedness") contributes the meaning of 'specific direction.' The preposition בְּ, with its wide range of uses, can be reduced to a sense of 'static location or orientation,' whether in the capacity of *location* ("look among the nations"), *manner* ("he drags them in his net"), *cause* ("through them his portion is rich"), or *matter* ("I rejoice in YHWH"). Finally, לְ is similarly diverse in its applications, just like בְּ. It realizes *extent* ("justice does not go out to forever"), *cause* ("all of him comes for violence"), *matter* ("wait for it"), or *location* ("to the light your arrows went"), but nonetheless there is a core sense of "general direction."

Since the results of the above analysis mostly confirm the meanings advanced by van der Merwe et al. (see the literature survey above), we should ask what can be done with systemic organization to express the relationships of the meanings of these prepositions? My tentative proposal for such a system begins with three initial options: *comparison*, *location*, and *direction*. *Comparison* branches off into two choices: *equivalence* (כְּ) and *difference* (מִן). *Location* presents two initial choices: *general* and *specific*. Here, the *general* option leads directly to בְּ, which provides a rather unspecialized indicator of location (whether spatially or metaphorically applied to cause or matter). The *specific* option branches out into two more choices. The first is between *distance*, realized by מִן (this also metaphorically extended to causation), and *location upon*, realized by עַל. The third initial choice is *direction*, which opens up a choice between either *general* (realized by לְ) or *specific* (realized by אֶל).

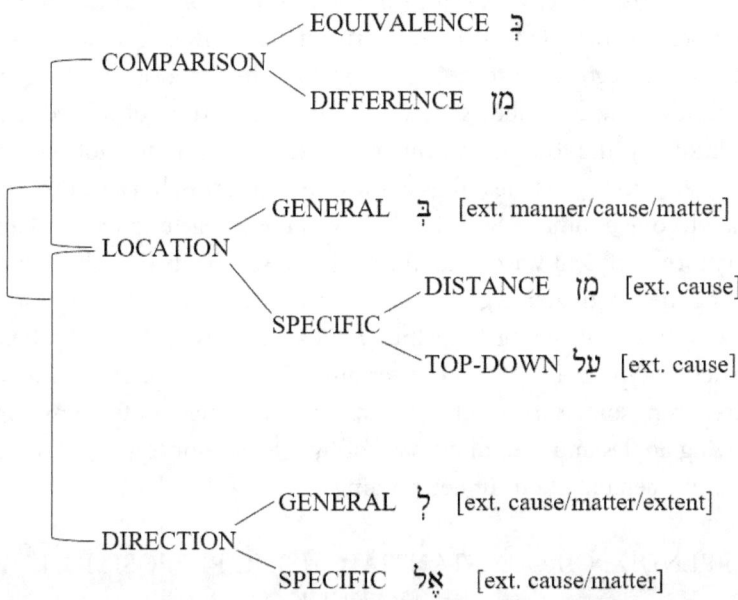

Figure 1. System: Comparison, Location, and Direction

There is certainly room for discussion about possible ways to improve this network. There are doubtless other ways that these minimal categories could be related to each other. The most significant cause for concern in this model is probably the fact that מִן appears in two different places. While the present study started from the principle of monosemic bias and tried to model the prepositions according to a monosemic meaning as much as possible, מִן resisted this; while a network conceivably could have been constructed that ended in the most generic meaning of מִן (some kind of "difference" perhaps), the opposing semantic categories suggested by the other prepositions led to מִן being realized in multiple places.

CONCLUSION

In order to arrive at a system of minimal core meanings for the most common Hebrew prepositions, this study followed a couple of simple steps. Comparing the different forms when utilized within the same categories in Halliday's system of circumstantial meanings allowed for the detection of their unique nuances, and with these unique nuances in view, a system network was formulated. While some of these conclusions were anticipated in the modern reference grammars, the use of Halliday's categories of meaning to compare the prepositions is a genuine innovation, as it allows for the convenient sorting of related texts. Additionally, the tool of systemic organization allows for not only the understanding of the meanings of the different forms, but also how they relate to one another. With this tool in mind, exegetes and translators can more confidently ascertain the degree of specificity of each form, allowing them a greater degree of accuracy in determining when multiple possibilities of meaning (and thus English glosses) exist, and when a particular type of usage is more certain. While no stage of this process is free from some sort of subjectivity, the employment of these multiple viewing angles and the submission of hypotheses for testing allows for the advancement of our understanding.

APPENDIX: CIRCUMSTANTIALS USING PREPOSITIONS IN HABAKKUK

Note: Only circumstantials employing the six main prepositions in view in this study are listed below:

Clause	MT	Translation	Circumstantial type	Prep
1:4b	וְלֹא־יֵצֵא לָנֶצַח מִשְׁפָּט	and justice does not go out endlessly	*Extent: spatial*	לְ
1:5a	רְאוּ בַגּוֹיִם	look among the nations	*Location: spatial*	בְּ
1:5e	כִּי־פֹעַל פֹּעֵל בִּימֵיכֶם	for [I am] working a work in your days	*Location: temporal*	בְּ
1:7b	מִמֶּנּוּ מִשְׁפָּטוֹ וּשְׂאֵתוֹ יֵצֵא	from him his justice and his authority will go out	*Location: spatial*	מִן
1:8d	וּפָרָשָׁיו מֵרָחוֹק יָבֹאוּ	his horsemen come from afar	*Location: spatial*	מִן
1:8e	יָעֻפוּ כְּנֶשֶׁר חָשׁ לֶאֱכוֹל	they fly like an eagle rushing to eat,	*Manner: comparison*	כְּ

1:9a	כֻּלֹּה לְחָמָס יָבוֹא	all of him comes for violence.	Cause: reason	לְ
1:9c	וַיֶּאֱסֹף כַּחוֹל שֶׁבִי	and he amasses captives like sand.	Manner: comparison	כְּ
1:10b	וְרֹזְנִים מִשְׂחָק לוֹ	and princes are a joke to him	Cause: behalf	לְ
1:12c	יְהוָה לְמִשְׁפָּט שַׂמְתּוֹ	you, O YHWH, have appointed them to judge	Cause: purpose	לְ
1:12d	וְצוּר לְהוֹכִיחַ יְסַדְתּוֹ	and you, O rock, have established them to correct.	Cause: purpose	לְ
1:13b	וְהַבִּיט אֶל־עָמָל לֹא תוּכָל	and you cannot look on wickedness	Matter	אֶל
1:14a	וַתַּעֲשֶׂה אָדָם כִּדְגֵי הַיָּם כְּרֶמֶשׂ לֹא־מֹשֵׁל בּוֹ	you made men like the fish of the sea, like creeping things without a ruler over them	Manner: comparison	כְּ
1:15a	כֻּלֹּה בְּחַכָּה הֵעֲלָה	he brings all of them up with a hook	Manner: means	בְּ
1:15b	יְגֹרֵהוּ בְחֶרְמוֹ	he drags them out with his net	Manner: means	בְּ
1:15c	וְיַאַסְפֵהוּ בְּמִכְמַרְתּוֹ	he gathers them in his dragnet	Location: spatial	בְּ
1:16a	עַל־כֵּן יְזַבֵּחַ לְחֶרְמוֹ	therefore, he sacrifices to his net	Cause: behalf	לְ
1:16c	כִּי בָהֵמָּה שָׁמֵן חֶלְקוֹ	for through them his portion is rich	Cause: reason	בְּ
2:1a	עַל־מִשְׁמַרְתִּי אֶעֱמֹדָה	I will take my stand at my watchpost	Location: spatial	עַל
2:1b	וְאֶתְיַצְּבָה עַל־מָצוֹר	and station myself on the tower	Location: spatial	עַל
2:2d	וּבָאֵר עַל־הַלֻּחוֹת	make plain on tablets	Location: spatial	עַל
2:3b	וְיָפֵחַ לַקֵּץ	it hastens to the end	Extent: temporal	לְ
2:3e	חַכֵּה־לוֹ	wait for it	Matter	לְ
2:4b	לֹא־יָשְׁרָה נַפְשׁוֹ בּוֹ	his life/throat is not right within him	Location: spatial	בְּ

2:4c	וְצַדִּיק בֶּאֱמוּנָתוֹ יִחְיֶה	and the righteous will live by his faith	*Manner: quality*	בְּ
2:5e	וַיֶּאֱסֹף אֵלָיו כָּל־הַגּוֹיִם	he gathers for himself all nations	*Cause: behalf*	אֶל
2:5f	וַיִּקְבֹּץ אֵלָיו כָּל־הָעַמִּים	and collects as his own all peoples.	*Cause: behalf*	אֶל
2:6a	הֲלוֹא־אֵלֶּה כֻלָּם עָלָיו מָשָׁל יִשָּׂאוּ	will not all of these take up a taunt-song against him,	*Cause: behalf*	עַל
2:7c	וְהָיִיתָ לִמְשִׁסּוֹת לָמוֹ	and you will become plunder for them.	*Cause: behalf*	לְ
2:8b	יְשָׁלּוּךָ כָּל־יֶתֶר עַמִּים מִדְּמֵי אָדָם	all the remainder of the peoples will loot you— Because of human bloodshed (etc.)	*Cause: reason*	מִן
2:10a	יָעַצְתָּ בֹּשֶׁת לְבֵיתֶךָ קְצוֹת־עַמִּים רַבִּים	you have devised a shameful thing for your house by cutting off many peoples;	*Cause: behalf*	לְ
2:11a	כִּי־אֶבֶן מִקִּיר תִּזְעָק	surely the stone will cry out from the wall	*Location: spatial*	מִן
2:11b	וְכָפִיס מֵעֵץ יַעֲנֶנָּה	and the beam will answer it from the framework	*Location: spatial*	מִן
2:13b	וְיִיגְעוּ עַמִּים בְּדֵי־אֵשׁ	peoples toil for fire	*Cause: purpose*	בְּ
2:13c	וּלְאֻמִּים בְּדֵי־רִיק יִעָפוּ	and nations grow weary for nothing	*Cause: purpose*	בְּ
2:14a	כִּי תִּמָּלֵא הָאָרֶץ לָדַעַת אֶת־כְּבוֹד יְהוָה כַּמַּיִם יְכַסּוּ עַל־יָם	for the earth will be filled with the knowledge of the glory of YHWH, as the waters cover the sea.	*Manner: comparison*	כְּ
2:16a	שָׂבַעְתָּ קָלוֹן מִכָּבוֹד	you are filled with disgrace rather than honor.	*Manner: comparison*	מִן

2:16d	תִּסּוֹב עָלֶיךָ כּוֹס יְמִין יְהוָה	the cup in the LORD's right hand will come around to you	Location: spatial	עַל
2:16e	וְקִיקָלוֹן עַל־כְּבוֹדֶךָ	and disgrace [is] on your glory	Location: spatial	עַל
2:17b	וְשֹׁד בְּהֵמוֹת יְחִיתַן מִדְּמֵי אָדָם	and the devastation of beasts terrified you, from human bloodshed (etc.)	Cause: reason	מִן
2:18c	כִּי בָטַח יֹצֵר יִצְרוֹ עָלָיו לַעֲשׂוֹת אֱלִילִים אִלְּמִים	for the one fashioning his product trusts in it, when he fashions speechless idols	Location: spatial	עַל
2:19d	וְכָל־רוּחַ אֵין בְּקִרְבּוֹ	and there is no breath at all inside it	Location: spatial	בְּ
2:20a	וַיהוָה בְּהֵיכַל קָדְשׁוֹ	but YHWH is in his holy temple	Location: spatial	בְּ
3:2c	בְּקֶרֶב שָׁנִים חַיֵּיהוּ	in the midst of years, revive it	Location: temporal	בְּ
3:2d	בְּקֶרֶב שָׁנִים תּוֹדִיעַ	in the midst of years, declare	Location: temporal	בְּ
3:2e	בְּרֹגֶז רַחֵם תִּזְכּוֹר	in wrath, remember compassion	Extent: temporal[46]	בְּ
3:3a	אֱלוֹהַּ מִתֵּימָן יָבוֹא	God came from Teman	Location: spatial	מִן
3:3b	וְקָדוֹשׁ מֵהַר־פָּארָן	and the holy one from Mount Paran	Location: spatial	מִן
3:4a	וְנֹגַהּ כָּאוֹר תִּהְיֶה	[the] brightness is like the light	Manner: comparison	כְּ
3:4b	קַרְנַיִם מִיָּדוֹ לוֹ	rays/horns (are) from his hand to him	Location: spatial / Location: spatial	מִן / לְ
3:5a	לְפָנָיו יֵלֶךְ דָּבֶר	before him goes pestilence	Location: spatial	לְ
3:5b	וְיֵצֵא רֶשֶׁף לְרַגְלָיו	and plague goes out from his feet	Location: spatial	לְ
3:8a	הֲבִנְהָרִים חָרָה יְהוָה	did YHWH rage against the rivers?	Cause: behalf	בְּ

---

46. This categorization is uncertain.

3:8b	אִם בַּנְּהָרִים אַפֶּךָ	was your anger against the rivers?	*Cause: behalf*	בְּ
3:8c	אִם־בַּיָּם עֶבְרָתֶךָ	was your wrath against the sea?	*Cause: behalf*	בְּ
3:8d	כִּי תִרְכַּב עַל־סוּסֶיךָ מַרְכְּבֹתֶיךָ יְשׁוּעָה	that you rode your horses, on your chariots of salvation?	*Location: spatial*	עַל
3:11b	לְאוֹר חִצֶּיךָ יְהַלֵּכוּ	to the light your arrows went	*Location: spatial*	לְ
3:11c	לְנֹגַהּ בְּרַק חֲנִיתֶךָ	your spear (went) to the great lightning	*Location: spatial*	לְ
3:12a	בְּזַעַם תִּצְעַד־אָרֶץ	in fury you marched the earth	*Manner: quality*	בְּ
3:12b	בְּאַף תָּדוּשׁ גּוֹיִם	in anger you treaded the nations	*Manner: quality*	בְּ
3:13a	יָצָאתָ לְיֵשַׁע עַמֶּךָ לְיֵשַׁע אֶת־מְשִׁיחֶךָ	you went out for the salvation of your people, for the salvation of your anointed	*Cause: purpose*	לְ
3:13b	מָחַצְתָּ רֹּאשׁ מִבֵּית רָשָׁע עָרוֹת יְסוֹד עַד־צַוָּאר	you crushed the head from the house of the wicked, laying open from base to neck	*Location: spatial*	מִן
3:14a	נָקַבְתָּ בְמַטָּיו רֹאשׁ פְּרָזָיו	you pierced with his arrows the head of his warriors	*Manner: means*	בְּ
3:14c	עֲלִיצֻתָם כְּמוֹ־לֶאֱכֹל עָנִי בַּמִּסְתָּר	their exaltation (is) like (those who) eat the poor in secret	*Manner: comparison*	כְּ
3:15a	דָּרַכְתָּ בַיָּם סוּסֶיךָ חֹמֶר מַיִם רַבִּים	you treaded on the sea (with) your horses, (on) the heap of mighty waters	*Location: spatial*	בְּ
3:16c	לְקוֹל צָלֲלוּ שְׂפָתַי	at the sound my lips quiver	*Cause: reason*	לְ
3:16d	יָבוֹא רָקָב בַּעֲצָמַי	rottenness enters my bones	*Location: spatial*	בְּ

3:16f	אֲשֶׁר אָנוּחַ לְיוֹם צָרָה לַעֲלוֹת לְעַם יְגוּדֶנּוּ	(when) I will rest for the day of distress to come up, for the people who attack us	Extent: temporal	לְ
3:17b	וְאֵין יְבוּל בַּגְּפָנִים	and there is no fruit on the vines	Location: spatial	בְּ
3:17e	גָּזַר מִמִּכְלָה צֹאן	the flock is divided from the fold	Location: spatial	מִן
3:17f	וְאֵין בָּקָר בָּרְפָתִים	and there is no herd in the stalls	Location: spatial	בְּ
3:18a	וַאֲנִי בַּיהוָה אֶעְלוֹזָה	and I, in YHWH I will exult	Matter	בְּ
3:18b	אָגִילָה בֵּאלֹהֵי יִשְׁעִי	I will rejoice in the God of my salvation	Matter	בְּ
3:19b	וַיָּשֶׂם רַגְלַי כָּאַיָּלוֹת	he makes my feet like the deer's	Manner: comparison	כְּ
3:19c	וְעַל בָּמוֹתַי יַדְרִכֵנִי	on my high places he makes me walk	Location: spatial	עַל

BIBLIOGRAPHY

Althann, R. "Approaches to Prepositions in Northwest Semitic Studies." *JNSL* 20 (1994) 179–91.

Arnold, Bill T., and John H. Choi. *A Guide to Biblical Hebrew Syntax*. Cambridge: Cambridge University Press, 2003.

Blau, Joshua. *Phonology and Morphology of Biblical Hebrew*. LSAWS 2. Winona Lake, IN: Eisenbrauns, 2010.

Bompiani, Brian A. "Prepositions." In *"Where Shall Wisdom Be Found?" A Grammatical Tribute to Professor Stephen A. Kaufman*, edited by Hélène M. Dallaire et al., 37–64. Winona Lake, IN: Eisenbrauns, 2017.

Chomsky, William. "The Ambiguity of the Prefixed Prepositions מ, ל, ב, in the Bible." *JQR* 16 (1970) 87–89.

Dahood, Mitchell Joseph. *Psalms III: 101-150*. AB 17A. New Haven: Yale University Press, 1970.

———. "'Weaker than Water': Comparative *beth* in Isaiah 1,22." *Bib* 59 (1978) 91–92.

Fewster, Gregory P. *Creation Language in Romans 8: A Study in Monosemy*. LBS 8. Leiden: Brill, 2013.

Fuller, David J. "Clausal Circumstantials at the Discourse Level: 'Macro-Exegesis' and the Book of Habakkuk." Paper presented at the Ontario/Quebec Regional Meeting of the Evangelical Theological Society, Cambridge, ON, September 30, 2017.

———. *A Discourse Analysis of Habakkuk: The Earth Will Be Filled with the Knowledge of the Glory of YHWH*. SSN 72. Leiden: Brill, 2019.

———. "Enigmatic Enemies and the Development of Faith: A Discourse Analysis of Habakkuk." PhD diss., McMaster Divinity College, 2018.

Futato, Mark D. "The Preposition 'Beth' in the Hebrew Psalter." *WTJ* 41 (1978) 68–83.

Gordon, Cyrus H. *Ugaritic Grammar: The Present Status of the Linguistic Study of the Semitic Alphabetic Texts from Ras Shamra.* AnOr 20. Rome: Pontifical Biblical Institute, 1988.

Haber, Esther. "Significance of the Interchanging of the Mono-Consonantal Prepositions in Biblical Hebrew: Rabbinic and Comparative Semitic Evidence." *Maarav* 16 (2009) 29–37.

Halliday, M. A. K. *Halliday's Introduction to Functional Grammar.* Revised by Christian M. I. M. Matthiessen. 4th ed. London: Routledge, 2014. (IFG4)

———. *An Introduction to Functional Grammar.* London: Arnold, 1985. (IFG1)

———. "Some Notes on 'Deep' Grammar." In *On Grammar,* edited by Jonathan Webster, 106–17. Collected Works of M. A. K. Halliday 1. New York: Continuum, 2002.

Hardy, Humphrey Hill, II. "Diachronic Development in Biblical Hebrew Prepositions: A Case Study in Grammaticalization." PhD diss., University of Chicago, 2014.

Jenni, Ernst. *Die hebräischen Präpositionen Band 1: Die Präposition Beth.* Stuttgart: Kohlhammer, 1992.

———. "Preposition: Biblical Hebrew." In *Encyclopedia of Hebrew Language and Linguistics. Vol. 3, P–Z,* edited by Geoffrey Khan, 208–12. Leiden: Brill, 2013.

Joüon, P., and T. Muraoka. *A Grammar of Biblical Hebrew.* SubBi 27. Rome: Gregorian and Biblical, 2016.

Kautzsch, E. *Gesenius' Hebrew Grammar,* edited by A. E. Cowley. 2nd ed. Oxford: Clarendon, 1910.

Lyle, Kristopher A. "A Cognitive Semantic Assessment of עִם and אֵת's Semantic Potential." MA thesis, University of Stellenbosch, 2012.

———. "A New Methodology for Ascertaining the Semantic Potential of Biblical Hebrew Prepositions." *HS* 54 (2013) 49–67.

Merwe, C. H. J. van der, et al. *A Biblical Hebrew Reference Grammar.* BLH 3. Sheffield: Sheffield Academic, 1999.

Pardee, Dennis. "The Preposition in Ugaritic (Part I)." *UF* 7 (1975) 329–78.

Porter, Stanley E. "Greek Prepositions in a Systemic Functional Linguistic Framework." *BAGL* 6 (2017) 17–43.

Reed, Jeffrey T. *A Discourse Analysis of Philippians: Method and Rhetoric in the Debate over Literary Integrity.* JSNTSup 100. Sheffield: Sheffield Academic, 1997.

Sarna, Nahum M. "Interchange of the Prepositions *Beth* and *Min* in Biblical Hebrew." *JBL* 78 (1959) 310–16.

Toffelmire, Colin M. *A Discourse and Register Analysis of the Prophetic Book of Joel.* SSN 66. Leiden: Brill, 2016.

Waltke, Bruce, and Michael P. O'Connor. *An Introduction to Biblical Hebrew Syntax.* Winona Lake, IN: Eisenbrauns, 1990.

3

Chaining and Wrapping
The Quantitative and Qualitative Economies of Greek Syntax

Ryder A. Wishart

INTRODUCTION

IN THIS PAPER, I describe two syntactic phenomena: chaining and wrapping.[1] Together, these comprise the most significant values of the conjunctive potential of Greek structure—a potential that should not be mistaken for *conjunctions* as a part of speech.[2] Traditionally, conjunction in Greek has been understood as the relating of syntactic units either by coordinating or else subordinating conjunctions (along with anacoluthon, where no conjunction is present, apposition, and perhaps also interjection and ellipsis). I will argue in this paper that the

---

1. This brief paper comprises a lightly revised documentation of the presentation given at the Bingham Colloquium. It can be considered a sketch of an important way that Greek syntax might be reconceived in pedagogy as more than simply categorizations of grammatical features. While there have been many changes to the specifics of how best to model the syntactic formations in this paper since its presentation at the 2018 Bingham Colloquium, this formulation remains a pedagogically useful and simplifying abstraction for considering the layering of various structures in Greek syntax.

2. *Conjunction* in this sense is similar to Tesnière's (*Elements*, 46) notion of "relations" between semantic units (in his case these are essentially content words with their modifiers, though I would not so delimit the units being related by relations).

traditional notion captures many of the instances of conjunction we observe in Hellenistic Greek but misses some very common syntactic constructions that can likewise be understood as instances of structural conjunction.[3] This includes the use of most particles, such as prepositions and adverbs, and also ὁ-items.

In the first part of this paper, I will outline how conjunction as a structural possibility relates to the use of conjunctions in Greek more generally, relying mainly on M. A. K. Halliday's distinction between structural and semantic cohesion in his systemic-functional model of linguistics. In the second part of the paper, I will offer an outline of chaining and wrapping, which are related to the more familiar coordinating/subordinating or paratactic/hypotactic distinctions, but with several differences. Together, I will argue, chaining and wrapping allow for the quantitative and qualitative augmentation of Greek syntactic units of all classes.[4]

TRADITIONAL FORMULATION OF GREEK CONJUNCTION

Greek syntax can be considered from either a structure-oriented perspective or else from a semantics-oriented perspective.[5] Semantically, Greek syntax consists in meaningful configurations, understood in traditional terminology as "subject and predicate" formations (often simply a predicating structure in Greek) or as "process and participant" formations (whether or not the process and participant[s] are explicit). Various forms of the subject–predicate distinction have been part of the grammatical tradition in general for as long as grammar has been analyzed, but its most influential articulation can be traced to the Port-Royal grammarians.[6] Port-Royal grammar analyzes language as the

---

3. For some examples of the traditional conception, see Blass, *Grammar*, 259–86; Robertson, *Grammar*, 426, 951–53; Wallace, *Basics*, 293–96. Wallace notes several possible classifications of sentential conjunction and organizes his treatment around types of conjunctions.

4. This wording ("quantitative" and "qualitative" economies) is taken from the English translation of Tesnière (*Elements*, 73), who says, "The functions assured by empty words [i.e., function as opposed to content words] are of two types. They serve to diversify the structure of the sentence by affecting economy, the first type in terms of quantity and the second in terms of quality." The concepts of chaining and wrapping I present here are especially influenced by Tesnière.

5. Cf. Tesnière, *Elements*, 33.

6. The key work to consult is Arnauld and Lancelot, *General and Rational Grammar*.

manifestation of essentially logical relationships, and the subject–predicate distinction forms the core of their analysis of the sentence. Though this distinction has been challenged and complicated in the centuries since, its usefulness for analysis of Greek clauses is clear insofar as Greek clauses canonically comprise a finite verb whose subject is encoded via inflection, and whose predicate is indicated by the lexical content of the verb, its stem, and other relevant properties.[7] Along similar lines, the traditional notion of transitivity is concerned with the inclusion of additional participants in a process configuration. The involvement of subject/object participants has been the subject of an enormous amount of linguistic research.

This semantic perspective does not exhaust the levels of analysis that can accurately describe Greek syntax, however, as the logico-semantic makeup of Greek predication structures is always communicated by means of a single linear flow of structural syntactic units. By adopting Halliday's metafunctional model, which distinguishes between the ideational, interpersonal, and textual metafunctions in language, we can better understand the relationship between the semantic and the structural in Greek syntax.[8]

In Halliday's systemic-functional model, the three metafunctions operate simultaneously on the same spans of text, with the clause rank as the nexus of this functionality. In other words, a single clause may have three distinct analyses depending on which metafunction is in view. In Greek, the semantic configurations that comprise the subject–predicate relationship are best understood as first of all interpersonal in nature. The units which realize the interpersonal metafunction in Greek syntax are, in other words, the Subject and Predicator, together with any Complements. The Adjuncts of a clause realize ideational meanings, such as location, agency, time, purpose, cause, etc. Adjuncts do not necessarily enter the modal relationships of the Greek clause (though they often do), because their ideational meanings are not bound to be real-

---

7. On the oscillating history of this basic understanding of syntax, see Graffi, *200 Years of Syntax*.

8. This distinction and the divergent analyses implied by it are reminiscent of Lamb's (*Outline*) central claim that the various strata of language, in this case something like semantics and lexicogrammar, have distinct tactics. This point is obscured by the widespread use of syntax to refer to any configuration beyond the level of the word. The key reference work for Halliday's model, as it has been revised and expanded by his student Christian M. I. M. Matthiessen, is Halliday, IFG4.

ized by the same syntactic units as the interpersonal meanings usually are.

In distinction from both of these essentially semantic metafunctions, the structure of Greek text is almost entirely constrained by the textual metafunction.[9] In other words, the interpersonal and ideational semantic meanings are deployed by means of the textual metafunction.

Halliday and Ruqaiya Hasan consider a text to be a semantic unit, which coheres internally on the basis of something other than structure, because structure usually extends only so far as units such as the clause or sentence.[10] Since a text can be larger than any linguistic structure, and yet it holds together, it must be held together by something other than structural relations, namely by semantic (or logico-semantic) ones. I would like to argue that the same distinction between structural and semantic units holds below the level of the complete text as well, at least in Greek. In other words, below the level of the text there are both semantic and structural units.[11] The semantic units of Greek include the clause as a predicative configuration and the lower-rank units that make up the constituents of the clause. The structural units of Greek include dependency nodes that operate within a hierarchy, beginning with finite verbs, and extending down to adverbs and other non-inflecting forms (see below).

Greek syntax can therefore be seen in two ways. First, Greek syntax creates the possibility for interaction between semantic units realizing ideational and interpersonal meanings. Secondly, Greek syntax constrains these possibilities, "packaging" them, so to speak, in the realization of textual meanings. While cohesion refers, according to Halliday and Hasan, to the "non-structural text-forming relations" of a language,[12] syntax can be understood as the domain of *structurally constrained* semantic relations. Thus, while conjunction more generally has to do with the unfolding of text, and thus is concerned with logico-

9. Counter examples can be found in parenthesis and its more general type, anacoluthon. Blass, *Grammar*, 279; Robertson, *Grammar*, 433–35.

10. Halliday and Hasan, *Cohesion in English*, 6–7. In fact, the *sentence* is the unit almost universally accorded a primary place in any model of syntax.

11. Halliday and Hasan (*Cohesion in English*, 8) argue that cohesive relations are present within sentences and not just between them. This fits with the notion that semantic relationships hold both above and below the sentence, but it is also true that below the sentence there will almost always be structural relations.

12. Halliday and Hasan, *Cohesion in English*, 7.

semantic relations, *syntactic* conjunction, or conjunction on the level of syntactic units, has to do with the structurally signalled and structurally constrained relations between units below the level of the text. Thus, conjunction as it relates to syntax remains a structural phenomenon.

In traditional grammars, systematic analysis of syntactic conjunction has resulted in essentially unanimous acceptance of the basic and comprehensive distinction between coordinating and subordinating connections.[13] In other words, virtually all connections in Greek syntax can and have been described as either coordinating or subordinating. This traditional distinction, however, misses some of the syntactic constructions that should be understood as being instances of structural conjunction, including many non-inflecting forms as well as what Ronald Peters describes as "ὁ-items."[14]

In summary so far, syntactic conjunction is a structural phenomenon constrained by the textual metafunction that packages ideational and interpersonal meanings. While a text is a semantic unit that coheres on the basis of semantic meanings, syntactic units are both structural and semantic and therefore must be analyzed not only in terms of logico-semantic conjunction but also structural conjunction. Next, therefore, I will offer an outline of syntactic conjunction in Greek that aims to be more wide-ranging as well as cognizant of the distinction between the complementary structural and semantic perspectives.

SYNTACTIC CONJUNCTION IN GREEK

There are two fundamental methods of syntactic conjunction in Greek. The first, chaining, is fundamentally *coordinating* insofar as it connects syntactic units by giving them equal status within a dependency structure. Chaining has the structural configuration of at least two units (X) compounded together (represented graphically by at least two places: XX). For example, consider Rev 6:10, in which the martyred saints describe the Lord as ὁ ἅγιος καὶ ἀληθινός ("the holy and true one"). In this case, the particle καί signals the chaining. By joining these two adjectives together, chaining enables the quantitative augmentation of this syntactic unit, the nominal group. Almost all chaining is structurally signalled,

---

13. E.g., Blass, *Grammar*, 259–86; Robertson, *Grammar*, 426, 951–53; Wallace, *Basics*, 293–96.

14. Peters, *Greek Article*. These items include especially the article and relative pronoun.

even in cases of parenthesis and anacoluthon more generally, where a syntactic unit is in some sense "set off" from its co-text as not fitting into adjacent structures (see an example below). There are nevertheless many cases of conjunction that are not structurally signalled.

It is important to keep in mind that chaining and wrapping are not simply labels for the structural signals we see, such as conjunctions and other particles. This is clear insofar as not every instance of καί, for example, is coordinating—these are the so-called adverbial uses of καί, which are functioning conjunctively beyond the level of their immediate syntactic context as the realization of logico-semantic meanings, even though they can also be seen as adverbial modifiers of the verbal element.

The second kind of relation can be described as wrapping, and it has the structural configuration of two and only two units (X) in an internal–external, or differential relationship (represented graphically as X[X]), where the internal unit is related to other external parts of the text only indirectly, through the mediation of the external unit, the wrapper. Consider again the example of Rev 6:10, where the article signals that the entire unit it modifies functions as a single nominal. The article "wraps" the chained nominal group, so that it interfaces with its context as a single nominal group with exactly the properties of the article. By determining the relationship with which the wrapped unit interfaces with its context, wrapping enables the qualitative augmentation of a syntactic unit. Consider another example from Matt 25:29 (ὃ ἔχει ἀρθήσεται ἀπ' αὐτοῦ, "what he has will be taken from him"). In this example the relative pronoun wraps the verb ἔχει such that it relates externally to ἀρθήσεται as a nominal Subject (i.e., "what he has" is the subject of the verb "will be taken"), with the wrapper itself relating internally as the Complement of ἔχει (interestingly, the form ὅ, which is ambiguous for being nominative or accusative, is not necessarily disambiguated by context here—it appears to be either one case or the other depending on whether the internal or external relation is considered).

The idea of wrapping is an adaptation of Tesnière's notion of transfer (French *translative* in his work). Transfer is a linguistic mechanism for changing the class of any unit. For Tesnière, there are three kinds of structural relationship that can be observed in languages in general: connection, junction, and transfer.[15]

15. Tesnière (*Elements*, 325) writes, "Connection, junction, and transfer are thus the

Connection is essentially a dependency relationship. These relationships are constrained by a class hierarchy (which is not exactly the same as Halliday's rank structure).[16] In Greek this class hierarchy might be: (1) verbal cluster (canonically, a finite verb primary with satellites); (2) nominal cluster (canonically, a nominal primary with satellites); and (3) adverb cluster (canonically, a non-inflecting primary with satellites).

The units belonging to these classes can be augmented quantitatively, through junction, and qualitatively, through transfer. Junction formulates complexes between units of the same class.[17] Usually junction involves connecting units with καί or some other particle. Transfer changes the class of an element in the dependency tree.[18] In other words, transfer involves using one class as another. A good example of transfer is the participle, which involves a verbal root functioning structurally as a nominal.

In this way, it is clear that the wrapping function is not simply a form of subordination. Subordination is primarily a matter of taxis, or the logical ordering of clauses. While there are subordinating conjunctions in Greek, the concept of subordination is not precisely the same as the concept of wrapping. The wrapper, as such, is not necessarily a constituent of the wrapped unit. Sometimes, however, it is, as in the case of a relative pronoun that relates outwardly as a nominal but inwardly as a clause constituent, such as Subject.

Let us consider some more complicated examples. Rev 6:10 reads:

Ἕως πότε, ὁ δεσπότης ὁ ἅγιος καὶ ἀληθινός, οὐ κρίνεις καὶ ἐκδικεῖς τὸ αἷμα ἡμῶν ἐκ τῶν κατοικούντων ἐπὶ τῆς γῆς;

Here we see several instances of chaining and wrapping. The chained units could be annotated using square brackets in this way (coordinating particles are underlined):

Ἕως πότε, ὁ δεσπότης ὁ [ἅγιος καὶ ἀληθινός], οὐ [κρίνεις καὶ ἐκδικεῖς] τὸ αἷμα ἡμῶν ἐκ τῶν κατοικούντων ἐπὶ τῆς γῆς;

The wrapped units (with underlined wrappers) can be annotated using round brackets as follows:

---

three big bosses that preside over all facts of structural syntax."

16. Tesnière, *Elements*, 56–59. Cf. Halliday, IFG4, 84–86.
17. Tesnière, *Elements*, 325–62.
18. Tesnière, *Elements*, 365–414.

Ἕως (πότε), ὁ (δεσπότης) ὁ (ἅγιος καὶ ἀληθινός), οὐ (κρίνεις καὶ ἐκδικεῖς) τὸ (αἷμα ἡμῶν) ἐκ (τῶν (κατοικούντων ἐπὶ (τῆς (γῆς))));

Note that chained units, units quantitatively augmented by what Tesnière would call junction, still function as a single unit. This is clear when observing how wrapping units modify both chained units simultaneously, as in ὁ (ἅγιος καὶ ἀληθινός). The article modifies both nominals that it wraps. It is also clear that wrapping is not precisely the same as Tesnière's notion of *translatif*, since a particle like οὐ can modify the wrapped, chained unit, (κρίνεις καὶ ἐκδικεῖς), but the negative particle does not change the class of the wrapped unit. It only changes its polarity.

We can also see that the units themselves are clearly delimited by these structural markers. We should keep in mind that while structurally these units are quantitatively and qualitatively augmented, the wrappers can also sometimes function within the unit they are wrapping, which is especially noticeable with ὁ-items. Consider this example from Ephesians, which also gives an example of a syntactic unit which interrupts the syntax, in this case what we might call a parenthesis. Ephesians 2:5–6 reads:

καὶ ὄντας ἡμᾶς νεκροὺς τοῖς παραπτώμασιν συνεζωοποίησεν τῷ Χριστῷ—χάριτί ἐστε σεσῳσμένοι—καὶ συνήγειρεν καὶ συνεκάθισεν ἐν τοῖς ἐπουρανίοις ἐν Χριστῷ Ἰησοῦ

The unit ὄντας ἡμᾶς νεκροὺς τοῖς παραπτώμασιν, which is wrapped by the initial participle, is not only wrapped so that the entire unit functions as a nominal, but ὄντας also functions within the wrapped unit as a Predicator. Relative pronouns almost always function *externally* as wrappers and *internally* as something else, whether Subject, Complement, or something else.

One of the clearest instances of the wrapping function is ὅτι. Consider this example from Rom 10:9:

ὅτι (ἐὰν ὁμολογήσῃς ἐν τῷ στόματί σου κύριον Ἰησοῦν, καὶ πιστεύσῃς ἐν τῇ καρδίᾳ σου ὅτι (ὁ θεὸς αὐτὸν ἤγειρεν ἐκ νεκρῶν,) σωθήσῃ)

The entire verse is wrapped with the initial ὅτι, and then the Complement of πιστεύσῃς is wrapped with the second ὅτι. Note as well that ὅτι, in both cases, does not have an "internal" function within the unit it wraps. It merely marks the wrapped unit as having the functional potential of a nominal in its context.

Wrapping can also occur with ostentatious wordings such as direct discourse (i.e., discourse that involves a shift in the point of reference). For example, note Luke 15:27 (ὁ εἶπεν αὐτῷ ὅτι Ὁ ἀδελφός σου ἥκει, "He said to him that 'Your brother has come'"). The direct discourse in this verse is wrapped with the word ὅτι. This wording evidently involves direct discourse rather than indirect discourse, since the referent being spoken to shifts from αὐτῷ ("him") to σου ("you"), and the wrapper ὅτι marks this shift. A marker is not necessary, however, as in the example of Mark 7:6 (ὁ εἶπεν αὐτοῖς Καλῶς ἐπροφήτευσεν Ἠσαΐας περὶ ὑμῶν τῶν ὑποκριτῶν, "He said to them, 'Well did Isaiah prophesy about you hypocrites'"). In this case, there is a shift in point of reference making direct discourse clear again, but this verse lacks a marker around the wrapped content. Direct discourse functions in its context as a nominal. The word ὅτι would mark this nominalization explicitly, but it is not strictly necessary to effect a change in the functional potential of the wrapped wording.

We can observe various levels of wrapping in Eph 2:11–13:

> Διὸ μνημονεύετε ὅτι ποτὲ ὑμεῖς τὰ ἔθνη ἐν σαρκί, οἱ λεγόμενοι ἀκροβυστία ὑπὸ τῆς λεγομένης περιτομῆς ἐν σαρκὶ χειροποιήτου, ὅτι ἦτε τῷ καιρῷ ἐκείνῳ χωρὶς Χριστοῦ, ἀπηλλοτριωμένοι τῆς πολιτείας τοῦ Ἰσραὴλ καὶ ξένοι τῶν διαθηκῶν τῆς ἐπαγγελίας, ἐλπίδα μὴ ἔχοντες καὶ ἄθεοι ἐν τῷ κόσμῳ. νυνὶ δὲ ἐν Χριστῷ Ἰησοῦ ὑμεῖς οἵ ποτε ὄντες μακρὰν ἐγενήθητε ἐγγὺς ἐν τῷ αἵματι τοῦ Χριστοῦ.

This example includes a verbal cluster with multiple *wrapped* complements. There are also additional non-structural cohesive features (e.g., ποτέ and νυνί), which do not create hierarchical structures via the chaining or wrapping functions. In other words, they are not constituents, so they do not relate to the structure at all. The two instances of ὅτι wrap almost all of this verse, creating two complements, but wrapping happens for other wordings as well. Consider the wording τῷ καιρῷ ἐκείνῳ χωρὶς Χριστοῦ ("in that time apart from Christ"). The initial dative nominal group is wrapped by the article, such that the entire group functions as a nominal (and in fact all the dependents are nominals as well). The final nominal, Χριστοῦ, is wrapped by a preposition, such that the class of the resulting whole is adverbial. Compare this wording with the following: ἐν τῷ αἵματι τοῦ Χριστοῦ ("in/by the blood of Christ"). In this latter case, the initial dative nominal group is the one wrapped by a preposition, such that ἐν τῷ αἵματι τοῦ Χριστοῦ functions as an adverbial, and the final word Χριστοῦ is wrapped by an article and functions as an oblique nominal that is dependent on what precedes it. Throughout the entire example we also see instances of marked chaining, too, such as ἀπηλλοτριωμένοι . . . καὶ ξένοι ("excluded . . . and strangers"). Within this chained unit, the participle ἀπηλλοτριωμένοι also exhibits the wrapping phenomenon, marked by the nominal ending, which effectively wraps the process in a nominal class, such that ἀπηλλοτριωμένοι functions as a nominal in its context (i.e., the predication of ἦτε). As this example illustrates, chaining quantitatively augments units, while wrapping qualitatively augments units in terms of their functional potential in context.

Looking at chaining, in Gal 5:19–23, we see an example of chaining that only has one explicit marker of chaining (the marker is underlined below) across two different chains:

> φανερὰ δέ ἐστιν τὰ ἔργα τῆς σαρκός, ἅτινά ἐστιν πορνεία, ἀκαθαρσία, ἀσέλγεια, εἰδωλολατρία, φαρμακεία, ἔχθραι, ἔρις, ζῆλος, θυμοί, ἐριθεῖαι, διχοστασίαι, αἱρέσεις, φθόνοι, μέθαι, κῶμοι, <u>καὶ</u> τὰ ὅμοια τούτοις . . . Ὁ δὲ καρπὸς τοῦ πνεύματός ἐστιν ἀγάπη, χαρά, εἰρήνη, μακροθυμία, χρηστότης, ἀγαθωσύνη, πίστις, πραΰτης, ἐγκράτεια· κατὰ τῶν τοιούτων οὐκ ἔστιν νόμος.

This passage involves two lists, both chaining together multiple vices or virtues. That these units are chained is clear, but the characteristic markers (e.g., καί or τε) are lacking almost entirely.

CONCLUSION

The patterns I am calling chaining and wrapping describe some of the traditional conjunctive patterns in Greek grammar usually referred to as paratactic and hypotactic, or coordinating and subordinating. At the same time, these chaining and wrapping functions also capture patterns that do not fall into traditional descriptions of Greek's conjunctive systems. Chaining and wrapping are best understood, then, as textual patterns often involving structural markers that allow for the quantitative and qualitative augmentation of Greek syntactic units of all ranks. Here, I have attempted to show how the system of conjunction can be realized through structure, but also how certain structures can be multivalent, operating in the service of multiple metafunctional systems.

BIBLIOGRAPHY

Arnauld, Antoine, and Claude Lancelot. *General and Rational Grammar: The Port-Royal Grammar*. Janua Linguarum 208. The Hague: Mouton, 1975.

Blass, Friedrich. *Grammar of New Testament Greek*. Translated by Henry St. J. Thackeray. London: Macmillan, 1898.

Graffi, Giorgio. *200 Years of Syntax: A Critical Survey*. Amsterdam Studies in the Theory and History of Linguistic Science 3. Studies in the History of the Language Sciences 98. Amsterdam: Benjamins, 2001.

Halliday, M. A. K. *Halliday's Introduction to Functional Grammar*. Revised by Christian M. I. M. Matthiessen. 4th ed. London: Routledge, 2014. (IFG4)

Halliday, M. A. K., and Ruqaiya Hasan. *Cohesion in English*. English Language Series 9. London: Longman, 1976.

Lamb, Sydney. *Outline of Stratificational Grammar*. Washington, DC: Georgetown University Press, 1966.

Peters, Ronald D. *The Greek Article: A Functional Grammar of ὁ-Items in the Greek New Testament with Special Emphasis on the Greek Article*. LBS 9. Leiden: Brill, 2014.

Robertson, A. T. *A Grammar of the Greek New Testament in the Light of Historical Research*. 4th ed. Nashville: Broadman, 1934.

Tesnière, Lucien. *Elements of Structural Syntax*, edited by Timothy John Osborne and Sylvain Kahane. Amsterdam: Benjamins, 2015.

Wallace, Daniel B. *The Basics of New Testament Syntax: An Intermediate Greek Grammar*. Grand Rapids: Zondervan, 2000.

4

A Multi-Dimensional Model of the System of Conjunction for the Greek of the New Testament

ZACHARY K. DAWSON

INTRODUCTION

IN AN ARTICLE PUBLISHED in 2007, Stanley E. Porter and Matthew Brook O'Donnell make the sweeping claim that "the study of the Greek conjunctions has been hindered methodologically."[1] They go on to explain that even works that are linguistically informed suffer from approaches that are either too atomistic or are skewed by supposed Semitic influence, so they conclude that "the failure to see the conjunctions as one of the systems of the [Greek] language seriously impedes analysis."[2] They then go on to identify three main aspects of conjunctions that can open new avenues for analysis: these include (1) how conjunctions

---

1. Porter and O'Donnell, "Conjunctions," 4.

2. Porter and O'Donnell, "Conjunctions," 5. An exception, however, is Stephanie Black's work, which is informed by a mixture of functionalist and cognitive linguistic models (*Sentence Conjunctions*). While not being as methodologically hindered as others, Black's work, however, is still limited in its scope and corpus; she only considers the use of five conjunctions and asyndeton in the Gospel of Matthew. Randall Buth is one of the main advocates for Semitic influence in the use of Greek conjunctions; see, for example, Buth, "Semitic Καί"; "Οὖν"; Buth, "Edayin/Tote."

function "vertically" to join segments of texts of varying lengths at multiple levels of discourse (i.e., words, word groups, clauses, and clause-complexes), an area of research that they find woefully underdeveloped across the literature;[3] (2) how conjunctions function "horizontally" to establish continuity-discontinuity in discourse;[4] and (3) how conjunctions function also "horizontally" to establish logico-semantic relations between spans of texts.[5]

Identifying the multiple ways that conjunctions function in discourse is vital for further developing our understanding of them, but to achieve a comprehensive systemization of conjunctions for New Testament Greek, we first need a linguistic model capable of handling all the systems at work in a language, because, as I will demonstrate in this chapter, conjunctions play a role in several of them. The goal of this essay, then, is to continue to overcome more of the methodological limitations that restrict analysis of the Greek system of CONJUNCTION[6] by devel-

---

3. Porter and O'Donnell, "Conjunctions," 4. Daniel Wallace, for instance, defines conjunctions as "linking words" and identifies their coordinating and subordinating functions at various levels, such as "sentence to sentence" and "paragraph to paragraph" (*Greek Grammar*, 667–68). However, Wallace then organizes Greek conjunctions into what can only be arbitrarily chosen semantic categories (i.e., substantival, adverbial, and logical) because Porter and O'Donnell clearly demonstrate how these categories direct Wallace to misinterpret several conjunctions in his consideration of John 3:16 ("Conjunctions," 4). Porter and O'Donnell also find that even linguistically informed works have not gone far beyond acknowledging a hierarchy of inter-sentential conjunctions, such as with the work of Cynthia Westfall, who maps conjunctions principally according to a cline of emphasis (*Discourse Analysis*, 82). Cf. the hierarchical chart of inter-sentential conjunctions in Westfall, "Method," 85. Since Porter and O'Donnell's article, other works that approach Greek conjunctions from a modern linguistic framework have taken a step backward by only discussing conjunctions (or "connectives") in terms of linking clauses together. For example, Steven Runge states, "Greek connectives play a functional role in discourse by indicating how the writer intended one clause to relate to another, based on the connective used" (*Discourse Grammar*, 18). This statement is rather surprising because the intention of Runge's *discourse* grammar is to move beyond the clause and sentence levels, and conjunctions play an important role in organizing discourse above these levels. Runge's account of "connectives" serves more as a reorganized account of Stephen Levinsohn's work on the most frequently occurring conjunctions in the New Testament; see Levinsohn, *Discourse Features*, 71–131.

4. Porter and O'Donnell, "Conjunctions," 10–11.

5. Porter and O'Donnell, "Conjunctions," 11–12.

6. In this essay, I am adopting the convention used by systemic-functional linguists of using small caps for the names of grammatical systems and italics for the names of systemic options within those systems. Also, while I agree with the way Porter and O'Donnell have modeled conjunctions for Greek, there is an assumption that they

oping a more discriminating model that is able to describe the various logico-semantic relationships that "obtain between text spans of varying extent, ranging from clauses within clause complexes to longer spans of a paragraph or more."[7] Further, in adapting the insights of Systemic Functional Linguistics (SFL), the system of CONJUNCTION for Greek will be modeled according to the generally accepted division between *external* and *internal* conjunction. This division enables description of how the CONJUNCTION system relates meanings across all the functions of language—experiential, textual, and interpersonal.

APPROACHING CONJUNCTION FROM AN EXPLICIT THEORY OF LANGUAGE

In SFL, the modeling of CONJUNCTION goes beyond the categorization of all the words that traditionally belong to the word class of conjunctions and their role in structural connectivity[8]—it aims to identify all the possible ways that two segments of text can be connected to each other.[9] However, work on CONJUNCTION in SFL is not without its diversity.

---

make that I believe is yet another hindrance to the study of Greek conjunctions. As seen in the quotation above, there is the assumption that a whole system of the Greek language corresponds neatly to the sub-set of lexical items belonging to the traditional word class of conjunctions. While it may be pragmatically expedient to bracket out other linguistic resources that are not formally defined as conjunctions, this does not mean that other lexical resources of the Greek language, such as words classed as adverbs, conjunctive adjuncts, and even some prepositions can have conjunctive functions in discourse, which would indicate that the system that Porter and O'Donnell identify extends beyond conjunctions as traditionally defined. The system of CONJUNCTION as I define it incorporates conjunctive resources other than conjunctions, even though I, too, will be giving primary attention to words classed as conjunctions, but with some consideration of adverbs and other particles out of necessity.

7. Halliday, IFG4, 609.

8. Historically, scholarly work on New Testament Greek grammar has been limited to this kind of an approach. J. D. Denniston's reference book on particles, which focused on Classical literature, established an exhaustive taxonomy of Greek conjunctions, which he exemplified with numerous examples (*Greek Particles*). Works that focused particularly on New Testament particles following Denniston's standard work tended to rely on his descriptive categories for conjunctions. See, for example, Thrall, *Greek Particles*, 41–67. See also Blomqvist, *Greek Particles*, 17–18, where he explicitly states that he adopts Denniston's categories. For a more detailed and insightful history of the development of the study of conjunctions in New Testament, see Black, *Sentence Conjunctions*, 19–22.

9. Thompson, "But Me Some Buts," 765. Cf. Halliday and Hasan, *Cohesion in English*, 227.

For instance, some works, especially those by Halliday, take a strictly grammar-based approach and focus mainly on how conjunctions and other conjunctive components function to link clauses together.[10] The primary concern of this approach is to systematize the lexico-grammatical resources of a language that are used to create cohesion in text. It is principally oriented to the textual metafunction of language but also draws on the logical metafunction to address logico-semantic relationships between text spans of varying lengths. Others have developed the SFL model of CONJUNCTION to address not only how texts create cohesion, but also how CONJUNCTION functions to stage and develop discourse, to relate activity sequences,[11] and to negotiate claims in discourse.[12] In other words, systemicists have shown how CONJUNCTION functions textually to create cohesion, experientially to construe relations between real-world activities, and interpersonally to negotiate value positions. All these uses are mediated through the logico-semantic relations between text segments by means of the logical metafunction of language. The result is a complete account of the system of CONJUNCTION in English mapped onto each metafunction of language. Getting to this stage of development, however, requires detailed consideration of the stratum of semantics in the SFL model, and so I will turn now to detail the framework needed for understanding this multi-dimensional model of CONJUNCTION.

Functions of Language

There are several systemicists (and those who have been influenced by SFL) who emphasize that the primary use of language is essentially to exercise social control, whether this refers to the negotiation of goods and services, information, value orientations, or power and status. Jay Lemke, for example, claims "the primary function of language, and of all semiosis, is to create, sustain and change social reality."[13] Norman Fairclough similarly states, "Discourse as an ideological practice constitutes, naturalizes, sustains and changes significations of the world from diverse positions in power relations"; he conceptualizes the social func-

---

10. See Halliday and Hasan, *Cohesion in English*, 226–73; Halliday, IFG4, 609–22.
11. Martin and Rose, *Working with Discourse*, 115–54.
12. Thompson, "But Me Some Buts."
13. Lemke, "Interpersonal Meaning," 86. See also Lemke, *Textual Politics*, 19–36.

tion of language entirely in terms of power and domination.[14] In their linguistic model of social context, J. R. Martin and David Rose explain that "ideology is understood more generally as relations that permeate every level of semiosis; there is no meaning outside power."[15] However, others who work within SFL find this description to be somewhat overdrawn. For instance, Halliday and Webster explain that language, in addition to being used to gain social control, can also be used simply to communicate ideas or to express one's emotions.[16] Therefore, they intentionally draw upon the more tempered theory of language developed in the 1930s by Karl Bühler, who theorized that language has three functions: a conative, expressive, and representational function, which "can be thought of as, respectively, language as social control, language as expressive of speakers' feelings [i.e., state of mind], and language as communication of ideas," and utterances can be mixtures of these three functions.[17] Once it has been acknowledged that language has more than one function, though, admittedly, the function of social control (e.g., persuasion) is often dominant,[18] then it needs to be explained how these various functions interact with one another. One way that this multipurposive view of language can be reconciled is by suggesting that differ-

---

14. Fairclough, *Discourse and Social Change*, 67. See also Fairclough, *Critical Discourse Analysis*, 56–68; *Language and Power*. Fairclough is a major proponent and developer of Critical Discourse Analysis (CDA), a form of discourse analysis concerned with how language functions to gain, maintain, and exercise power; it is primarily concerned with political discourse. It draws heavily on the social sciences but makes use of a linguistic model that is largely informed and adapted from SFL. Fairclough details his modifications to the SFL model in a few places. See Fairclough, *Discourse and Social Change*, 64–65, 71; Fairclough, *Analysing Discourse*, 5–6. CDA has not been widely used in biblical studies, perhaps due largely to its ideological baggage and fatalistic stance that all language is motivated by power. However, there are a few instances in which insights from CDA have been adapted for biblical studies, but in a more tempered way; see Porter, "Is Critical Discourse Analysis Critical?"; Dawson, "Rules of 'Engagement.'"

15. Martin and Rose, *Genre Relations*, 17.

16. Halliday and Webster, *Text Linguistics*, 3–4.

17. Halliday and Webster, *Text Linguistics*, 4. Cf. Bühler, *Theory of Language*, 30–39. See also Porter, *Linguistic Analysis*, 317–20, for a more detailed description of Bühler's organon model of language, as well as an overview of Bühler's influence on certain modern linguists, including systemic-functional linguists.

18. See Halliday and Webster, *Text Linguistics*, 5. Social control often carries a pejorative connotation, but this is not necessary. For example, a parent verbally chastening a misbehaving child would be considered an instance where the exertion of authority is in the best interest of the child and necessary for moral development.

ent components or segments of text can have different functions, or at least a function that is more prominent than the others. In other words, whereas the function of one segment of text or one grammatical element might serve primarily to convey information, another part of the same text might function to persuade or exercise control in some way.

To continue using Bühler's functions of language for a moment, we can expect most utterances to communicate conative, expressive, and representational meanings simultaneously. Representational meanings are those that construe a writer's interpretation of "real world" events—that is, the linguistic coding of experience that readers will interpret as the content of an utterance.[19] In SFL terms, this corresponds to the experiential metafunction of language, or what an utterance is "about."[20] Additionally, processes are also related together in certain ways in language. So, in the example, *If I go to the store, then I will buy milk*, two processes, "go" and "buy," are related by *if . . . then*, a conditional. This is a kind of construing of experience, but one that requires a composite unit (in this case a dependent and independent clause) where the experience is realized by a logical connection between two wordings. This exemplifies the logical metafunction of language, and, as seen in this example, the logical metafunction is most salient at the level of clause-complex (i.e., the combination of two or more clauses into one unit that shares interdependence).[21] Taken together the experiential and logical metafunctions are combined into the more general ideational metafunction. However, in dealing with the system of CONJUNCTION, it is necessary to distinguish their differences. Furthermore, while construing experience, a language user also enacts relationships and expresses forms of involvement with his or her interlocutors; this includes both the conative and expressive functions of language, both of which correspond with SFL's interpersonal metafunction. The interpersonal notion of "clause as exchange" addresses that even at the clausal level every utterance can be categorized as either a proposition or a proposal whereby language users negotiate goods and services or information based on a clause's speech function.[22] In SFL, the equivalent of Bühler's expressive function

19. Halliday and Webster, *Text Linguistics*, 6–7.
20. Halliday and Webster, *Text Linguistics*, 7.
21. Thompson, *Introducing Functional Grammar*, 187–88.
22. Halliday and Matthiessen, *Introduction to Functional Grammar*, 30. Speech functions modeled in SFL for English do not correspond one-to-one with Greek. This

has been modeled most extensively in J. R. Martin and P. R. R. White's theory of appraisal, especially in the systems of attitude and graduation.[23]

SFL's textual metafunction, however, does not have a correspondent in Bühler's model. Perhaps this is because it is purely linguistic—that is, it only pertains to the internal aspect of the operation of language, and therefore is understood as the means by which the social functions of language are achieved.[24] However, because of this, the textual metafunction is essential for the ideational and interpersonal metafunctions to operate effectively; the structural and cohesive features of textual meaning ensure that instances of language produce texts, where "text" is defined as "any coherent passage of language in use, whether spoken or written."[25]

Meaning beyond the Clause: Clause Complexes and Conjunction

From Clause Complexing to Conjunction

Halliday and Matthiessen identify the clause complex as the most extensive semantic domain of grammatical structure.[26] Systemicists define a clause complex as "the grammatical and semantic unit formed when two or more clauses are linked together in certain systematic and meaningful ways."[27] The two semantic systems that this definition presumes are the systems of TAXIS and LOGICO-SEMANTICS.[28] The system of TAXIS sys-

---

has been shown especially by Porter, "Systemic Functional Linguistics," 20–32. Cf. Dawson, "Language as Negotiation," 373–74n50. Several recent suggestions have been made about how to model speech functions for Greek with respect to verbal Mood, the most delicate system being modeled by Stanley Porter ("Systemic Functional Linguistics," 20–32), but see also Dawson, "Language as Negotiation," 373–80; Land, "Jesus before Pilate," 238–40.

23. See Martin and White, *Language of Evaluation*, 42–91, 135–59. Attitude has to do with how feelings are encoded in text, and graduation has to do more specifically with how language users can vary the intensity of their language. See also White, "Evaluative Semantics"; Lemke, "Resources." For Greek, the system of appraisal is modeled in Dvorak, "'Prodding with Prosody'"; Dvorak, *Interpersonal Metafunction*.

24. Halliday and Webster, *Text Linguistics*, 10.

25. Halliday and Webster, *Text Linguistics*, 9.

26. Halliday, IFG4, 609.

27. Eggins, *Introduction*, 255.

28. In addition to the systems of TAXIS and LOGICO-SEMANTICS, the system of RECURSION is also operative in clause complexing, which consists of the binary option to either stop or go on—that is, the choice of whether to stop or continue a grammatical

tematizes the types of interdependent relationships between clauses in a clause complex; a clause complex can share a combination of paratactic (i.e., equal status) or hypotactic (i.e., unequal status) relationships that create clause nexuses, and these facilitate the development of text and guide understanding.[29] This system is also pertinent to CONJUNCTION because CONJUNCTION is realized in three kinds of grammatical contexts: paratactic, hypotactic, and cohesive.[30] Greek has a relatively large number of conjunctions used in paratactic contexts, the most frequent being καί.[31] Greek conjunctions used in hypotactic contexts often signal relations of result, purpose, time, comparison, among others.[32] Cohesive conjunction, on the other hand, refers to the logico-semantic relations that operate outside the tactic system and thus extend beyond the level of clause complex to larger spans of texts such as paragraphs.[33] The lexico-grammatical resources that realize cohesive CONJUNCTION are often called "discourse markers"[34] because they mark off boundaries and signal how the text is to be understood as a coherent whole.[35]

The system of LOGICO-SEMANTICS, the second system operative in clause complexing, describes the type of meaning relationship between linked clauses.[36] The choices here are also binary: clauses can be related through *projection* (i.e., reported or indirect speech/thought) or *expansion*. In Greek, indirect speech is realized by three main grammatical constructions: the infinitive construction, the ὅτι construction, and the participle construction.[37] Direct quotation, however, usually must be

---

unit. Cf. Halliday, IFG4, 438.

29. Halliday, IFG4, 609.

30. Martin and Rose, *Working with Discourse*, 120.

31. The most common conjunctions used in independent clauses are discussed in Porter, *Idioms*, 204–17.

32. See Porter, *Idioms*, 230–43.

33. Halliday, IFG4; Martin and Rose, *Working with Discourse*, 121; Thompson, *Introducing Functional Grammar*, 225.

34. See Porter and O'Donnell, "Conjunctions," 5. Louw and Nida provide an entire semantic domain for "discourse markers" in their lexicon (*Greek–English Lexicon*, 1:811–13), most of which are conjunctions. Others (cf. Runge, *Discourse Grammar*, 17) refer to this type of conjunction with the label "connective." See Halliday, IFG4, 609n3.

35. Thompson, *Introducing Functional Grammar*, 225.

36. Eggins, *Introduction*, 259.

37. McKay, *New Syntax*, 99–105. This system is left undeveloped in Hunt, "Meaning in Bulk."

deduced by context alone.[38] In modeling expansion for Greek, Benjamin B. Hunt adopts the same logico-semantic options developed by Halliday: *elaboration, extension,* and *enhancement*.[39] *Elaboration* is described in terms of how a clause elaborates on the meaning of another to further specify, clarify, or otherwise describe it;[40] an equal symbol (i.e., =) is often used to signify this kind of relationship.[41] *Extension* refers to how a clause extends the meaning of another by adding something new to it;[42] this relationship is signified by an addition symbol (i.e., +).[43] And with *enhancement* "one clause (or subcomplex) enhances the meaning of another by qualifying it in one of a number of possible ways: by reference to time, place, manner, cause or condition;"[44] the symbol for this relationship is that of multiplication (i.e., x).[45] The values *projection* and *expansion* thus serve as entry conditions to two of the main sub-systems of CONJUNCTION.

While similar and complementary in several respects, clause complexing and conjunction are two distinct parts of the grammar. Conjunction, for instance, is not confined to the level of clause complex; it refers to "the combining of any two textual elements into a potentially coherent complex semantic unit."[46] Within clauses, both conjunctions and prepositions function "junctively" to add meanings recursively, and between clauses and clause complexes, conjunctions and adverbs especially link segments into coherent texts. Once an inventory is compiled of all the lexico-grammatical resources that can function conjunctively—these are not necessarily limited to lexemes but also include word groups (i.e., conjunctive adjuncts)—the conjunctive relations of Greek can be systematized in full. For now, I will only be describing CONJUNCTION as it relates to the relations between clauses and clause complexes, which means that the system detailed below can only be considered partial in its description because it is rank-specific. Moreover, Halliday

---

38. McKay, *New Syntax*, 97–98.
39. Hunt, "Meaning in Bulk," 395. Cf. Halliday, IFG4, 460–508.
40. Halliday, IFG4, 461.
41. Eggins, *Introduction*, 279.
42. Halliday, IFG4, 471.
43. Eggins, *Introduction*, 279.
44. Halliday, IFG4, 476.
45. Eggins, *Introduction*, 279.
46. Thompson, *Introducing Functional Grammar*, 225.

explains the differences between clause complexing and conjunction in the following way:

> A key difference between clause complexing and cohesive conjunction is that while the clause complexing specifies (i) the nature of the logico-semantic relation, (ii) the degree of interdependency, and (iii) the clausal domains being related through the formation of univariate structure, cohesive conjunction only specifies (i)—the nature of the logical-semantic relation. In this sense, cohesive conjunctions are "clue words" ... providing listeners and readers with information about (i) that may also allow them to infer (ii) and (iii).[47]

As a result, the model illustrated below is principally concerned with describing the kinds of logical relations between clauses and between clause complexes. The nature of such relations, however, needs to be discussed further.

Types of Conjunction

The system of CONJUNCTION in Greek is a system used to create logico-semantic relations in texts across all the functions of language—experiential, textual, and interpersonal; it is comparable in this regard to English. In other words, when logico-semantic relations between clauses are realized by conjunctive resources in the lexico-grammar, they function as links between experiential meanings, between textual meanings, and/or between interpersonal meanings.[48] This gives rise to a system of conjunctive ORIENTATION, which enables a choice between *external* and *internal* conjunction.

---

47. Halliday, IFG4, 609.

48. The SFL literature is mixed on this issue. Halliday and Hasan interpret conjunction based on ideational and interpersonal meanings (*Cohesion in English*, 240–41). Martin and Rose divide conjunction between ideational and textual meaning in their chapter modeling the system of conjunction (*Working with Discourse*, 116), though they also discuss the notion of concession elsewhere, which is based on the interpersonal function of conjunctions and adverbs (*Working with Discourse*, 56–58). This inconsistency is problematic in their work because they fail to explain how to understand all three types of conjunction in relation to one another. Thompson, to my knowledge, is the only systemicist who has attempted to bring all three types of conjunction under one multi-dimensional analysis (see "But Me Some Buts"). However, in his introduction to the field he accounts for conjunction inconsistently, claiming that only ideational and textual meanings are possible (Thompson, *Introducing Functional Grammar*, 227).

The conjunctive orientation that interacts with experiential meanings is called *external* conjunction; "it is a relation between meanings in the sense of representations of 'contents' (our experience of) external reality."[49] An example of *external* conjunction is found in Mark 1:23 (καὶ εὐθὺς ἦν ἐν τῇ συναγωγῇ αὐτῶν ἄνθρωπος ἐν πνεύματι ἀκαθάρτῳ καὶ ἀνέκραξεν, "and immediately there was in their synagogue a man with an unclean spirit, *and* he cried out"). The conjunction καί here functions to link the ideational processes of a man being in the synagogue and the man crying out by means of *expansion*, more specifically, by means of the *additive* use of καί (see below).

The conjunctive orientation that interacts with the interpersonal and textual metafunctions is called *internal* conjunction. Interpersonally, conjunction is "a relation between meanings in the sense of representations of the speaker's own 'stamp' on the situation—his choice of speech role and rhetorical channel, his attitudes, his judgments and the like"—for the purpose of connecting moves in an unfolding interaction or negotiation of claims.[50] The label *negotiating* has been chosen to designate this kind of *internal* conjunction. An example of *internal* conjunction relating interpersonal meanings is found in Gal 2:15–16a: ἡμεῖς φύσει Ἰουδαῖοι καὶ οὐκ ἐξ ἐθνῶν ἁμαρτωλοί εἰδότες [δὲ] ὅτι οὐ δικαιοῦται ἄνθρωπος ἐξ ἔργων νόμου ("we by birth are Jews and not from among Gentile sinners, *but* seeing that a person is not righteous by works of the law . . ."). In this example, the conjunction δέ signals an *adversative* relationship with the previous clause.[51] The interpersonal move is an assertion–concession whereby the writer counters some expectation in the context to negotiate a belief or value position. Without considering more of the surrounding context, the move here can be generally explained as a conclusion contrary to the addressees' projected expectation that Jews are made righteous by works of the law.[52]

---

49. Halliday and Hasan, *Cohesion in English*, 240.

50. Halliday and Hasan, *Cohesion in English*, 240. See also Thompson, "But Me Some Buts," 774–75.

51. The use of the conjunction δέ itself is not enough to conclude that an adversative relationship is being realized because δέ can be used to realize other types of relations. Additional contextual constraints, therefore, must guide interpretation, and since a comparison is set up between Jews and Gentiles, the adversative relationship is reasonably deduced because a Jewish reader would closely associate righteousness with the law (Torah), whereas someone outside Judaism would not.

52. I use the term *projected* here in the sense that Paul is attributing or assuming

Textually, *internal* conjunction functions to connect steps in an unfolding argument, not linking events in the field of experience but linking logical steps internal to the text itself.[53] The label *organizing* has been chosen to designate this type of *internal* conjunction. In many instances, internal clausal relations can be construed as either textual or interpersonal, and they can often be construed as both simultaneously. Even conjunctions functioning as discourse markers—a specifically textual function—often carry with them interpersonal implications. For instance, the conjunction ἀλλά often signals a textual relationship of development between clauses, but with an adversative implication that points to some kind of negotiation of a value position.[54] Thus, some conjunctive relations may be multivariate regarding their orientation.

Expectancy and Counter-Expectancy

Another aspect of logico-semantic relations that needs to be introduced here is the notion of EXPECTANCY, which I model as a distinct sub-system in the larger network of CONJUNCTION. The theoretical principles underlying the whole notion of expectancy are Mikhail Bakhtin's intertextual concepts of heteroglossia and dialogism. Heteroglossia refers to the polyphony of "voices" that express the various ideological stances present in a culture, whether this entails the promoting or demoting of beliefs and values or the stylization of one's way of representing reality.[55] When language users speak or write, their meanings are constrained by this heteroglossic backdrop, and so they inevitably take these other "voices" into account, whether to affirm, refute, or otherwise respond to them in some way, and this phenomenon is referred to as dialogism.[56] As texts unfold, CONJUNCTION helps to manage the readers' or listeners'

---

that his addressees might have this belief, or perhaps that there are some—not necessarily his addressees—who promote this view by means of their stated beliefs or actions. Whether or not they had this belief is beside the point, because either way they are inter-subjectively positioned as having this belief. On the notion of inter-subjectivity, see White, "Dialogue and Inter-Subjectivity," 68–73.

53. Thompson, "But Me Some Buts," 775; Martin and Rose, *Working with Discourse*, 117.

54. See Louw and Nida, *Greek–English Lexicon*, 1:811.

55. Bakhtin, *Speech Genres*, 91. See also Bakhtin, "Discourse in the Novel," 263; Frow, *Genre*, 48; Dawson, "Books of Acts," 20–21.

56. See Holquist, *Dialogism*, 69–70; Lemke, "Interpersonal Meaning," 85; Dawson, "Books of Acts," 21.

expectations about what is to happen.[57] This can take the form of linking the logical steps in an argument or a series of statements in the telling of a story. Most often, the logico-semantic relations between clauses follow along the lines of expectancy—they can be labeled as *expectant* with regard to the relationship they share with their preceding co-text. However, *counter-expectant* realizations signal important junctions where the writer or speaker accounts for some "voice" and opposes it in some way. From a strictly interpersonal standpoint, counter-expectancy readjusts the expectations of addressees so as to reposition them in terms of the writer or speaker's value position.[58] In English, the conjunction "but" is perhaps the most common resource for accomplishing this linguistic move. In the Greek of the New Testament markers of contrast and concession are important resources for realizing *counter-expectant* relations.

Summary

To sum up this section, Geoff Thompson explains the three orientations of conjunctive relations succinctly in the following way:

> The choice from the three major types of conjunction reflects whether the speaker at that point in the communicative event is operating with a model of potential connection between stretches of the discourse that is primarily oriented toward language as representation (experiential), as exchange (interpersonal), or as message (textual). That is, at any moment the speaker may be more concerned to foreground 'real-world' connections, or to enact awareness of, and/or guide, the hearer's reactions to what is being said, or to make explicit the organization of what is being said.[59]

This set of options constitutes the sub-system of ORIENTATION in the overall system of CONJUNCTION that I have been detailing. This system is simultaneous with the choice between *projection* and *expansion*, so its values can be selected alongside values from the systems of PROJECTION TYPE, EXPANSION TYPE, and EXPECTANCY. The following figure depicts the system of CONJUNCTION as I have modeled it so far.

---

57. Martin and Rose, *Working with Discourse*, 117.
58. See Martin and Rose, *Working with Discourse*, 56–57.
59. Thompson, "But Me Some Buts," 775.

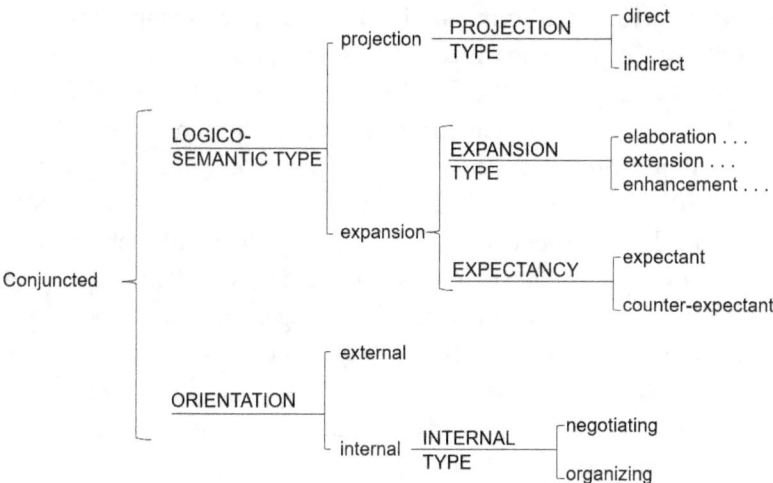

Figure 1. The Initial Systems of CONJUNCTION for Greek

THE GREEK SYSTEM OF CONJUNCTION AND LEXICO-GRAMMATICAL RESOURCES

In the previous section, the system of CONJUNCTION was modeled to account for three main sub-systems that function in the CONJUNCTION system, but also to clarify how the logico-semantic relations are understood as experiential, interpersonal, and textual in their orientation. To model the system of CONJUNCTION so that it can be applied with precision to Greek texts, the logico-semantic notion of expansion needs to be developed to a further point of delicacy.

There are various suggestions among systemicists about how to classify the phenomena that are grouped together by Halliday as expansions. Halliday and Hasan, for example, suggest four: additive, adversative, causal, and temporal.[60] These categories are interpreted broadly and developed to varying points of delicacy for both external and internal conjunction. They are described principally as a cohesive system of language, but are also used to describe coherence in general terms.[61] Martin's system of CONJUNCTION, on the other hand, eliminates the cat-

---

60. Halliday and Hasan, *Cohesion in English*, 238–73.
61. Halliday, "Text Semantics," 225.

egory of "adversative," grouping it with options of "comparison."[62] He also situates "contrary to expectation" as an option within his sub-categories of "consequence."[63] Below I have adopted a scheme for organizing the CONJUNCTION system in Greek based mainly on classifications of Greek conjunctions, but also with consideration of certain particles and adverbs. While others might suggest alternative schemes, the system detailed below is dependent largely on Porter's *Idioms*. Where information on lexico-grammatical resources is missing from Porter's grammar, I have consulted Louw and Nida's *Greek–English Lexicon*. Due to space constraints, there are many lexico-grammatical resources that are left undeveloped here, such as other word classes (e.g., concessive participles) or conjunctive adjuncts made up of multiple words (e.g., κατ' ἐκεῖνον τὸν καιρὸν, "about that time" [Acts 12:1]).

The System of Expansion Type

The system of EXPANSION TYPE has only ever been roughly explained for New Testament Greek in a couple of articles by Jeffrey Reed; no work to my knowledge has advanced this discussion beyond his work.[64] In his explanation, Reed essentially adopts Halliday's categories of elaboration, extension, and enhancement and provides lexico-grammatical resources in Greek that fit into Halliday's sub-categories of each of these types of expansion. While Reed's work begins to organize some Greek resources, in no way can it be claimed that expansion has been adapted for Greek, other than to say that Greek words have been plugged into the categories that Halliday has modeled for English. As a result, many of the categories Reed suggests are questionable, and there are other categories for which he has not accounted. This is not to say that Reed's work lacks value or innovation, but rather that he does not provide the right starting place for expansion to be modeled in terms of Greek, nor does he model such resources in a rigorous manner. Thus, in the following section, Reed will serve as an appropriate discussion partner as the system of EXPANSION TYPE is modeled for Greek.

---

62. Martin and Rose, *Working with Discourse*, 125.

63. Martin and Rose, *Working with Discourse*, 132.

64. See Reed, "Discourse Analysis," 205–8 (this section is duplicated in Reed, "Cohesiveness of Discourse," 33–36).

Elaboration

With *elaboration* a clause functions to elaborate on the meaning of another, whether this is to clarify, specify, or further describe it in some way. The semantics of Greek conjunctions and conjunctive adverbs are relatively poor when it comes to elaboration, though there are other lexico-grammatical resources that can realize this type of relation.[65] This is because elaboration, from the perspective of clause complexing, is usually hypotactically constructed by means of relative pronouns, which, in SFL, are often dealt with as part of cohesion.[66] However, the explanatory use of the conjunction γάρ and the use of ὅτι and ἵνα in the opening of content clauses are exceptions. Γάρ is the only conjunction, according to Porter's grammar, that elaborates to explain further;[67] in other words, it can function to clarify the meaning of another clause. It is appropriate, then, to designate *clarification* as a systemic type of elaboration in Greek. Other conjunctive adverbs that function to clarify include ὅλως and ὄντως. Contrary to Reed, who sub-divides these adverbs under the category of clarification even further to make use of Halliday's category "verificative," it is probably better not to force these Greek words to this level of delicacy because they do not occur frequently enough in the New Testament to model them confidently them as such.[68] Content clauses function appositionally to other units (e.g., Subject, Complement, Predicator, etc.) in that they restate their content in more elaborate terms.[69] We are thus left with

---

65. Some of these are suggested in Reed, "Cohesiveness of Discourse," 34, including γέγραπται and ῥητῶς, which are odd and perhaps even questionable examples given that γέγραπται is a verb and can only be said to be conjunctive by means of formulaic or pragmatic effect, and given that ῥητῶς is a rather obscure term used only once in the New Testament (1 Tim 4:1).

66. See Halliday and Hasan, *Cohesion in English*, 31–87. Elaboration can also be realized through paratactic constructions in Greek. One of the main types of elaboration that Halliday and Matthiessen identify is apposition; this is the case with his explanation of clause complexing, but also with conjunction (*Introduction to Functional Grammar*, 462, 612–13). Greek can also realize apposition in clause complexing through resources such as intensive pronouns, such as the example in Rev 20:19 that Hunt identifies ("Meaning in Bulk," 402), where the clausal relationship is paratactic. However, pronouns are bracketed out of the lexico-grammatical resources considered here, though a case could be made that relative pronouns function in essentially the same way as content clauses in Greek, which are included in my analysis because of the conjunctions ὅτι and ἵνα.

67. Porter, *Idioms*, 207.

68. Reed, "Cohesiveness of Discourse," 34.

69. See Porter, *Idioms*, 237–39.

organizing ELABORATION TYPE according to the options of *clarifying* and *appositional*, as shown in Figure 2.

Figure 2. The System of ELABORATION TYPE for Greek

EXTENSION TYPE

In *extension*, a clause adds something new to another, which extends its meaning in some way.[70] In Martin's model, extension is reconceived as addition; this differs from Halliday's model in that it treats extension differently for internal and external conjunctions (e.g., "additive" for external versus "staging" for internal).[71] This is an important development in Martin's work, the insights of which bear relevance for internal conjunction in Greek as well. However, for the sake of space, in this essay when types of systemic options diverge due to their different orientations, I have consistently modeled the network in terms of *external* conjunction (so, with respect to the ideational metafunction). Therefore, when considering specific *internal* instances of *extension*, as with other types of internal relations, one might need to rework the system network to represent accurately the systemic options of logico-semantic relationships as they pertain to the other metafunctions. This is one area that is in need of further modeling.

Additionally, the semantic options of Greek cannot be schematized in exactly the same way that either Halliday or Martin schematizes English. In Halliday's model, there are three main categories of extension: *addition, variation*, and *alternation*.[72] *Variation* and *alternation* in Greek are

---

70. Contrary to Reed, who explains extension in terms of hypotactic relations (secondary clauses). Extension can be realized by both paratactic and hypotactic constructions ("Cohesiveness of Discourse," 34). It is strange that Reed would specify "extending" relations as hypotactic when he includes conjunctions, such as καί, δέ, ἀλλά, and others that are clearly used to create paratactic relations.

71. Martin and Rose, *Working with Discourse*, 124, 134.

72. Halliday, IFG4, 471. Reed unhelpfully conflates variation and alternation in his diagram, making variation the parent category of alternation ("Cohesiveness of Discourse," 34–35); this confuses the semantic distinctions between these categories in Halliday's model, which are also applicable to Greek.

not as lexically distinctive as they are in English; instead, they are realized through a subset of conjunctive resources, some of which are contrastive in their basic semantic value, as the discussion below will show. These are observations that Reed does not make, which is reflective of his overdependence on Halliday's scheme for English. Martin's model, on the other hand, is too simplistic for Greek because he dispenses with the distinction between *variation* and *alternation* entirely.[73] In Greek, these two are distinct semantic options, even if they are not always clearly distinguishable by lexical choice. In modeling the network of EXTENSION TYPE, I apply these considerations, which results in suggesting *addition, alternation,* and *variation* as the three main systemic options in Greek, which can then be developed to greater degrees of delicacy.

Another systemic variable that operates alongside the types of extension involves the system of CONTRAST. Conjunctions often have contrastive semantic values, which factor into their logico-semantic relations. This systemic variable is not entirely independent of extension; for example, *adversative* relations have an inherent *contrastive* feature, but *additive* and *alternative* relations do not, though they still construe *contrastive* relations in some cases. I will discuss this more fully below.

In *addition*, segments of text are simply joined to each other without any causal, temporal, or otherwise specified relationship.[74] In Halliday's model, *addition* divides into three sub-categories: *positive* addition, *negative* addition, and *adversative*.[75] Positive addition is signaled principally by *and*, while negative addition is signaled by the conjunction *nor*. These categories conveniently correspond well with Greek, where *positive* addition is realized through conjunctions such as καί, δέ, and τέ, and *negative* addition is realized by οὐδέ and μηδέ. Because *positive* and *negative* meanings are options for other types of conjunctive relations as well, the system of POLARITY is represented in my network as simultaneous with EXPANSION TYPE. Sometimes, *additive* relations can

---

73. See Martin and Rose, *Working with Discourse*, 124.
74. Halliday, IFG4, 472.
75. Halliday, IFG4, 472–73. Here I am following Halliday's categories rather than Martin's because several of Greek's main conjunctions are adversative in their basic semantic meaning, and several other Greek conjunctions can often be construed as adversative, even if this sense is not their most common use.

take on a contrastive meaning, and this may even be slight, such as with the conjunction δέ.[76]

The basic meaning of *adversative* conjunction is "contrary to expectation."[77] According to Halliday and Hasan, "The expectation may be derived from what is being said, or from the communication process, the speaker-hearer situation, so . . . we find cohesion on both the external and internal planes."[78] In the Greek system, conjunctions such as ἀλλά, δέ, εἴτε, ἤ, καί,[79] μέν, ὅμως, οὖν (on occasion),[80] and πλήν all function adversatively in this sense,[81] each countering expectations in some way.[82]

With *variation*, the content of "one clause is presented as being in total or partial replacement of [the content of] another."[83] Halliday subdivides this category to account for both total replacement (i.e., *replacive*) and partial replacement (i.e., *subtractive*). In Greek, however, the same conjunctive resources can be used in both of these logico-semantic relations; context is the determining factor to decide on whether a clausal relationship realizing *variation* is either whole or partial. Compare the following parallel Gospel passages:

- καὶ τοὺς ἄρτους τῆς προθέσεως ἔφαγον, ὃ οὐκ ἐξὸν ἦν αὐτῷ φαγεῖν οὐδὲ τοῖς μετ' αὐτοῦ εἰ μὴ τοῖς ἱερεῦσιν μόνοις ("and he [David] ate the consecrated bread, which it was not lawful for him to eat nor those with him but instead only the priests") (Matt 12:4)

- καὶ τοὺς ἄρτους τῆς προθέσεως λαβὼν ἔφαγεν καὶ ἔδωκεν τοῖς μετ' αὐτοῦ, οὓς οὐκ ἔξεστιν φαγεῖν εἰ μὴ μόνους τοὺς ἱερεῖς ("and taking the consecrated bread he [David] ate, and he gave it to those who were with him, which is not lawful to eat except by the priests") (Luke 6:4)

---

76. See Louw and Nida, *Greek–English Lexicon*, 1:790.

77. Halliday and Hasan, *Cohesion in English*, 250.

78. Halliday and Hasan, *Cohesion in English*, 250.

79. Porter notes that the adversative uses of καί are often overlooked (*Idioms*, 211). Cf. Dana and Mantey, *Manual Grammar*, 250–52.

80. Cf. Dana and Mantey, *Manual Grammar*, 257–58.

81. See Porter, *Idioms*, 205–15.

82. See Dawson, "Language as Negotiation," 381–82.

83. Halliday, IFG4, 473.

In the Matthew passage, there is a varying relation realized by εἰ μή, but it is the content of the related clauses interpreted in accordance with the conjunctive element εἰ μή that requires this instance of *variation* to be construed as *replacive*; those who are permitted to eat the bread are not David and his companions *but instead* the priests. In Luke's parallel passage, on the other hand, the *variation* type, realized also by εἰ μή, is *subtractive* (again, determined by the content); it is not lawful for anyone (implied) to eat *except* the priests. There are certain conjunctive options, however, that tend to be exclusively *replacive* in Greek, such as with ἀλλὰ μᾶλλον, ἀλλ' ἤ, and δὲ μᾶλλον. Also, with the help of the adverb ἐκτός, εἰ μή can realize *subtraction* in Greek without further need of considering the content of the related clauses.[84] An example is found in 1 Cor 14:5: μείζων δὲ ὁ προφητεύων ἢ ὁ λαλῶν γλώσσαις, ἐκτὸς εἰ μὴ διερμηνεύῃ ("the one who prophesies is of greater value than the one who speaks in tongues, *unless* someone interprets").

In *alternation* one clause functions as an alternative to another.[85] In English these are often construed by "either . . . or" and "on the one hand . . . on the other hand" constructions. This logico-semantic relation can be realized in Greek through several conjunctive resources, the most apparent ones perhaps being μέν . . . δέ, μέν . . . ἀλλά, ἤ . . . ἤ, and their related constructions.[86] The adverb μᾶλλον, as a contrastive marker, can indicate an alternative relationship with δέ as well: νῦν δὲ γνόντες θεόν, μᾶλλον δὲ γνωσθέντες ὑπὸ θεοῦ ("but now knowing God, but rather, being known by God") (Gal 4:9).[87]

Based on this discussion, the network below represents the semantic options available in the Greek system of EXTENSION TYPE.

---

84. See Louw and Nida, *Greek–English Lexicon*, 1:796.
85. Halliday, IFG4, 473.
86. See Louw and Nida, *Greek–English Lexicon*, 1:795–96. There are instances where the μέν . . . δέ construction relates clauses additively (e.g., Matt 13:8), and so these constructions should not be understood as exclusive to the realizations I have selectively identified them with here. Cf. Louw and Nida, *Greek–English Lexicon*, 1:791.
87. See Louw and Nida, *Greek–English Lexicon*, 1:794–96, where the contrastive meanings of conjunctions that realize other kinds of *alternative* relations are apparent in their definitions.

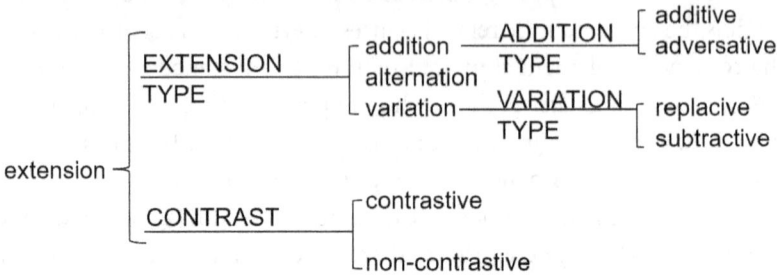

Figure 3. The System of Extension Type for Greek

Enhancement Type

Halliday defines enhancement as follows: "In enhancement one clause (or subcomplex) enhances the meaning of another by qualifying it in one of a number of possible ways: by reference to time, place, manner, cause or condition."[88] In Martin's model these categories are addressed as systems of TIME and CONSEQUENCE (comparable to Halliday and Hasan's earlier categories of temporal and causal),[89] though he also adds the system of COMPARISON, which would be best categorized under enhancement in Halliday's model.[90] In English, hypotactic enhancing clauses are traditionally called adverbial clauses because they function much like adjuncts to specify aspects of the main clause, such as why and how an event happened (i.e., circumstantial information).[91] Paratactic enhancing clauses in English function much like basic coordination (i.e., extension), but with an additional circumstantial component to them.[92] These are often difficult to tell apart such as with the use of *and* in narrative texts, which can sometimes be paraphrased as "and then" when a causal or temporal connection logically relates two paratactic clauses. In such cases, the relation is enhancing rather than extending. The same is true for καί, δέ, and τέ in Greek, making the extension/enhancement

---

88. Halliday, IFG4, 476.
89. Halliday and Hasan, *Cohesion in English*, 256–67.
90. See Martin and Rose, *Working with Discourse*, 125–32, 135–41.
91. Thompson, *Introducing Functional Grammar*, 198.
92. Reed, in the same way as with extension, makes the mistake of referring to enhancing relations exclusively in terms of hypotactic relations ("Cohesiveness of Discourse," 34).

line blurry at times.[93] In Greek, as in English, enhancement is a much more intricate system than both elaboration and extension; it includes the majority of hypotactic (dependent) clausal relationships that are linked to a main clause by a conjunction (or adverb), including purpose, result, causal, inferential, temporal, and comparative clauses, as well as conditional clauses and clauses that qualify another based on the logico-semantic categories of means and location. The Greek conjunctions that realize the logico-semantic relations of each of these types of clauses are usually schematized according to three main categories: *spatio-temporal, causal-conditional,* and *manner*.[94]

Before discussing types of spatio-temporal relations, it will be helpful to demonstrate how this type of relation functions in relation to orientation. In English, conjunctive relations do not only realize temporal relations between "real-world" events—that is, the ways in which textually sequential processes are related to each other temporally in an experiential sense (successive, simultaneous, etc.)—but also between sequential components of an argument (interpersonal) by means of adverbs such as *next, finally, first . . . second . . . third*,[95] which also function to organize texts by signaling new stages (textual).[96] Greek temporal clauses are also versatile in this respect. For example, the conjunctive adverb πρῶτον, among several other conjunctions and adverbs, commonly realizes the internal relation of *ordering*.[97] Spatial (i.e., *locative*) relations, on the other hand, usually realize external relations but with

---

93. See Louw and Nida, *Greek–English Lexicon*, 1:789, where these conjunctions are placed under the label "Sequential Addition."

94. This scheme differs from Reed's in a few ways. First, Reed does not include a system of MANNER, which is where I locate the sub-systems of MEANS and COMPARISON. Second, Reed does not account for MEANS at all in his diagram. As a result, the third way our schemes differ is that he situates COMPARISON as parallel with SPATIO-TEMPORAL and CAUSAL-CONDITIONAL, where I do not (see Reed, "Cohesiveness of Discourse," 35).

95. See Halliday and Hasan, *Cohesion in English*, 261–67.

96. Martin and Rose, *Working with Discourse*, 137–39.

97. An example from the New Testament where temporal relations are used to construe an internal relation can be found in Rom 1:8, where Paul textually signals the opening of the thanksgiving section of his letter (vv. 8–15) with the adverb πρῶτον. Regarding this verse, Porter states, "Paul begins with the word 'first', using an indicator of priority, as well as a linking conjunction . . . that ties this unit to the opening" (*Letter to the Romans*, 50). On the relation of Ordering, see Martin and Rose, *Working with Discourse*, 139. This semantic option is omitted from the networks developed in this paper because it is specific to internal conjunction of the organizing (textual) type.

some exceptions.[98] Some lexico-grammatical resources in Greek are, when translated into English, inadvertently made to suggest internal temporal relations. This often happens with the translation of inferential conjunctions and particles, such as οὖν and ἄρα:[99] e.g., Τί οὖν ἐροῦμεν; ("What then are we to say?" Rom 6:1, NRSV). But these resources are better treated as realizing *cause* in Greek, since they pertain to drawing conclusions more than signaling internal temporal relations. Given these considerations, and because the semantic options differ in spatio-temporal relations based on orientation, the modeling of these types of relations will be limited to external conjunction when the systemic options diverge due to orientational differences.

Spatio-temporal conjunction is organically divided into the subcategories of *locative* and *temporal*.[100] Locative clauses are realized by adverbs such as ὅθεν, ὅπου, and οὗ,[101] and they can be systematized into three types: locations of *extent, point,* and *somewhere*. Relations of *extent* realize the meaning of "up to or as far as a goal";[102] common expressions include ἕως and ἄχρι.[103] Next, relations of *point* indicate some point of origin such as "from inside," "from outside," or even "from where"; common expressions include ὅθεν, ἔσωθεν, and ἔξωθεν. Conjunctions and adverbs of *somewhere* realize a locative relation that is unrestricted or undetermined; common expressions include ὅπου and οὗ.

---

98. The adverb ὅθεν, for example, is used inferentially in Hebrews six times (2:17; 3:1; 7:25; 8:3; 9:18; and 11:19) and in 1 John 2:18, where a basis is drawn from using a spatial metaphor (see Halliday, IFG4, 617). Spatial metaphors are often used in English to realize relations that have nothing to do with actual spatial location, such as with the phrase, "on these grounds."

99. English translations often render these terms as "then," which is a resource of internal temporal relations in English (see Halliday and Hasan, *Cohesion in English*, 243, 263).

100. The system of Spatio-Temporal relations is one adapted directly from Halliday's model. Reed and I both adopt this scheme, but it is odd that Reed would retain Halliday's spatial component when he only considers temporal relations in his diagram; see Reed, "Cohesiveness of Discourse," 35. If Reed's diagram were representative of the resources of Greek conjunction, then one would simply refer to this system as "temporal." However, spatial relations are realized in Greek in several ways, and accounting for these improves Reed's initial consideration of this system.

101. See Porter, *Idioms*, 239–40.

102. Louw and Nida, *Greek–English Lexicon*, 1:722.

103. The adverb μέχρι has a similar meaning to these two terms, but it is omitted here due to its never being used to join clauses together in the New Testament; it is only used as an enhancing resource in intra-clausal relations.

Greek conjunctions and adverbs also organize into a certain level of delicacy in the system of TEMPORAL TYPE, which defines two features: *serial* and *simultaneous*.[104] Serial relations pertain to events or circumstances that occur either before or after one another and can be further divided into more delicate realizations—categories I will refer to as *successive* and *preceding*. *Successive* clauses are construed as experientially sequential, and this sequential relationship can be specified further as either *sometime*, *immediate*, or *punctiliar*, where *sometime* indicates an event happening after another without specificity of when or how soon afterwards the event occurs, *immediate* indicates instant succession, and *punctiliar* indicates a current circumstance that implies some difference from prior circumstances. Some of the same conjunctions are used for relations of *sometime* and *immediate*, such as ὅτε and ὅταν, and so other contextual factors must be considered. Some adverbs, however, can be more discriminating, such as εὐθέως, which realizes *immediate* succession. *Punctiliar* relations are realized principally by the adverb νῦν. Types of conjunction that realize *preceding* relations can also be further specified as either *sometime* or *terminal*, and these relations can be realized through a variety of temporal conjunctions and adverbs. *Terminal* relations refer to the "'time up to which' some event may have occurred (up to a given point or until another event is transpiring)."[105] Resources include ἕως (ἕως οὗ, ἕως ὅτου) and ἄχρι. *Sometime*, with *preceding* relations, can be realized through conjunctions such as πρίν. *Simultaneous* relations can be realized by the temporal use of ὡς and ἅμα.[106]

The CAUSAL-CONDITIONAL TYPE system pertains to causal relations in a broad sense; one clause will give information for why something happened in another clause (or larger span of text). In Greek this type of relation can be realized through a variety of options, including *causal* clauses of various types (*obligative*, *inferential*, *purpose*, *result*, and *reason*) and *conditional* clauses whether they belong to the traditionally defined classes or whether they are *concessive*.

So then, *causal* relations divide between general and specific types. *General* causal relations indicate a simple cause and effect relation be-

---

104. While I identify many of the same types of temporal relations as Reed, I diverge substantially from his scheme in how these should be systemically organized.

105. Porter, *Idioms*, 241.

106. See Porter, *Idioms*, 242. This is not the usual use of ὡς, and its "simultaneous" usage can only be determined by context.

tween clauses and can either be *obligative* or *inferential*; in other words, clauses are causally related because they must follow each other experientially (e.g., *because I dropped the ball, it hit the floor*) or interpersonally (e.g., *John received an A on the exam. Therefore, he must have studied hard*), where a claim is negotiated.[107] Conjunctions that can be used to realize these relations include *inter alia* ὅτι, διότι, καθότι, οὖν, and γάρ. *Purpose, result*, and *reason* make up the options for *specific* causal relations, where *purpose* contains the added feature of intention, *result* contains the feature of consequence or "an action which results from a previous action,"[108] and *reason* contains the feature of basis or conscious decision. The conjunction ἵνα is used to realize both *purpose* and *result* relations, but *result* "is expressed in subordinate clauses mainly by means of ὥστε with the infinitive."[109] Reason is often realized by the conjunction γάρ, but is also realized by many of the same resources as general causes (i.e., *obligative*), such as ὅτι, διότι, εἰ, ἐπεί, and ἐπειδή among others, making the distinction blurry at times.[110]

Moreover, there is at times overlap between the *general* and *specific* types of causal relations in Greek. Cause/reason is only one instance where the distinction between these categories is blurred. It may be that some contexts call for an either/or decision between cause or reason, but as Louw and Nida have suggested, "there are numerous contexts in which one may interpret the relation as either cause or reason *or a blend of the two*."[111] A similar need to combine *general* and *specific* types is found, for instance, with the particle ἄρα, which Louw and Nida define as "a marker of result as an inference from what has preceded."[112] To complexify matters even more, there are several resources that often ap-

---

107. Porter indicates that the labels "causal" and "inferential" can be used interchangeably, but according to the scheme used here they should be clearly distinguished (*Idioms*, 237). I have substituted "causal" in the sense used by Porter and others here with "obligative" to maintain a clear distinction between causal relations more broadly and their more specified types. "Obligative" was chosen because it communicates the necessity in one event following another due to their causal relation.

108. Porter, *Idioms*, 234.

109. McKay, *New Syntax*, 127.

110. See Louw and Nida, *Greek–English Lexicon*, 1:779–82, who also state "Though in some languages a very important distinction is made between an external physical cause of an event and the reason for an event based upon a decision by a conscious being, this distinction is not made lexically in Greek" (779).

111. Louw and Nida, *Greek–English Lexicon*, 1:779 (emphasis mine).

112. Louw and Nida, *Greek–English Lexicon*, 1:783.

pear to blend *specific* types of causal relations, such as ὡς and ἵνα, which tend to realize relations with both *purpose* and *result*. This speaks to the potential of semantic blending with Greek conjunctions, which seems to require an option of whether to blend otherwise distinct semantic options into a single conjunctive relation. This option is not exclusive to causal relations, but can cross boundaries of enhancement types, such as with the conjunctions ὡς and καθώς, which can blend *causal* relations with relations of *manner*.[113]

Conditional clauses in Greek are traditionally divided into four classes, and these are realized by means of conjunctions such as εἰ and ἐάν. Whereas conditional relations can function both externally and internally, their interpersonal function is dominant, which can be observed in the definitions ascribed to them, especially by Porter (however, I am not implying that this is intentional on Porter's part): "a first class conditional makes an assertion *for the sake of argument*";[114] "a third class conditional . . . is more tentative and simply projects some action or event *for hypothetical consideration*."[115] Because conditional relations are further divided by other semantic features, such as the Greek Mood system rather than conjunctions, I have not developed this system to a further point of delicacy.

The system of POLARITY could be considered operative in conditions; this would be consonant with the categories of positive and negative conditionals that Reed suggests in his categories.[116] However, the particle ἄν, which often (but not always) appears in the apodosis, is the major distinctive of the second class rather than the negative particle μή.[117] As a result, Reed's categories, which are a strict adoption of Halliday's categories of positive and negative conditionals,[118] need to be further

---

113. See Louw and Nida, *Greek–English Lexicon*, 1:784–85.

114. Porter, *Idioms*, 256 (emphasis mine).

115. Porter, *Idioms*, 262 (emphasis mine).

116. Reed, "Cohesiveness of Discourse," 35.

117. Porter, *Idioms*, 260.

118. See Halliday, IFG4, 614. Reed also considers *concessive* a type of conditional in Greek. However, the same resources that Reed lists for concessive conditionals could also be interpreted as concessive causals. Take, for instance, the use of καίπερ in Heb 5:8 (καίπερ ὢν υἱός, ἔμαθεν ἀφ' ὧν ἔπαθεν τὴν ὑπακοήν, "even though he was a son, he learned obedience through what he suffered"). Is the relation between "being a son" and "learning obedience by suffering" conditional or causal in this instance? It is probably better understood as causal ("even though") rather than conditional ("even then")

considered for the nuances of conditional relations realized in Greek. Maintaining the descriptions of the various classes is one way to do this.

Another type of conditional relation is *concessive*. Like the option of *adversative* in the system of EXTENSION TYPE, concessive relations are inherently *counter-expectant*; they relate two clauses by indicating a concessive condition despite other circumstances that would lead one to reasonably expect some other condition. Resources include καίπερ, καίτοι, κἄν, ὅμως (μέντοι), some of which blend with other logico-semantic relations (e.g., ὅμως can imply an additional aspect of *similarity*).[119] Some of these resources are also *emphatic* (κἄν, καίτοιγε), where EMPHASIS is modeled as a simultaneous system alongside EXPANSION TYPE.[120]

The system of MANNER pertains to how a clause explains how some circumstance in another clause happened; it is divided in Greek between *means* and *comparison*. Resources that realize *means* include ὅπως, καθώς, ὡς, πόθεν, among others. *Comparison* relates clauses based on *similarity* or *difference* with other processes or circumstances. *Difference* is realized by negation, such as with ὡς μή in 1 Cor 7:30. *Comparison* overlaps with *means* regarding the conjunctions used to realize this relation; they include ὡς, ὥσπερ, καθώς, καθό, καθά, and καθάπερ, among others.[121]

This concludes the systematizing of the system of EXPANSION TYPE. A representation of the system as outlined here is illustrated in Figure 4.

---

because "being obedient" is consequentially tied to "being a son," which is causal-concessive rather than conditional-concessive. In any case, since concessive conjunctions and adverbs realize multiple kinds of expansion, the system of EXPECTANCY, with the binary choices of *expectant* and *concessive*, is best modeled as parallel in relation to the system of CAUSAL-CONDITIONAL TYPE. Cf. Martin and Rose, *Working with Discourse*, 132, where they map expectant and concessive realizations of causal, means, conditional, and purpose relations for English.

119. Louw and Nida, *Greek–English Lexicon*, 1:786–87.

120. Other emphatic conjunctions and particles include ἀλλά, γέ, δή, καί, μέν, μήν, οὖν, πέρ-words, πού, πώς, and τοί-words, among others (see Porter, *Idioms*, 204–17).

121. See Porter, *Idioms*, 242.

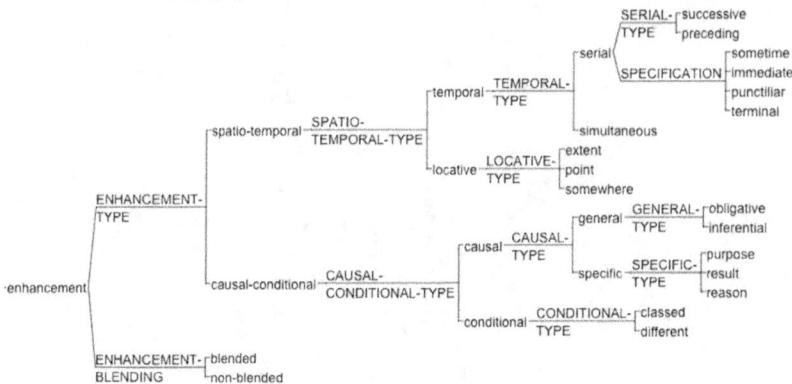

Figure 4. The System of Expansion Type for Greek

CONCLUSION

In this study I have modeled the Greek system of CONJUNCTION according to the various ways that logico-semantic relationships can be realized by the lexico-grammatical resources of Greek conjunctions, adverbs, and other particles. The model itself is therefore more adaptive than adoptive of the English-based SFL model, and so this study stands in contrast to previous attempts to model CONJUNCTION for Greek. Moreover, new methodological possibilities for analyzing conjunctive relations have been mapped by introducing the distinction between *internal* and *external* conjunction. The exegetical payoff for such a model has significant potential for future research, not least with the ways analysis of CONJUNCTION helps to describe the coherent unfolding of texts as series of logically constructed relations of experiential, interpersonal, and textual meanings. The final proposal is presented in Figure 5.

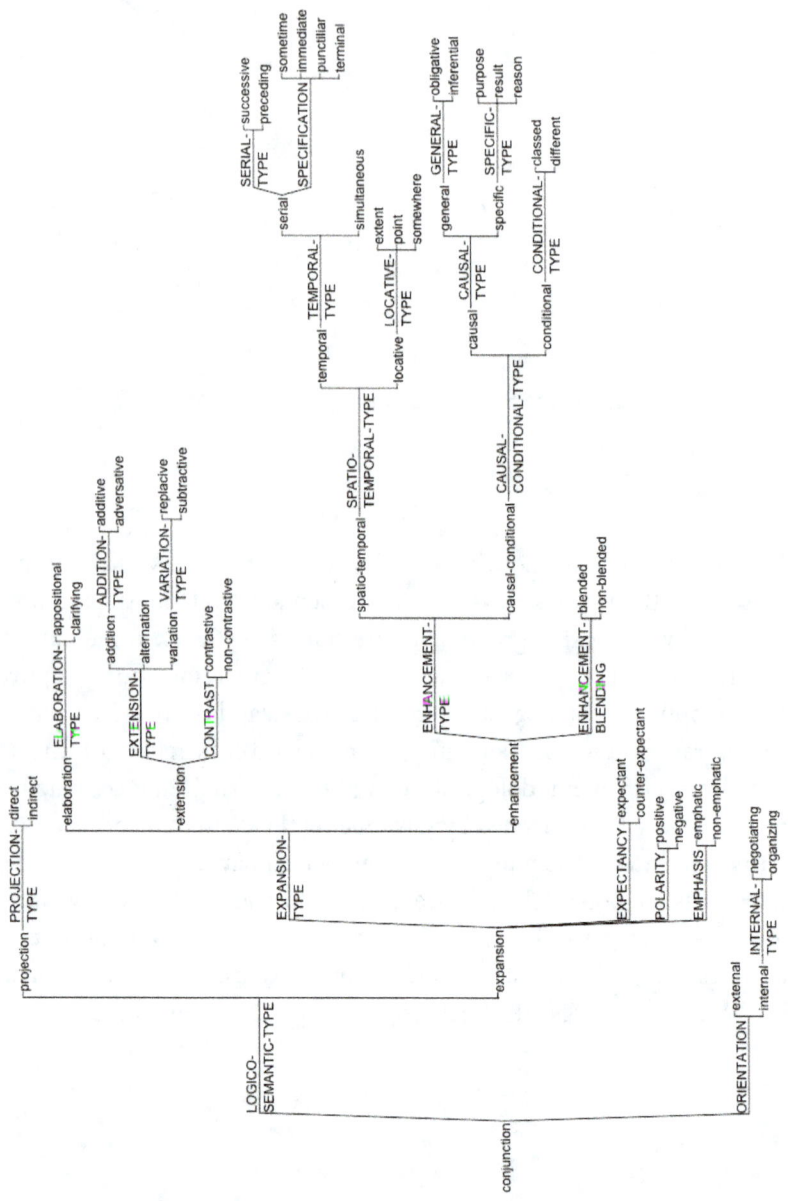

Figure 5. The Overall System of CONJUNCTION for Greek

BIBLIOGRAPHY

Bakhtin, Mikhail M. "Discourse in the Novel." In *The Dialogic Imagination: Four Essays by M. M. Bakhtin*, edited by Michael Holquist, 259–422. Translated by Caryl Emerson and Michael Holquist. University of Text Press Slavic Series 1. Austin: University of Texas Press, 1981.

———. *Speech Genres and Other Later Essays*, edited by Caryl Emerson and Michael Holquist. Translated by Vern W. McGee. Austin: University of Texas Press, 1968.

Black, Stephanie L. *Sentence Conjunctions in the Gospel of Matthew: καί, δέ, τότε, γάρ, οὖν and Asyndeton in Narrative Discourse*. JSNTSup 216; SNTG 9. London: Sheffield Academic, 2002.

Blomqvist, Jerker. *Greek Particles in Hellenistic Prose*. Lund: Gleerup, 1969.

Bühler, Karl. *Theory of Language: The Representational Function of Language*. Translated by D. F. Goodwin. Philadelphia: Benjamins, 1990.

Buth, Randall. "Edayin/Tote—Anatomy of a Semiticism in Jewish Greek." *Maarav* 5–6 (1990) 33–48.

———. "Οὖν, Δέ, Καί, and Asyndeton in John's Gospel." In *Linguistics and New Testament Interpretation: Essays on Discourse Analysis*, edited by David Alan Black et al., 144–61. Nashville: Broadman and Holman, 1992.

———. "Semitic Καί and Greek Δέ." *START* 3 (1981) 12–19.

Dana, H. E., and Julius R. Mantey. *A Manual Grammar of the Greek New Testament*. Toronto: Macmillan, 1957.

Dawson, Zachary K. "The Books of Acts and *Jubilees* in Dialogue: A Literary-Intertextual Analysis of the Noahide Laws in Acts 15 and 21." *JGRChJ* 13 (2017) 9–40.

———. "Language as Negotiation: Toward a Systemic Functional Model for Ideological Criticism with Application to James 2:1–13." In *Modeling Biblical Language: Selected Papers from the McMaster Divinity College Linguistics Circle*, edited by Stanley E. Porter et al., 362–90. LBS 13. Leiden: Brill, 2016.

———. "The Rules of 'Engagement': Assessing the Function of the Diatribe in James 2:14–26 Using Critical Discourse Analysis." In *The Epistle of James: Linguistic Exegesis of an Early Christian Letter*, edited by James D. Dvorak and Zachary K. Dawson. LENT 1. Eugene, OR: Pickwick, 2019.

Denniston, J. D. *The Greek Particles*. Revised by K. J. Dover. 2nd ed. 1950. Reprint, London: Gerald Duckworth, 1996.

Dvorak, James D. *The Interpersonal Metafunction in 1 Corinthians 1–4: The Tenor of Toughness*. LBS 19. Leiden: Brill, 2021.

———. "'Prodding with Prosody': Persuasion and Social Influence through the Lens of Appraisal Theory." *BAGL* 4 (2015) 85–120.

Eggins, Suzanne, *An Introduction to Systemic Functional Linguistics*. 2nd ed. London: Bloomsbury, 2004.

Fairclough, Norman. *Analyzing Discourse: Textual Analysis for Social Research*. New York: Routledge, 2003.

———. *Critical Discourse Analysis: The Critical Study of Language*. 2nd ed. Harlow, UK: Pearson, 2010.

———. *Discourse and Social Change*. Cambridge: Polity, 1992.

———. *Language and Power*. 3rd ed. New York: Routledge, 2015.

Frow, John. *Genre*. 2nd ed. The New Critical Idiom. London: Routledge, 2015.

Halliday, M. A. K. *Halliday's Introduction to Functional Grammar*. Revised by Christian M. I. M. Matthiessen. 4th ed. London: Routledge, 2014. (IFG4)

———. "Text Semantics and Clause Grammar: How Is a Text Like a Clause?" In *On Grammar*, edited by Jonathan J. Webster, 219–59. Collected Works of M. A. K. Halliday 1. London: Continuum, 2002.

Halliday, M. A. K., and Ruqaiya Hasan. *Cohesion in English*. English Language Series 9. London: Longman, 1976.

Halliday, M. A. K., and Jonathan J. Webster. *Text Linguistics: The How and Why of Meaning*. Equinox Textbooks and Surveys in Linguistics. Sheffield: Equinox, 2014.

Holquist, Michael. *Dialogism: Bakhtin and His World*. New Accents. London: Routledge, 1990.

Hunt, Benjamin B. "Meaning in Bulk: The Greek Clause Complex and 1 Peter 1:1–12." In *Modeling Biblical Language: Selected Papers from the McMaster Divinity College Linguistics Circle*, edited by Stanley E. Porter et al., 391–414. LBS 13. Leiden: Brill, 2016.

Land, Christopher D. "Jesus before Pilate: A Discourse Analysis of John 18:33–38." In *Modeling Biblical Language: Selected Papers from the McMaster Divinity College Linguistics Circle*, edited by Stanley E. Porter et al., 233–49. LBS 13. Leiden: Brill, 2016.

Lemke, Jay L. "Interpersonal Meaning in Discourse: Value Orientations." In *Advances in Systemic Linguistics: Recent Theory and Practice*, edited by Martin Davies and Louise Ravelli, 82–104. Open Linguistics Series. London: Pinter, 1992.

———. "Resources for Attitudinal Meaning: Evaluative Orientations in Text Semantics." *Functions of Language* 5 (1998) 33–56.

———. *Textual Politics: Discourse and Social Dynamics*. Critical Perspectives on Literacy and Education. Abingdon: Taylor & Francis, 1995.

Levinsohn, Stephen H. *Discourse Features of New Testament Greek: A Coursebook on the Information Structure of New Testament Greek*. 2nd ed. Dallas: SIL International, 2000.

Louw, Johannes P., and Eugene A. Nida. *Greek-English Lexicon of the New Testament Based on Semantic Domains*. 2 vols. 2nd ed. New York: United Bible Societies, 1989.

Martin, J. R., and David Rose. *Genre Relations: Mapping Culture*. Equinox Textbooks and Surveys in Linguistics. London: Equinox, 2008.

———. *Working with Discourse: Meaning Beyond the Clause*. Open Linguistics Series. 2nd ed. New York: Continuum, 2007.

Martin, J. R., and P. R. R. White. *The Language of Evaluation: Appraisal in English*. New York: Palgrave Macmillan, 2005.

McKay, K. L. *A New Syntax of the Verb in New Testament Greek: An Aspectual Approach*. SBG 5. New York: Peter Lang, 1994.

Porter, Stanley E. *Idioms of the Greek New Testament*. 2nd ed. BLG 2. Sheffield: Sheffield Academic, 1994.

———. "Is Critical Discourse Analysis Critical? An Evaluation Using Philemon as a Test Case." In *Discourse Analysis and the New Testament: Approaches and Results*, edited by Stanley E. Porter and Jeffrey T. Reed, 47–70. JSNTSup 170. Sheffield: Sheffield Academic, 1999.

———. *The Letter to the Romans: A Linguistic and Literary Commentary*. NTM 37. Sheffield: Sheffield Phoenix, 2016.

———. *Linguistic Analysis of the Greek New Testament: Studies in Tools, Methods, and Practice*. Grand Rapids: Baker Academic, 2015.

———. "Systemic Functional Linguistics and the Greek Language: The Need for Further Modeling." In *Modeling Biblical Language: Selected Papers from the McMaster Divinity College Linguistics Circle*, edited by Stanley E. Porter et al., 9–47. LBS 13. Leiden: Brill, 2016.

Porter, Stanley E., and Matthew Brook O'Donnell. "Conjunctions, Clines and Levels of Discourse." *FN* 20 (2007) 3–14.

Reed, Jeffrey T. "The Cohesiveness of Discourse: Towards a Model of Linguistic Criteria for Analyzing New Testament Discourse." In *Discourse Analysis and the New Testament: Approaches and Results*, edited by Stanley E. Porter and Jeffrey T. Reed, 28–46. JSNTSup 170. SNTG 4. Sheffield: Sheffield Academic, 1999.

———. "Discourse Analysis." In *Handbook to Exegesis of the New Testament*, edited by Stanley E. Porter, 189–217. 1997. Reprint, Leiden: Brill, 2002.

Runge, Steven E. *Discourse Grammar of the Greek New Testament: A Practical Introduction for Teaching and Exegesis*. Lexham Bible Reference Series. Peabody, MA: Hendrickson, 2010.

Thompson, Geoff, "But Me Some Buts: A Multidimensional View of Conjunction." *Text* 25 (2005) 763–91.

———. *Introducing Functional Grammar*. 3rd ed. London: Routledge, 2014.

Thrall, Margaret Eleanor. *Greek Particles in the New Testament: Linguistic and Exegetical Studies*. NTTS 3. Grand Rapids: Eerdmans, 1962.

Wallace, Daniel B. *Greek Grammar beyond the Basics: An Exegetical Syntax of the New Testament*. Grand Rapids: Zondervan, 1996.

Westfall, Cynthia Long. *A Discourse Analysis of the Letter to the Hebrews: The Relationship between Form and Meaning*. LNTS 297. London: T. & T. Clark, 2005.

———. "A Method for the Analysis of Prominence in Hellenistic Greek." In *The Linguist as Pedagogue: Trends in the Teaching and Linguistic Analysis of the Greek New Testament*, edited by Stanley E. Porter and Matthew Brook O'Donnell, 75–94. NTM 11. Sheffield: Sheffield Phoenix, 2009.

White, P. R. R. "Dialogue and Inter-Subjectivity: Reinterpreting the Semantics of Modality and Hedging." In *Dialogue Analysis VII: Working with Dialogue*, edited by Malcolm Coulthard et al., 67–80. Tübingen: Max Niemeyer, 2000.

———. "Evaluative Semantics and Ideological Positioning in Journalistic Discourse: A New Framework for Analysis." In *Mediating Ideology in Text and Image*, edited by Inger Lassen et al., 37–67. Amsterdam: Benjamins, 2006.

5

"It's Probably Untrue, but It Wouldn't Matter Anyway"

Εἰ καί Conditions in the Greek New Testament

Mark Proctor

This essay examines the structure and interpretive significance of the Greek New Testament's twenty-two εἰ καί conditions.[1] It seeks to demonstrate how the presence of an adverbial καί at the head of a first class condition effectively signals that neither its satisfaction nor dissatisfaction nullifies the claim in the apodosis; for "here the protasis is treated as a matter of indifference."[2] Whereas second class conditions mark the apodosis as inaccurate and, as a consequence, indicate the protasis is likewise untrue, εἰ καί conditions instead uphold their apodoses regardless of whether one affirms or denies their protases. While the protasis of an εἰ καί condition normally presents a contrary-to-fact notion, such need not always be the case. What seems clear, however, is that the New Testament writers deploy the εἰ καί structure in part to indicate they would concede the truth of the protasis only with reluctance. Such is in keeping with the normal additive effect that adverbial καί has on the meaning of whatever discourse unit it modifies.

This understanding of the meaning of εἰ καί conditions differs greatly from the opinion of those who treat their protases like concessive

---

[1]. This essay has been previously published as Proctor, "'It's Probably Untrue.'"
[2]. Robertson, *Grammar*, 1026; see also Denniston, *Greek Particles*, 302.

clauses. For Chamberlain, the protasis of an εἰ καί condition "*concedes something to be true, but treats it as a matter of indifference.*"[3] Having suggested that εἰ καί with the indicative can express "an admitted fact" and so mean "even though," Denniston admits a mere three pages later that εἰ καί can also mean "'if indeed,' 'if really' ('though I should be surprised if it were so')."[4] This essay suggests that Denniston's second meaning for εἰ καί is not only more faithful to Greek idiom but also obviates the need for positing the first by allowing for the protasis's unlikely satisfaction. The forcefulness of εἰ καί conditions thus seems to lie in their ability to add rhetorical strength to the apodosis's claim *via* the inclusion of a benign exception in the protasis that the language user presents as exaggerated, inconsequential, and likely false. Hence, what a second-class condition does to deny the truth of its apodosis (and by extension also its protasis), an εἰ καί condition does instead to affirm the same while casting doubt on the protasis. Approaching the Greek New Testament's examples of εἰ καί conditions with such an understanding generates a number of potential ways to improve the NRSV, which the National Council of Churches asked the SBL to update in 2017.

SEMANTICS OF FIRST- AND SECOND-CLASS CONDITIONS

Conditional sentences announce a supposition in a grammatically dependent clause (the protasis), the satisfaction of which validates an assertion finding expression in the structure's independent companion clause (the apodosis).[5] The protasis of every conditional sentence conceals an indirect question that language receivers must answer by whatever means available (contextual clues, common sense, rationality, conven-

---

3. Chamberlain, *Exegetical Grammar*, 201 (emphasis mine).
4. Denniston, *Greek Particles*, 300, 303.
5. Dana and Mantey, *Manual Grammar*, 286; Burton, *Syntax*, 100. Brooks and Winbery say the following about subordination of the protasis: "Conditional clauses [i.e., protases] function as part of the predicate in that they give a condition under which the action of the verb can take place or a reason or cause for the action of the verb taking place or not taking place" (*Syntax*, 181–82). Wallace's commentary on the relationship between the protasis and apodosis is even more nuanced: "The apodosis is *grammatically independent, but semantically dependent*. That is, it can stand on its own as a full-blown sentence . . . but it depends for its 'factuality' on the fulfillment of the protasis . . . The protasis . . . is *grammatically dependent, but semantically independent*. That is, it does not form a complete thought . . . but its fulfillment is independent of whether the apodosis is true" (*Greek Grammar*, 684).

tion, sentiment, appeals to authority, etc.). In the event that a language receiver agrees to consider the conditional structure and responds to its query in the *if* clause affirmatively, the assertion in its apodosis follows as a matter of logical necessity per *modus ponens* reasoning. While rejecting the protasis does not defeat the apodosis, that claim nevertheless experiences some level of argumentative frustration whenever grounds for granting the antecedent go wanting; for the number of possible scenarios under which the apodosis might hold true consequently goes down. Only in the event that the protasis's claim constitutes a necessary condition for its consequent's fulfillment could one justifiably deny the latter whenever the former fails, but this consideration falls outside of the logic of the conditional argument itself.

First-Class Conditions

Sorting Greek conditions on the basis of the language user's mood selection in the protasis most commonly yields four conditional "classes."[6] The distinctive feature of first-class conditions involves the use of εἰ ("if") with any tense of the indicative in the protasis. Instead of following some scripted style in the "then" clause, the New Testament writers simply utilized whatever verb their meaning required and the resultant expression remained identical with what the writer would have asserted apart from the conditional formula.[7] In the words of Robertson, the form of the apodosis for first class conditions "all depends on what one is after, whether a mere statement, prediction, command, prohibition, suggestion, [or] question."[8] Hence, what makes a first-class condition semantically distinct is the protasis's ability to oblige an audience's assent to its apodosis whenever the supposition in the "if" clause holds true. Put simply, the "if" clause of any first-class condition worth considering introduces a potential caveat for readers that when true logically requires affirmation of the "then" clause.

---

6. First- (e.g., Porter, *Verbal Aspect*, 305) and third-class (e.g., 277) conditions are most numerous, with second-class conditions finishing a distant third (e.g., 47). While the Greek New Testament offers no complete example of a fourth-class condition, a number of mixed conditions contain one or more elements of this structure. Porter's modal understanding of the future tense leads him to identify a fifth-class condition, one combining εἰ with the future indicative in the protasis (see 312–16).

7. Zerwick, *Biblical Greek*, 102.

8. Robertson, *Grammar*, 1008.

Although some mistakenly assume use of the indicative in the protasis of first-class conditions points to something necessarily factual or real, one should remember the purely hypothetical nature of such statements when assessing their meaning. The force of the indicative in the "if" clause of a first-class condition extends no further than the *presentation* of the protasis as real. As Kijne writes, "When *ei* with the indicative is used, it implies that the truth or otherwise of the condition is regarded as in principle 'determined,' i.e., is *represented* as a fact (although the speaker does not commit himself as to whether he believes the condition is true or not)."[9] Turner goes so far as to describe indicative verbs in the protases of conditional sentences as examples of the "unreal" indicative.[10] So as Burton assiduously points out, a first class condition's protasis "simply states a *supposition* which refers to a particular case in the present or past, implying *nothing* as to its fulfilment."[11] Burton then adds that while the protases of many first class conditions do, in fact, suppose conditions the writer considers true or factual, the "fact of fulfilment lies . . . not in the conditional sentence, but in the context."[12]

In fairness to the New Testament writers, the hypothetical nature of the first-class conditional form likewise expresses no doubt about the factual status of the supposition, but instead remains semantically indifferent. "A conditional proposition of itself asserts *merely* the connection between what is enunciated by its two clauses."[13] A first class condition "does not imply either that the speaker believes that the condition stated is true or that he believes it is not true."[14] Robertson puts it thus, "The form of the condition has to do only with the *statement*, not with the absolute truth or certainty of the matter."[15] For these reasons, Boyer claims a first class condition "implies absolutely nothing as to 'relation to reality.' It is saying that the result (the apodosis) is as sure as the condition (the protasis)."[16]

---

9. Kijne, "Greek Conditional Sentences," 223 (emphasis mine).
10. Moulton and Turner, MHT3, 91.
11. Burton, *Syntax*, 102.
12. Burton, *Syntax*, 102.
13. Zerwick, *Biblical Greek*, 101 (emphasis mine).
14. Greenlee, "'If,'" 40.
15. Robertson, *Grammar*, 1006.
16. Boyer, "First Class Conditions," 82.

A first-class condition's protasis thus expresses a potential claim in the form of an indirect question for the sake of argument. Even in cases where the supposition articulates something both writer and reader regard as true, the structure's semantics still require the latter's judgment about the accuracy of the protasis for affirming the apodosis. Dana and Mantey thus note that Greek writers employed first class conditions whenever they "wished *to assume* or *to seem to assume* the reality of [the] premise."[17] "Very often ... this form is used in cases where the fulfilment or non-fulfilment of the condition is in fact known or supposed; but this circumstance is to be gathered from the context; the grammatical form is indifferent to it."[18] According to Boyer, only 115 (37 percent) of the New Testament's first class conditions suppose something that unquestionably corresponds with reality, while 36 (12 percent) suppose something obviously false. He regards the truth value of the protases in the remaining 155 New Testament examples as "undetermined."[19]

Readers must, therefore, base their decision about the reliability of the protasis on considerations purely external to the conditional structure itself. As a consequence, translating εἰ in the protasis of any first class condition (*especially* when the protasis's truth is beyond doubt) with the English gloss 'since' or 'because' yields two unfortunate effects: (1) it forecloses on the reader's opportunity to weigh in on the protasis's status; and (2) it makes the writer appear bullish by transforming the condition's "if" clause from a diplomatic appeal for audience judgment into an argumentative ground for their agreement. As Mathewson and Emig point out, "translating class 1 conditions with 'since' obscures the rhetorical effect of the conditional. The function of the class 1 conditional is to leave the judgment as to its truthfulness up to the reader or hearer."[20] Zerwick expresses a similar concern when he says "it is an astonishing fact that even scholars sometimes ... forget ... εἰ even in a 'real' condition still means 'if' and not 'because.'"[21] For this reason, Wallace rightly concludes "the first class condition should *never* be translated *since*."[22]

17. Dana and Mantey, *Manual Grammar*, 289 (emphasis mine).
18. Zerwick, *Biblical Greek*, 102–3.
19. Boyer, "First Class Conditions," 76.
20. Mathewson and Emig, *Intermediate Greek Grammar*, 236–38.
21. Zerwick, *Biblical Greek*, 104.
22. Wallace, *Greek Grammar*, 690n12.

Second-Class Conditions

What grammarians refer to as second class conditions are actually a marked variety of first-class conditions, for they too use εἰ with the indicative in the protasis. The distinction between the two classes lies in the second's provision of lexical and grammatical signals that the language user expects a negative answer to the protasis's indirect question precisely because the apodosis's assertion is contrary to fact. Whereas first class conditions task readers with judging whether a consequent follows from its antecedent via an affirmative response to an open-ended indirect question in the protasis, second class conditions instead present complete *modus tollens* arguments in summary fashion: If one considers a conditional statement ("If *p* then *q*") and finds the consequent untrue (*not-q*), one can logically negate the antecedent (*not-p*). Put simply, second class conditions deploy linguistic markers within the first-class conditional structure to signal the counterfactual status of the consequent, and in so doing indicate the only appropriate response to the protasis's question is negative. Second class conditions thus present the consequent as contrary to fact, and so enable readers to deny the antecedent. As a result, both components of the conditional structure in a second-class condition present untrue notions.

The mechanisms second class conditions use to this end are both lexical and grammatical, involving (a) use of the conditional particle ἄν with the indicative in the apodosis to point up the assertion's contingency; (b) the employment of secondary tense forms (aorist, imperfect, or pluperfect) for the main verbs of both protasis and apodosis; and (c) the use of μή rather than οὐ in examples with negated protases. Moulton characterizes ἄν as "a very marked peculiarity of Greek" and "a kind of leaven in a Greek sentence: itself untranslatable, it may transform the meaning of a clause in which it is inserted."[23] While some grammarians regard ἄν as a modal particle capable of making indicative verbs carry subjunctive or optative meanings, Goodwin comes closer to the truth when he says that whenever ἄν appears in construction with the secondary tenses of the indicative mood it indicates that "the action of the verb is dependent on some circumstances or condition, expressed or implied."[24] This is why Porter prefers to think of ἄν as a "conditional" or

---

23. Moulton, MHT1, 165.
24. Goodwin, *Greek Grammar*, 277 (see also 285).

"idealization" marker that "presupposes no reference to reality."[25] When it appears with a secondary tense form in the apodosis of a second class condition, ἄν basically marks the apodosis's idea as something that would have taken place had the protasis happened, yet did not; i.e., ἄν negates the apodosis.[26] For this reason, Porter suggests that "the *major distinctive* of this class is provided by the apodosis with the conditional particle (ἄν) ... The conditional particle in the apodosis is a grammatical indicator that the speaker is asserting for argument (but may not believe) that the protasis is contrary to fact."[27] Since the imperfect, aorist, and pluperfect are best suited to address temporally past and background matters and since a second class condition denies the truth of the claims in both parts of its conditional structure, selection of a secondary tense for both the protasis and apodosis seems natural. Finally, negation with μή in a second-class condition's protasis is one of but a few instances where this particle appears with the indicative. When one considers that protases of second-class conditions express only what *might* have been, this use of μή becomes understandable; for as Moorehouse notes, μή serves to negate the "notional or ideal" and οὐ the "concrete or actual."[28]

Whereas Boyer is right to say, "the second-class conditional sentence ... states a condition which as a matter of fact has not been met and follows with a statement of what would have been true if it had,"[29] these structures do not present their apodoses as false because their protases are untrue, since doing so would commit the logical fallacy of de-

25. Porter, *Verbal Aspect*, 166.
26. Robertson, *Grammar*, 922; Moulton, MHT1, 200.
27. Porter, *Verbal Aspect*, 260 (emphasis mine). While I am inclined to agree with Porter, Boyer points out that a full quarter of the New Testament's forty-seven examples of second-class conditions lack the particle (see, e.g., Matt 26:24; Mark 14:21; Luke 19:42; John 9:33; 15:20c, 22, 24a; 18:36; 19:11; Acts 26:32; 1 Cor 12:17, 19; Gal 4:15). One such example concerns Synoptic parallels (Mark 14:21/Matt 26:24). Another lacks an explicit apodosis (Luke 19:42). One concerns the singular omission of ἄν in B (Vaticanus) (John 18:36). Tense selection in the apodosis of the example in John 15:20c (τηρήσουσιν) does not fit the profile of a second-class condition. And finally, the trio of examples in 1 Cor 12:17 and 19 contain verbless clauses and their apodoses pose questions rather than make assertions. While Boyer explains the particle's routine absence by suggesting its omission is "characteristic of *koine* Greek" ("Second Class Conditions," 82n6), perhaps the exceptions I note from his list of "examples" reveals the problem to be a far less critical concern. One might also simply deny that the remaining "exceptions" constitute genuine examples of the second-class conditional form.
28. Moorehouse, *Studies*, 40n1.
29. Boyer, "Second Class Conditions," 83.

nying the antecedent. Rather, the falsehood of a second-class condition's protasis derives from the "contrary to fact" status of its apodosis. Hence, a second-class condition effectively denies that its apodosis could follow as a matter of logical necessity from the satisfaction of its protasis by using the particle ἄν to characterize the apodosis's content as "contrary to fact." As a direct logical consequence, the supposition of the protasis in such a construction is equally untrue per *modus tollens* reasoning.

So, whereas the protases of first-class conditions present audiences with unmarked or "open" indirect questions to resolve for themselves and by so doing oblige acceptance of their apodoses whenever those questions receive affirmative answers, second-class conditions instead make a pair of negative declarative statements by using the conditional form and *modus tollens* reasoning to present both apodosis and protasis as contrary to fact. To this extent, second class conditions are akin to marked rhetorical questions of fact, which deploy οὐ and μή to anticipate what in the language user's estimation count as appropriate answers. This of course does not mean that the ideas finding expression in second class conditions are, in reality, contrary to fact, only that the language user presents them as such to foreclose on debate.

THE SEMANTICS OF EI KAI CONDITIONS

Young's intermediate grammar illustrates how vigorous grammarians can become when discussing the New Testament's most frequently occurring conjunction by listing fourteen possible meanings.[30] Of the meanings Young lists for καί, those finding routine discussion in similar works include its supposed temporal ("when"), consecutive ("then," "and so," "as a result"), circumstantial ("since," "seeing that"), final ("so that"), adversative ("but," "and yet"), and relative ("who," "which," "that") nuances. Since this multiplicity of meanings is not sustainable on anything but contextually determined pragmatic grounds, this essay suggests a simpler model. Wherever it occurs, καί always signals simple addition in one of two distinct ways: either (1) by conjoining one coordinate discourse component with another like a conjunction, or (2) by accentuating the meaning of a single discourse element (word, phrase, or even clause) like an adverb. The particle thus performs a solitary semantic

---

30. Young, *Intermediate New Testament Greek*, 187–89.

function (by signaling addition) in one of two pragmatic ways (be it conjunctive or adverbial).

Even though BDAG's entry for καί is nearly three pages long, it marshals discussion of its meaning under two main heads: καί can (1) act like a conjunction and mark the connection between coordinate elements of the same grammatical order (words, phrases, clauses, sentences, or even larger discourse units) thus meaning "and," or (2) behave like an adverb and point up "an *additive relation* that is not coordinate to connect clauses and sentences" thus meaning "also" or "even."[31] In both cases καί indicates that some form of addition or expansion is taking place, but whenever it behaves like an adverb the single item the language user modifies with καί receives amplification of or addition to its own meaning by virtue of the conjunction's presence. Hence, "the primary function of the adverbial καί is to indicate that the following component(s) should be intensified or emphasized, just as a spotlight focuses our attention on something."[32]

Detecting an Adverbial καί

Approaching καί with this understanding in place helps make detecting an adverbial καί more straightforward, for in the absence of a paired group of coordinate discourse elements for καί to conjoin, it must behave adverbially. This is why Funk remarks that "ascensive καί does not connect or contrast elements."[33] Syntax provides another strong indicator when καί carries an adverbial meaning provided it appears in something other than the clause-initial position, because "when καί is copulative, it comes first in sentence or clause."[34] Mathewson and Emig thus note that καί "usually occurs in postposition ... when it functions adverbially."[35]

---

31. BDAG 494–96. As concerns the first meaning, Runge observes that "καί does not mark a distinction of semantic continuity or discontinuity; it connects two items of equal status, constraining them to be closely related to one another" (*Discourse Grammar*, 24). A number of grammars add a third, adjunctive nuance to this list of meanings for καί, one that normally finds representation with the English gloss "also." Robertson compares this adjunctive meaning for καί with the English "too" and says it indicates an "addition to something already mentioned," but not without admitting "the difference between καί as 'and' and καί as 'also' is very slight" (*Grammar*, 1180–81).

32. Titrud, "Overlooked KAI," 4.

33. Funk, *Beginning-Intermediate Grammar*, 358.

34. Denniston, *Greek Particles*, 325.

35. Mathewson and Emig, *Intermediate Greek Grammar*, 262. See also Titrud,

Moule is consequently right to notice a potential difference in meaning between εἰ καί and καὶ εἰ. Whereas καί most naturally means "and" in the latter construction (and so would conjoin the conditional clause it introduces to what precedes in context), in the former καί must be adverbial.[36] This is not to say, however, that a clause-initial καί cannot be adverbial (e.g., Matt 8:9a), but such syntax makes this sort of adverbial καί harder to identify.[37]

Meaning of εἰ καί Conditions

In keeping with its normal function, the presence of an adverbial καί in a first-class condition's protasis effectively characterizes its claim as exceptional, out of the ordinary, exaggerated, or extreme. In commenting on the ascensive use of καί, Robertson suggests, "the thing that is added is out of the ordinary and rises to a climax like the crescendo in music."[38] Blass, moreover, adds that adverbial καί tends to appear naturally "in contexts that give rise to an interpretation of 'lowness of likelihood.'"[39] The inclusion of an adverbial καί in the protasis of a first class condition thus tags its idea not only as unlikely by virtue of its exaggerated status, but also as inconsequential for the satisfaction of the apodosis (which applies regardless). Hence, one could say that καί is to the protasis of an εἰ καί condition what ἄν is to the apodosis of a second-class condition; for whereas the latter mark their apodoses as false, the former present their protases as most likely untrue.

"Overlooked KAI," 8; Levinsohn, *Discourse Features*, 100.

36. Moule, *Idiom Book*, 167.

37. The Greek New Testament contains approximately twenty-four first-class conditions with protases beginning with καὶ εἰ (Matt 5:30; 11:14; 12:26–27; 18:9; 24:22; Mark 3:26; Luke 6:32; 16:12; 19:8; Rom 11:16; 13:9; 1 Cor 6:2; Phil 3:15; 4:8; 1 Tim 1:10; Heb 11:15; 1 Pet 1:17; 3:1; 4:18; Rev 11:5; 14:11; 20:15), and in all but 1 Pet 3:1 καί carries a conjunctive meaning. This verse advises wives to "accept the authority of your husbands, so that, *even if* (ἵνα καὶ εἰ) some of them do not obey the word, they may be won over without a word by their wives' conduct" (NRSV). The καί in question is technically not clause-initial since ἵνα precedes it, thereby enabling καί to function adverbially. Second, the writer's use of the indefinite pronoun τινες to supply an explicit subject for ἀπειθοῦσιν in the protasis combines with the optimism of the apodosis (see the future κερδηθήσονται) to confirm the protasis's unlikely status. Hence, the Greek New Testament's lone example of an adverbial καὶ εἰ condition is amenable to this article's thesis.

38. Robertson, *Grammar*, 1181.

39. Blass, *Constraints on Relevance*, 12.

Whereas translators and interpreters always seem to recognize the truth of an εἰ καί condition's apodosis on the basis of clear contextual data, common sense, or other reasoning, the likely falsehood of its protasis frequently evades detection. Consequently, English translations routinely treat the protases of εἰ καί conditions as concessive statements rather than indirect questions hinting at a negative answer, and so they gloss these two words in English with "even though" rather than "even if." They thereby transform the meaning of the Greek into something other than a conditional statement with a marked protasis and, in so doing, misrepresent the construction's function. The result is even more unfortunate than glossing εἰ with "since" in first class conditions with true protases. In that case at least the resultant translation accurately represents the writer's judgment, albeit at the expense of reader autonomy. The protases of εἰ καί conditions, however, express thoughts the language user wishes to present as false or would concede only begrudgingly. Therefore, translating εἰ καί with "even though" grossly misrepresents a New Testament writer's opinion about the condition's protasis by presenting its idea as something the writer acknowledges as true. In effect, the mechanism New Testament writers implemented to prompt their readers to deny the protasis's question (an adverbial καί) becomes in translation an ironic affirmation of its content.

EI KAI CONDITIONS IN THE NRSV

Approximately twenty-two of the Greek New Testament's ca. 305 first-class conditions (all of which pose exegetically significant issues) contain an adverbial καί in the protasis: Mark 14:29; Luke 11:8, 18; 18:4–5; 1 Cor 4:7; 7:21; 2 Cor 4:3, 16; 5:3, 16; 7:8–9 (x3), 12; 11:6, 15; 12:11; Gal 3:4 (see the footnote on Gal 3:4 below); Phil 2:17; Col 2:5; Heb 6:9; 1 Pet 3:14. While the NRSV's treatment of them varies, the editors frequently represent the protases of εἰ καί conditions as concessive statements.

Six Instances Where the NRSV Gets εἰ καί Right

At times the NRSV treats εἰ καί conditions appropriately. In Luke 11:17, for instance, Jesus predicates his *apologia* on the commonsense notion that "every kingdom divided against itself becomes a desert, and house falls on house." For this reason, the NRSV recognizes that the protasis of the εἰ καί condition that follows in v. 18a must be false for Jesus' argument to work: "*If* Satan *also* is divided against himself, how will his kingdom stand?" (emphasis mine).⁴⁰ Since divided kingdoms are inherently unstable, Jesus cannot possibly perform exorcisms on Beelzebul's authority.⁴¹

The NRSV renders εἰ καί appropriately three times in the Corinthian correspondence, the first of which is at 1 Cor 7:21 ("Were you a slave when called? Do not be concerned about it. *Even if* [ἀλλ' εἰ καί] you can gain your freedom, make use of your present condition now more than ever"). Here Paul's pessimism over the possibility of manumission for Christian slaves makes sense in light of the prospects for premature death in Greco-Roman antiquity. While nearly all slaves received "freedom" by age thirty, an average life expectancy of twenty-five years likely foreclosed on many slaves' survival to manumission (thereby validating Paul's use of ἀλλ' εἰ καί in this verse).⁴² Second Corinthians 4:3 provides

---

40. Jesus' response in Luke is rhetorically superior to what one finds in either Synoptic parallel. Whereas Mark 3:24–26 and Matt 12:26 leave the audience to determine whether or not Satan opposes himself in Jesus' ministry, Luke 11:18's deployment of the εἰ καί structure leaves nothing to chance by marking this counterintuitive notion as contrary to fact.

41. Were it not for the verse's quirky punctuation scheme ("Did you experience so much for nothing?—*if* it *really* was for nothing"), one might add Gal 3:4 to the list of instances where the NRSV gets things right with εἰ καί conditions. The verse's peculiar punctuation is likely attributable to the UBS3 text, which also inserts a mark of interrogation after Gal 3:4a. Replacing this question mark with a comma and relocating it to the end of the verse is preferable, because doing so eliminates the hiatus at the end of the verse by treating v. 4b as the protasis of an εἰ καί condition with a fronted interrogative apodosis. Since the likely referent for the cognate accusative τοσαῦτα in v. 4a is the Galatians' experience of Christlike sufferings, Paul knows his audience would be loath to admit they had experienced hardships for no reason (εἰκῇ) and so poses his question in a way that confirms his recognition of the value of their faithful endurance. The presence of the enclitic γε between εἰ and καί, moreover, helps Paul make this point stronger, for the particle "*emphasizes* the word with which it occurs" (Porter, *Idioms*, 208 [emphasis mine]; see also Robertson, *Grammar*, 1147–49; and Denniston, *Greek Particles*, 114). Gal 3:4 is thus akin to Luke 11:18a since it too presents an εἰ καί condition with an interrogative apodosis, the only difference being the order of presentation for the structure's twin components. Regarding either protasis as true generates conflicts with the surrounding contexts that undercut the reason for asking the questions their respective apodoses pose in the first place. One should also note that these are questions only by form, not by function; for both clearly anticipate answers and so make implicit assertions. If divided, Satan's kingdom cannot stand—but it is not divided and must be overcome by another means. If the Galatians suffered for Christ in vain, then they vainly suffered—but there is no such thing as vain Christian suffering.

42. Where I find the NRSV's treatment of this verse wanting lies instead in its over-

the second example: "And even if (εἰ δέ καί) our gospel is veiled, it is veiled to those who are perishing." The final paragraph of the preceding chapter contrasts the believer's unveiled contemplation of the Lord's glory with the visually challenged status of those appealing to the old Mosaic covenant. In 2 Cor 4:2, Paul renounces secret and shameful things, denies behaving in a tricky manner or falsifying God's word, and claims instead to have commended himself to everyone's conscience before God by means of an open disclosure of the truth. So, Paul offers his gospel in an unveiled format that any unimpaired person should be capable of seeing. If it should seem veiled to the perishing, their sad fate is due to the god of this world rather than Paul and his ministerial associates (v. 4). Hence, Heckert is correct to suggest that the adverbial καί in 2 Cor 4:3 "may be interpreted as constraining 'if our gospel is covered' to be processed in parallel with the earlier statement that the truth of the gospel was being proclaimed openly (v. 2)."[43] Finally, the NRSV recognizes Paul's reluctance to admit he grieved the Corinthians in sending the severe letter by representing εἰ καί with "even if" at 2 Cor 7:8a.

Given Paul's anticipation of a positive outcome to his trial in Phil 1:25, the protasis of the εἰ καί condition in 2:17 expresses a notion that in his estimation should prove contrary to fact. Since Paul apparently finds it unlikely that he will be "poured out as a libation over the sacrifice and the offering of your faith," the NRSV adequately represents the meaning of εἰ καί by translating the words with "even if." Rendering the text in such a manner reinforces the apodosis's presentation of Paul's continued joy as an unshakeable certainty his improbable death could not undo even in the unlikely event it transpired.

A final example comes from the General Epistles. Since the question preceding the εἰ καί condition appearing in 1 Pet 3:14a anticipates the answer "no one," the contrary to fact status of its protasis appears beyond dispute. 1 Pet 3:13 reads as follows in the NRSV: "Now who will harm you if you are eager to do what is good?" That this question

---

translation of the apodosis (μᾶλλον χρῆσαι). The content of vv. 22–23 clearly demonstrates Paul thinks believers should avoid slavery, yet the protasis of v. 21b acknowledges the unlikelihood of such an opportunity for believers who came to Christ as slaves. For this reason, Paul leaves the apodosis of v. 21 intentionally vague. All the imperative apodosis of this εἰ καί condition enjoins is for Corinthian slaves to "make the most" of whatever life affords them, be it the life of a slave or the rare but spiritually expedient opportunity to experience living as a freed person.

43. Heckert, *Discourse Function*, 61.

anticipates a negative response seems clear not only on common sense grounds, but grammatical grounds as well. The protasis's use of ἐάν with the subjunctive γένησθε and the selection of a future tense participle (ὁ κακώσων) to name the subject of the verbless apodosis both suggest the unlikelihood of the scenario the author envisions. The letter's author thinks it unlikely that the audience will experience any suffering on account of their righteous behavior, and the NRSV accordingly represents εἰ καί in v. 14a with the translation "even if." So, to the editors' credit, there are at least six instances where the NRSV renders εἰ καί conditions in a way commensurate with this article's thesis.

Thirteen Instances Where the NRSV Needs Improvement

In a number of other passages, however, the NRSV treats εἰ καί protases as concessive clauses, and does so in contexts where the statement's falsehood is clear, the aesthetic value of the passage suffers, or even both. In the Second Gospel's account of Jesus's after-dinner dialogue with the disciples on Mount Olivet, for instance, Jesus predicts the twelve "will all fall away" (Mark 14:27). Peter responds two verses later with an εἰ καί condition: "*Even though* all become deserters, I will not" (14:29). By representing the protasis of Peter's statement as a concessive clause, the NRSV portrays him as conceding the inevitable apostasy of his eleven colleagues. If, however, the protasis expresses what Peter takes to be an unlikely scenario, then Mark presents him instead as affirming not just his own loyalty but that of his cohorts also. The strong rhetoric in the subsequent dialogue confirms not only this understanding of the protasis's function, but the remaining disciples' solidarity with Peter: "Jesus said to him, 'Truly I tell you, this day, this very night, before the cock crows twice, you will deny me three times.' But he said vehemently, 'Even if I must die with you, I will not deny you.' And all of them said the same" (14:30–31). Hence, reading Mark 14:29's protasis as expressing a notion Peter deems unlikely greatly accentuates the dramatic irony resulting from the subsequent failure of the twelve.

In an effort to demonstrate the importance of being bold when petitioning God for others, Jesus tells the parable of the Friend at Midnight in Luke 11:5–8. The story tells of a man who, upon receiving a traveler into his home unexpectedly, goes to his friend in the middle of the night to request bread. While the drowsy neighbor initially objects (v. 7), Jesus suggests the petitioner's willingness to act in a socially unconventional manner will secure his request by convincing the neighbor to make good on his social obligation. The NRSV text of Luke 11:8 reads as follows: "I tell you, *even though* (εἰ καί) he will not get up and give him anything because he is his friend, at least because of his persistence (διά γε τὴν ἀναίδειαν αὐτοῦ) he will get up and give him whatever he needs."[44] While this rendering has Jesus claim that the host's status as a friend would not persuade his drowsy neighbor to rise and attend to his needs, such an understanding does not align with the importance of friendship obligations in ancient Levantine society. According to Stern, since ancient Jewish communities considered hospitality a sacred duty, it would be unthinkable for the neighbor to refuse this request: "Even if it meant rising off the straw mat on which husband, wife, and children slept huddled together, unlocking the creaky latch, opening the door, and waking the children, the neighbor would comply."[45] So if the presence of an adverbial καί instead points to the falsity of the protasis's suggestion, Jesus here recognizes that the shameless requester's status as a friend would secure the provisions he seeks. His description of the host's scandalous behavior in the apodosis thus combines with the protasis's implicit anticipation of the neighbor's compliance to illustrate just how obligatory looking after a neighbor's needs must have been. The host has a right to ask even in the way he does because the neighbor has an obligation to respond even though doing so inconveniences him. Put simply, the strong sense of obligation (on the neighbor's part) and feelings of entitlement (on the host's part) that were bound up in ancient friendship ties drives the plot of Jesus's story, a notion the NRSV text of Luke 11:8 misses by treating its protasis as an exception clause.[46]

---

44. "Shamelessness" provides a better gloss for ἀναίδειαν in v. 8 than the NRSV's "persistence." This alternative is etymologically sound (alpha privative + αἰδεῖα ⊠ ἀναίδεια = "without shame or proper regard for social convention") and helps distinguish this parable's subject matter (boldness in prayer) from that concerning the widow and the unjust judge in Luke 18:1-8 (persistence in prayer). Blomberg provides a brief but helpful discussion of the translation options for ἀναίδειαν in Luke 11:8, from which he wisely approves the NIV's "shameless audacity" (*Interpreting the Parables*, 376-77). Blomberg (*Interpreting the Parables*, 377) also observes that since "the other Lukan uses of διά + τό + εἶναι + an accusative subject ... usually equate the subject of the infinitive εἶναι with the subject of the sentence (Lk 2:4; 19:11; Acts 18:13; diff. 27:3)," τὴν ἀναίδειαν αὐτοῦ in Luke 11:8 most likely indicates a quality of the importunate host rather than his sleepy neighbor.

45. Stern, *Rabbi*, 201-2.

46. The NRSV's translation of v. 8 also misrepresents οὐ as negating the circum-

In Luke 18:1–8, Jesus tells his disciples a second parable on prayer to illustrate "their need to pray always and not to lose heart" (v. 1). Jesus begins the Widow and the Unjust Judge in v. 2 by characterizing the latter as a person "who neither feared God nor had respect for people" before moving on in v. 3 to describe the former's repeated appeal for justice. The NRSV text of vv. 4–5 states "for a while he refused; but later he said to himself, 'Though (εἰ καί) I have no fear of God and no respect for anyone, yet because this widow keeps bothering me, I will grant her justice, so that she may not wear me out by continually coming.'" By rendering v. 4c as a concessive clause, the NRSV aligns the judge's self-appraisal with Jesus's prior assessment of his character. Yet if this article's understanding of εἰ καί conditions is right, perhaps Luke aims instead to portray the judge as expressing a false opinion about himself. Put simply, the εἰ καί protasis of the judge's conditional statement presents as contrary to fact what Jesus knows to be true about him as the story's narrator. On the lips of this judge, the claim in v. 4c constitutes an ironic statement because it suggests he fears God and respects humanity when in fact he does not. As a consequence of the judge's apparent confusion, his characterization receives significant aesthetic improvement; for Jesus's audience is left to regard him not simply as an uncaring atheist, but as self-deluded. Luke's use of διά γε to introduce the apodosis perhaps confirms this interpretation, for the same construction appears in the previous example at 11:8a.

The NRSV text for 1 Cor 4:7 reads as follows: "For who sees anything different in you? What do you have that you did not receive? *And if* you received it (εἰ δὲ καὶ ἔλαβες), why do you boast as if it were not a gift?" While the NRSV preserves the conditional wording, it does so without glossing καί. Concluding, moreover, that v. 7c is concessive follows only in the event that Paul anticipates a positive response to v. 7b's question. Yet if Paul instead expects his interlocutor to admit to having received nothing at all, then it remains possible to read v. 7c as express-

---

stantial participle ἀναστάς "not get up," rather than δώσει, and tries to make up for this by supplying an object for the finite verb ("anything") that appears nowhere in the Greek text. Understanding the εἰ καί protasis of this conditional sentence as contrary to fact corrects both issues. Supposing the neighbor would refuse to give to the host thus presents Jesus's audience with what he presents as an unlikely circumstance. This scenario, moreover, takes the neighbor's rising up (ἀναστάς) for granted, which would be pointless if he wished to refuse the host's request. Would the neighbor perhaps express reluctance to assist in the middle of the night? Yes. Would he refuse to do so? No. Would he be quicker about doing so as a consequence of the manner of the request's delivery? Yes, and that is the parable's point.

ing a contrary to fact idea. Paul's progressive argumentative strategy in these sentences first solicits an admission on his conversation partner's part to having received nothing. The protasis of the εἰ καί condition that follows builds rhetorically on this embarrassing revelation by suggesting that even the possibility of a positive response to v. 7b's query would not have the effect of legitimating the interlocutor's boasting. The negated participle λαβών in v. 7d thus does not carry a concessive meaning ("why do you boast as if it were not a gift"), but instead acknowledges the interlocutor's negative reply to v. 7b's question ("why do you boast as someone not having received anything at all"). A paraphrase might clarify: "But even if you received anything at all (which you did not), why is it that you (as someone who admits to having received nothing at all) boast?" Such an understanding of 1 Cor 4:7 is in keeping with Paul's normal abuse of the interlocutor in other diatribal contexts, and his mocking sarcasm in the following verse indicates that this approach to the text is preferable.

Second Corinthians contains the highest concentration of εἰ καί conditions in the Greek New Testament, and the NRSV treats the majority of their protases as concession clauses. The problem with this approach to this letter's εἰ καί conditions is easy to recognize and emend in 5:16; 11:6; 12:11. While the NRSV treats it as a concession clause, regarding the protasis of the εἰ καί condition in 2 Cor 5:16 as contrary to fact fits better with Paul's not having been an earthly associate of Jesus (see 1 Cor 15:8). If, by "we," Paul here means himself and the Corinthians, his use of the first-person plural poses no obstacle. Including himself among those who like the twelve "knew Christ from a human point of view (κατὰ σάρκα)," however, makes no sense. The NRSV's rendering of 2 Cor 11:6 is equally off-the-mark. Paul's claim in the preceding verse ("I think I am not in the least inferior to these super-apostles") indicates he would disagree with the notion that he is "untrained in speech." One could make a similar point about the NRSV text for 2 Cor 12:11d: "For I am not at all inferior to these super-apostles, even though (εἰ καί) I am nothing." Paul clearly did not consider himself "nothing," but here seeks to indicate that were it so the "super-apostles" would therefore amount to "less than nothing." The εἰ καί conditional form of 2 Cor 12:11d thus helps Paul castigate his adversaries.

The εἰ καί conditions in 2 Cor 4:16b and 5:2–3 are more difficult. While the NRSV treats it as an exception clause, understanding the protasis of 2 Cor 4:16b as contrary to fact allows the eschatological optimism that Paul displays in texts like 1 Thess 4:17 and 1 Cor 15:51 to remain intact. On such a reading, Paul would here resist the idea that his outer nature (ὁ ἔξω ἡμῶν ἄνθρωπος) is subject to the sort of final destruction (διαφθείρεται) that Christ's daily rejuvenation (ἀνακαινοῦνται ἡμέρᾳ καὶ ἡμέρᾳ) of his inner nature (ὁ ἔσω ἡμῶν) would be unable to counteract. Such a reading is in concert with Paul's comments in vv. 7–11, which speak of "hard pressing" but not "crushing," of "being perplexed" but not "despairing," of "persecution" but not "abandonment," of "striking down" but not "destruction." Paul pairs references to death in vv. 10–12 with references to renewal of life, and the implication seems to be that (while he willingly acknowledges having sustained injury as a believer) he would be loath to admit in v. 16 that it could result in a state of utter destruction. Paul can be hurt without it resulting in his defeat precisely because whatever harm his outer nature incurs God renews daily from the inside out. Hence, there is plenty of room for understanding the protasis of 2 Cor 4:16b as contrary to fact.

The NRSV's punctuation scheme for 2 Cor 5:2–3 obscures v. 2's function as the construction's fronted apodosis: "For in this tent (ἐν τούτῳ) we groan, longing to be clothed with our heavenly dwelling—if indeed (εἴ γε καί), when we have taken it off, we will not be found naked." A number of important textual witnesses read ἐνδυσάμενοι 'having put on' in place of ἐκδυσάμενοι 'having disrobed' in v. 3. Metzger in his textual commentary summarizes the UBS committee's reflections on the variation unit: "Internal considerations ... decisively favor the latter reading, for with ἐνδυσάμενοι the apostle's statement is banal and even tautologous, whereas with ἐκδυσάμενοι it is characteristically vivid and paradoxical."[47] Metzger himself, however, demurs: "In view of its superior external support the reading ἐνδυσάμενοι should be adopted, the reading ἐκδυσάμενοι being an early alteration to avoid apparent tautology."[48] This article's suggestion about the meaning of the protasis in εἰ καί conditions offers a way to affirm ἐκδυσάμενοι as the *lectio difficilior* that does not involve appeal to Pauline paradox. If adverbial καί marks the protasis as contrary to fact, v. 3 aims only to make the common-sense observation that no one would ever mistake a naked person for a clothed one: "Indeed even if we should not be found naked once we

47. Metzger, *Textual Commentary*, 511.
48. Metzger, *Textual Commentary*, 511.

have disrobed (which would never happen), then we would groan in the meantime (ἐν τούτῳ) because we long to be clothed with our heavenly dwelling." This way of translating the verse discloses the contrary to fact nature of the protasis; for disrobing necessarily leaves one unmistakably naked. The conceptual link between v. 2 and v. 3 consists in the desire that undressed people with a concern for personal modesty have for clothing.

Second Corinthians 7:8–9 contains three εἰ καί conditions: "For even if (ὅτι εἰ καί) I made you sorry with my letter, I do not regret it (though [εἰ καί] I did regret it, for I see that I grieved you with that letter, though only briefly [εἰ καὶ πρὸς ὥραν]). Now I rejoice, not because you were grieved, but because your grief led to repentance; for you felt a godly grief, so that you were not harmed in any way by us." Separating the verse's three conditions into their respective components helps simplify critiquing the NRSV text, which incorrectly translates εἰ καί in conditions 2 and 3, which cuts off condition 2's protasis from its apodosis thereby obscuring the Greek text's structure, and which incorrectly presents Paul as the subject of ἐλύπησεν in condition 3:

> Condition 1: This condition appears in v. 8a.
>
> Protasis:
> Greek—Ὅτι εἰ καὶ ἐλύπησα ὑμᾶς ἐν τῇ ἐπιστολῇ
> NRSV—"For even if I made you sorry with my letter"
>
> Apodosis:
> Greek—οὐ μεταμέλομαι
> RSV—"I do not regret it"
>
> Condition 2: This condition begins with the protasis in v. 8b, is interrupted by the γάρ clause containing condition 3, and then v. 9a delivers its apodosis.
>
> Protasis:
> Greek—εἰ καὶ μετεμελόμην
> NRSV—"though I did regret it"
>
> Apodosis:
> Greek—νῦν χαίρω, οὐχ ὅτι ἐλυπήθητε ἀλλ' ὅτι ἐλυπήθητε εἰς μετάνοιαν
> NRSV—"Now I rejoice, not because you were grieved, but because your grief led to repentance"
>
> Condition 3: This condition forms a content clause providing βλέπω in v. 8c with an object.

Protasis:
Greek—εἰ καὶ πρὸς ὥραν
NRSV—"though only briefly"

Apodosis:
Greek—ἡ ἐπιστολὴ ἐκείνη . . . ἐλύπησεν ὑμᾶς
NRSV—"I grieved you with that letter"

The contrary to fact status of condition 1's protasis indicates that Paul is not responsible for grieving the Corinthians. That he also wishes to present condition 2's protasis as contrary to fact finds confirmation in condition 1's apodosis, where Paul likewise affirms absence of personal regret. The change of tense from the present in condition 1's apodosis to the imperfect in condition 2's suggests an affinity with second class conditions that the NRSV misses by treating v. 8b as a concession. Neither at the time of the severe letter's inscription (μετεμελόμην) nor at any point since (μεταμέλομαι) did Paul have reason to lament writing it, because no one can hold him directly responsible (note the switch from the first person active ἐλύπησα in v. 8a, to the third person active ἐλύπησεν with ἡ ἐπιστολὴ ἐκείνη as subject in v. 8b, to three occurrences of the second person [divine?] passive ἐλυπήθητε in v. 9) for thereby grieving his audience. While Paul recognizes that the letter prompted a negative experience for the audience, whatever pain the Corinthians endured as a consequence remains acceptable for four reasons: (1) it lasted less than an hour (εἰ καὶ πρὸς ὥραν); (2) it was of a godly or God-induced variety (κατὰ θεόν); (3) it resulted in their repentance; and (4) it is not ultimately attributable to Paul and his ministerial associates (ἐν μηδενὶ ζημιωθῆτε ἐξ ἡμῶν). The NRSV thus misses an important textual nuance by presenting Paul rather than the severe letter (ἡ ἐπιστολὴ ἐκείνη) as the subject of ἐλύπησεν in v. 8c. The protases of conditions 1–2, moreover, concede nothing about the Corinthians' experience of an unhealthy sort of grief nor Paul's regret as its supposed cause.

Whereas comments in the letter's thanksgiving confirm Paul's lack of familiarity with the Colossian church (see 1:4, 7, and 9), the statement he highlights with a disclosure formula in 2:1 affirms the apostle's desire for a closer relationship: "For I want you to know that I have great anxiety for you, and for those in Laodicea, and for all who have not seen me face to face." In light of this admission, the NRSV treats the εἰ καί protasis of the conditional statement that follows in Col 2:5 as a concession: "For *though* I am absent in body, yet I am with you in spirit, and I rejoice to see your morale and the firmness of your faith in Christ." Yet since the nearby context makes clear how Paul begrudges having never visited the Colossian congregation, perhaps it would be better to understand v. 5's protasis as suggesting such would not remain the case in perpetuity. Rendering Col 2:5a–b in the following manner would serve to help make the sense clear: "Even if I *should continue to remain* absent in body, I would still be with you in spirit."

The NRSV also treats the εἰ καί protasis in Heb 6:9 as a concession clause: "*Even though* (εἰ καί) we speak in this way, beloved, we are confident of better things in your case, things that belong to salvation." The five verses immediately preceding this condition provide the explicit referent for v. 9's οὕτως λαλοῦμεν, and in them the author speaks of the damning consequences that would result from a believer's fall from grace. It would prove impossible in this writer's estimation to restore such apostates to repentance; for in failing to maintain the faith they would once more shame and crucify God's Son to their own detriment, thereby proving themselves a most fallow sort of ground, one in need of a good burning (v. 7). As it stands, the NRSV's treatment of v. 9 portrays the pitiful scenario the writer describes in vv. 4–8 as regrettably realistic. While the author of Hebrews clearly defends the members of his beloved audience against any such negative characterization (see πεπείσμεθα δὲ περὶ ὑμῶν), the NRSV's way of handling v. 9's protasis nevertheless represents him as admitting that the content of vv. 4–8 sadly applies to at least some fallen Christians. Yet only in the event that v. 9's protasis constitutes a concessive clause does it become necessary to think of what precedes as having in the writer's perspective any actual referent. Put simply, reading Heb 6:9 in the way this article suggests allows the author to celebrate the fact that (to his knowledge) no truly enlightened believer has ever stumbled; i.e., vv. 4–8 remain delightfully hypothetical precisely because the New Testament writers used εἰ καί protases to introduce counterfactual claims rather than painful concessions.

Two εἰ καί Conditions with True Apodoses that Nevertheless Prove the Rule

While the εἰ καί conditions in 2 Cor 7:12 and 11:15 contain true protases, it is clear from their surrounding contexts that Paul would grant them only begrudgingly. The NRSV predictably treats the protasis of 2 Cor 7:12 as a concession clause: "So although (ἄρα εἰ καί) I wrote to you, it was not on account of the one who did the wrong, nor on account of the one who was wronged, but in order that your zeal for us might be made known to you before God." Here it seems impossible to deny that the protasis is true; for Paul did write the Corinthians. What makes his adoption of the εἰ καί conditional structure appropriate, however, is his reluctance to admit he did so to provoke their collective sorrow. As concerns 2 Cor 11:15, that Satan's messengers would masquerade as "ministers of righteousness" seems at face value unlikely, but that they could do so is clear enough from Satan's own impersonation of an angel of light (see 2 Cor 11:14). That Paul would be hesitant to acknowledge the likelihood of any such scenario justifies his implementation of the εἰ καί conditional structure in this passage.

CONCLUSION

This article tries to make a simple point: what the insertion of ἄν does to deny the claim in the apodosis of a second-class condition, the presence of an adverbial καί in the protasis of a first-class condition does to affirm it. The point of an εἰ καί condition is not that the protasis's satisfaction is a necessary condition for the apodosis, but that the assertion in the 'then' clause remains true even apart from such confirmation. In the same way that denying the antecedent does not logically defeat the consequent, so admission of the likely falsehood of the supposition in an εἰ καί condition allows its apodosis to remain true. As another marked variety of first-class conditions, εἰ καί conditions effectively accomplish the opposite of second class conditions by presenting conditional arguments that permit affirmation of their apodoses despite the likely dissatisfaction of their protases. Might the protasis of an εἰ καί condition present a true idea? Yes, but such is rare and runs counter to the aesthetic reasons for selecting such a conditional form in the first place. Despite the frequency with which the NRSV renders εἰ καί with "even though," the New Testament writers did not deploy such conditions for the sake of making concessions, but for the sake of denying the antecedent and affirming the consequent.

BIBLIOGRAPHY

Blass, Regina. *Constraints on Relevance in Koiné Greek in the Pauline Letters*. Nairobi: Summer Institute of Linguistics, 1993.

Blomberg, Craig L. *Interpreting the Parables*. 2nd ed. Downers Grove, IL: InterVarsity, 2012.

Boyer, James L. "First Class Conditions: What Do They Mean?" *Grace Theological Journal* 2 (1981) 75–114.

———. "Second Class Conditions in New Testament Greek." *Grace Theological Journal* 3 (1982) 81–88.

Brooks, James A., and Carlton L. Winbery. *Syntax of New Testament Greek*. Lanham, MD: University Press of America, 1979.

Burton, Ernest DeWitt. *Syntax of the Moods and Tenses in New Testament Greek*. 1900. Reprint, Eugene, OR: Wipf and Stock, 2003.

Chamberlain, William Douglas. *An Exegetical Grammar of the Greek New Testament*. 1941. Reprint, Grand Rapids: Baker, 1979.

Dana, H. E., and Julius R. Mantey. *A Manual Grammar of the Greek New Testament*. Toronto: Macmillan, 1957.

Denniston, J. D. *The Greek Particles*. Revised by K. J. Dover. 2nd ed. 1950. Reprint, London: Gerald Duckworth, 1996.

Funk, Robert W. *A Beginning-Intermediate Grammar of Hellenistic Greek*. 3rd ed. Salem, OR: Polebridge, 2013.

Goodwin, William W. *A Greek Grammar*. 2nd ed. London: St. Martin's, 1894.

Greenlee, J. Harold. "'If' in the New Testament." *BT* 13 (1962) 39–43.

Heckert, Jakob K. *Discourse Function of Conjoiners in the Pastoral Epistles*. Dallas: Summer Institute of Linguistics, 1996.

Kijne, J. J. "Greek Conditional Sentences." *BT* 13 (1962) 223–24.

Levinsohn, Stephen H. *Discourse Features of New Testament Greek: A Coursebook on the Information Structure of New Testament Greek*. 2nd ed. Dallas: SIL International, 2000.

Mathewson, David L., and Elodie Ballantine Emig. *Intermediate Greek Grammar: Syntax for Students of the New Testament*. Grand Rapids: Baker Academic, 2016.

Metzger, Bruce M. *A Textual Commentary on the Greek New Testament*. 2nd ed. Stuttgart: Deutsche Bibelgesellschaft, 1994.

Moorehouse, A. C. *Studies in the Greek Negative*. Cardiff: University of Wales, 1959.

Moule, C. F. D. *An Idiom Book of New Testament Greek*. 2nd ed. New York: Cambridge University Press, 1959.

Moulton, James Hope. *A Grammar of New Testament Greek: Volume I. Prolegomena*. 3rd ed. Edinburgh: T. & T. Clark, 1908. (MHT1)

Moulton, James Hope, and Nigel Turner. *A Grammar of New Testament Greek: Volume III. Syntax*. London: T. & T. Clark, 1963. (MHT3)

Porter, Stanley E. *Idioms of the Greek New Testament*. 2nd ed. BLG 2. Sheffield: Sheffield Academic, 1994.

———. *Verbal Aspect in the Greek of the New Testament, with Reference to Tense and Mood*. SBG 1. New York: Peter Lang, 1989.

Proctor, Mark A. "'It's Probably Untrue, but It Wouldn't Matter Anyway': Εἰ Καί Conditions in the Greek New Testament." *Neot* 53 (2019) 437–58.

Robertson, A. T. *A Grammar of the Greek New Testament in the Light of Historical Research*. 4th ed. Nashville: Broadman, 1934.

Runge, Steven E. *Discourse Grammar of the Greek New Testament: A Practical Introduction for Teaching and Exegesis*. Lexham Bible Reference Series. Peabody, MA: Hendrickson, 2010.

Stern, Frank. *A Rabbi Looks at Jesus' Parables*. Lanham, MD: Rowman & Littlefield, 2006.

Titrud, Kermit. "The Overlooked KAI in the Greek New Testament." *Notes on Translation* 5 (1991) 1–28.

Wallace, Daniel B. *Greek Grammar beyond the Basics: An Exegetical Syntax of the New Testament*. Grand Rapids: Zondervan, 1996.

Young, Richard A. *Intermediate New Testament Greek: A Linguistic and Exegetical Approach*. Nashville: Broadman & Holman, 1994.

Zerwick, Maximilian. *Biblical Greek: Illustrated by Examples*. Translated by Joseph Smith. Rome: Pontifical Biblical Institute, 2005.

6

Defining Definers
An Exploration into the Functions of Attributive Adjectives in Koine Greek

JAMES D. DVORAK

INTRODUCTION

IN HIS NOW CLASSIC *Idiom Book of the Greek New Testament*, C. F. D. Moule begins the chapter on adjectives by stating, "Precise definition of the adjective would, even if possible, not necessarily be very valuable."[1] Now, let it be noted that I have a tremendous amount of respect for Moule, and I have found his *Idiom Book* to be a valuable resource. Nevertheless, advances in linguistic research and the study of Greek since the 1959 publication of the second edition of his grammar have cleared a path for a more careful consideration of the functions and semantic contributions of all types of definers with a greater level of delicacy.[2] With this paper I wish to walk for a bit on this *Wanderweg* and to "think out loud," so to speak, about a relatively thin slice of definers, namely adjectives that stand in an attributive relationship with the nouns that they define (I may, however, comment on other classes of

---

1. Moule, *Idiom Book*, 93.

2. Formative for me has been Halliday's work on nominal groups (see IFG2, 180–96; see also Halliday, IFG3, 311–34, and IFG4, 364–96). See also Martin and Rose, *Working with Discourse*, 96–99.

words functioning as definers in this same syntactical arrangement [e.g., possessive pronouns, participles, and the like]). More to the point, I want to explore a bit more critically and systematically the delicacy with which we define "definition" as well as what it is that definers contribute not only to the semantics of the nominal groups in which they appear but also as their meaning affects the semantics of other units up the rank scale.

The basic perspective offered here is Hallidayan in essence, although along the way I will bring to bear other SFL-influenced models (e.g., critical discourse analysis, social semiotics, and other varieties of social-scientific criticism).[3] Yet I have found it to be the case that as researchers continue to fixate on the specific, minute details of any given object, process, or idea—which is precisely what we will do in this exploratory excursion—it becomes increasingly important to review the broader theoretical context in which those minute details may be understood. Thus, we will embark from a trailhead where the path is well-worn and the trail markers (i.e., key terms and tenets) are relatively easy to see. As we venture on, I suspect that we will encounter a few places where the trail is overgrown or, perhaps, has yet to be blazed. I realize that much of what I provide early on in this paper will likely seem commonsensical, since I will start with a view of the forest before narrowing my view to the bark located at a specific spot on a single tree. Nevertheless, I hope that such a review will keep us from unnecessarily venturing too far down any side trails. My intuition, however, based on reading a number of even the most recent Greek grammars, is that the lower ranking units receive the most attention, often with little or no reference to the semantic contribution they make to larger units or to the role(s) they play in the overarching social purpose of making and exchanging meaning as a means of acting towards or interacting with others.

---

3. See Fairclough, *Discourse and Social Change*; *Analyzing Discourse*; *Language and Power*; *Critical Discourse Analysis*; Lemke, *Textual Politics*; Hart, *Discourse, Grammar and Ideology*; Gee, *Introduction*; Simpson, *Language, Ideology and Point of View*; Hodge and Kress, *Social Semiotics*; Black, ed., *To Set at Liberty*; deSilva, *Honor, Patronage, Kinship and Purity*; Esler, ed., *Modelling Early Christianity*; Malina, *Christian Origins and Cultural Anthropology*; Meeks, *Origins of Christian Morality*; Neufeld and DeMaris, *Understanding the Social World of the New Testament*; Pilch, ed., *Social Scientific Models*; Pilch and Malina, eds., *Handbook*.

REVIEW OF THEORY

What initially drew my attention to SFL theory and grammar and what still holds my attention today is its foundational tenet that language is a *social semiotic*.[4] For Halliday this tenet encapsulates basically two notions. First, language or, more precisely, the lexicogrammatical system of language, "constitutes the 'reality' of [a given] culture,"[5] and is, thus, a system of "meaning potential."[6] The second notion is that humans make selections from this lexicogrammatical system in order to make *texts*, and these texts—the "actualization of the meaning potential"[7]—are the means by which and through which people behave toward or interact with one another in the multifarious situations that, as we often say, "life throws at them."[8]

As I have argued elsewhere, one of the primary social tasks for which people deploy language—and this is true even of the *inspired* biblical writers—is to negotiate values and ideologies (or in our discipline, theology), to present "the way things are" (or are not) and to orient others to "the way things ought to be" (or ought not to be).[9] These presentations and orientations are never neutral;[10] both their content and their intended effects (i.e., the sought after affinity or alignment of the readers to a certain set of values)[11] are shaped by the socially-rooted interests of

---

4. See the essays in Halliday, *Language as Social Semiotic*, esp. 108–26; see also the essays in Halliday, *Explorations*. See also Dvorak, "To Incline Another's Heart," 602–7; Dvorak, "Not Like Cain," 3–6.

5. Halliday, *Language as Social Semiotic*, 123.

6. Halliday, *Language as Social Semiotic*, 122. See Dvorak, "Not Like Cain," 4–6.

7. Halliday, *Language as Social Semiotic*, 122.

8. In more colloquial terms, Halliday characterizes this point by saying that language is "can do" translated into "can mean" which is, in turn, realized in the language system as "can say" or "can write," all of which is constrained by the contexts of culture and situation (see *Explorations*, 48–58). See also Malina's characterization (*Christian Origins and Cultural Anthropology*, 9), where he writes, "Language here takes on the nuance of a verb, 'to language' . . . To language is to mean; to language is what a speaker/writer and/or hearer/reader can do. To language is a social activity, a form of social interaction like buying and selling, marrying and bearing children, or ruling or being ruled."

9. Dvorak, "To Incline Another's Heart," 604–6.

10. Bakhtin, "Problem of Speech Genres," 84, who says, "There can be no such thing as an absolutely neutral utterance."

11. Hodge and Kress (*Social Semiotics*, 123) speak of "affinity"; Martin and White (*Language of Evaluation*, 95–97) use the language of "alignment" (as do I in Dvorak,

the people who produced them and the groups to which they belong.¹² Fairclough helpfully describes this as the "dialectical" function of discourse. On the one hand, discourse is shaped and constrained by the cultural and situational contexts in which it is produced and, therefore, it construes *reality* on the basis of those contextual constraints, yet, on the other hand, discourse is socially constitutive in that it *re*-construes the social world; it "contributes to the constitution of all those dimensions of social structure which directly or indirectly shape and constrain it: its own norms and conventions, as well as the relations, identities, and institutions which lie behind them."¹³ Since, as Hodge and Kress point out, "social control rests on control over the representation of reality which is accepted as the basis of judgement and action,"¹⁴ how reality is represented, what is included or left out, what identities and relationships are enacted in a text, who or what gets evaluated positively or negatively, what is emphasized or gets downplayed, and how it all gets packaged together into a coherent message all play into how the language user *simultaneously* generates solidarity with some people (i.e., affinity or alignment) *and* creates difference with others as she or he engages and interacts with them.¹⁵

According to Halliday, the kinds of meanings that people make in every linguistic interaction in this dialectical process may be organized around three distinct yet intimately interdependent categories. He labels these *ideational, interpersonal,* and *textual* meanings,¹⁶ but I have come to prefer Lemke's nomenclature and descriptions, as I have found them to be a bit clearer.¹⁷ The first is *presentational* meaning (= Halliday's

---

Interpersonal Metafunction). Both are terms that have to do with solidarity.

12. See Martin and White, *Language of Evaluation*, 92; Stubbs, "Matter of Prolonged Field Work," 1; Dvorak, *Interpersonal Metafunction*, 37–38.

13. Fairclough, *Discourse and Social Change*, 64. See also Fairclough, *Analysing Discourse*, 26–29. Halliday (*Language as Social Semiotic*, 191) says, "Since reality is a social construct, it can be reconstructed only through an exchange of meanings. Hence meanings are seen as constitutive of reality."

14. Hodge and Kress, *Social Semiotics*, 147.

15. See Hodge and Kress, *Social Semiotics*, 3, where they describe generating solidarity and creating difference as a "double and contradictory necessity."

16. Descriptions of the metafunctions saturate the Hallidayan corpus, but see Halliday, *Language as Social Semiotic*, 112–13. See also IFG4, 30–31 and Lemke, *Textual Politics*, 40–41.

17. Lemke, *Textual Politics*, 41. Halliday's descriptions have varied slightly over the years. See Martin, *English Text*, 487–501. Also, I prefer Lemke's more generalized

ideational meaning). This kind of meaning is involved in "the construction of [one's perspective of] how things are in the natural and social worlds by their explicit description as participants, processes, relations and circumstances standing in particular semantic relations to one another across meaningful stretches of text, and from text to text."[18] The next type is *orientational* meaning (= Halliday's *interpersonal* meaning), which is involved in "the construction of [one's] orientational stance toward present and potential addressees and audiences, and toward the presentational content of [one's] discourse, in respect of social relations and evaluations from a particular viewpoint, across meaningful stretches of text and from text to text."[19] Finally, the third type of meaning is *organizational* meaning (= Halliday's *textual* meaning). This type of meaning is involved in "the construction of relations between elements of the discourse itself, so that it is interpretable as having structure ... texture ... and informational organization and relative prominence across meaningful stretches of text and from text to text."[20]

Like every other social activity, meaning-making with language is "patterned activity,"[21] and for Halliday, the patterns or models of these three types of meaning are most clearly visible in clauses. Presentational meanings, he argues, are construed as models of experience, which he calls "figures" of happening, doing, sensing, saying, being, or having.[22] Each figure consists of a verbal process (often explicit but sometimes

---

approach that defines the kinds of meanings as primary and then investigates to see how all the different linguistic resources put to use contribute to the "construction, continuity, modulation and change across a text" and even intertextually "from text to text" (*Textual Politics*, 41). Fairclough uses a slightly different functional typology: identity, relational, and ideational. He says, "The identity function relates to the ways in which social identities are set up in discourse, the relational function to how social relationships between discourse participants are enacted and negotiated, the ideational function to ways in which texts signify the world and its processes, entities and relations. The identity and relational functions are grouped together by Halliday (1978) as the 'interpersonal' function. Halliday also distinguishes a 'textual' function which ... concerns how bits of information are foregrounded or backgrounded, taken as given or presented as new, picked out as 'topic' or 'theme', and how a part of text is linked to preceding and following parts of the text, and to the social situation 'outside' the text" (*Discourse and Social Change*, 64–65; see also *Analysing Text*, 26–28).

18. Lemke, *Textual Politics*, 41.
19. Lemke, *Textual Politics*, 41.
20. Lemke, *Textual Politics*, 41.
21. Halliday, "Categories," 42.
22. Halliday, IFG4, 213.

implied) and one or more participants (not necessarily human) that are involved in the process in some way.²³ Additionally, a figure may construe various circumstances related to the process, such as time, space, cause, manner, and a handful of others.²⁴ Halliday calls this kind of patterned activity "transitivity or experiential structuring."²⁵

Orientational meanings are construed as models of exchange or dialogue. An ancient Greek language user, according to Porter, could give, demand, project, wish, or enquire about information or about goods and services.²⁶ In doing any of these, the language user enacts in the text that she or he produces social roles both for her- or himself as well as the one(s) to whom the exchange is directed.²⁷ Orientational meanings are structured in the clause in two main blocks, a Mood block and a Residue block, each of which has additional components. The Mood block consists of the Subject (sometimes only implied or signaled by the personal ending of the verb), and the Residue consists of everything else in the clause—Predicator, Complement(s), and Adjunct(s). This kind of patterned activity Halliday calls "modal structuring."²⁸

Finally, organizational meanings are construed as quanta of information that are structured primarily into two major parts, which Halliday calls Theme and Rheme²⁹ but which OpenText calls Prime and Subsequent.³⁰ Prime is "who or what the clause is focused upon, realized by the first [word] group element in the clause,"³¹ and Subsequent is how the language user develops the Prime, if she or he chooses to do so, through the remaining group elements in the clause.³² The language user chooses the Prime as her or his point of departure and any Subsequent elements provide a means of guiding the addressee in de-

---

23. Halliday, IFG4, 213.
24. Halliday, IFG4, 213.
25. Halliday, IFG4, 361.
26. Porter, "Systemic Functional Linguistics," 29.
27. Halliday, IFG4, 135.
28. Halliday, IFG4, 361.
29. Halliday, IFG4, 89.
30. See "Clause Level." See also Dvorak, "Thematization," 19–21; Dvorak and Walton, "Clause as Message," 42–45.
31. Dvorak and Walton, "Clause as Message," 43.
32. Dvorak and Walton, "Clause as Message," 43.

veloping an interpretation of the message of the clause.[33] This kind of patterned activity Halliday calls "thematic structuring."[34]

Yet we must not forget that these meaningful patterns, even though most clearly recognizable at the clause level, are generated from the selections that a language user makes from the lexicogrammatical system, and that these selections are realized, for the most part, at units of rank lower than the clause. In other words, *clauses*, as we have just seen, are realized by a *configuration of word groups*, and each word group is realized by a *configuration of words*.[35] So it becomes necessary for us to consider these smaller units. Moreover, we must always keep before us a particularly important point made by Porter: "In discourse analysis, one can begin at the top or the bottom, but one must work through all the stages, from both directions, to provide full analysis."[36] One needs to identify and to interpret the smaller units that comprise the patterns of the larger units, yet at the same time one must also interpret those smaller units in light of the patterns of the larger units. This kind of cyclical analysis is called abductive or retroductive reasoning, which is "a process of logic of the discovery procedure of working from evidence to hypothesis, involving a back-and-forth movement of suggestion checking."[37]

DEFINING DEFINERS

With that broader perspective now salient, discussion may now be focused on the lower ranks of units. The unit that is one rank below the clause is the word group. SFL recognizes three main classes of word groups: the *nominal group*, which has as its pivotal element[38] a noun (including proper nouns) or pronoun as head term, along with any modifiers such as adjectives; the *verbal group*, which has as its pivotal element a finite verb (sometimes a non-finite verbal, as in the case of a participle in a genitive absolute structure); and the *adverbial group*,

---

33. Halliday, IFG4, 89.
34. Halliday, IFG4, 361.
35. Martin and Rose, *Working with Discourse*, 96. See also Halliday, "Categories," 43.
36. Porter, *Idioms*, 299.
37. Elliott, *What Is Social-Scientific Criticism?* 48; see also Dvorak, *Interpersonal Metafunction*, 43n209.
38. Fawcett defines "pivotal element" as an element that is typically present in a given class (Fawcett, *Theory of Syntax*, 196).

which has as its pivotal element an adverb (or another class of word or rank-shifted element that takes up an adverbial function).[39] Following Fawcett and Porter, I add prepositional group to this list, which has as its pivotal element a preposition,[40] although its head term is the nominal element that is specified by the preposition and not the preposition itself.[41] Thus, for example, using this basic model of group classes, we may label the groups in the clause ὅτε οἱ ἀληθινοὶ προσκυνηταὶ προσκυνήσουσιν τῷ πατρὶ ἐν πνεύματι καὶ ἀληθείᾳ ("when true worshipers will worship in spirit and [in] truth," John 4:23b) as shown in Table 1.

ὅτε	οἱ ἀληθινοὶ προσκυνηταὶ	προσκυνήσουσιν	τῷ πατρὶ	ἐν πνεύματι καὶ ἀληθείᾳ
Adverbial group	Nominal group	Verbal group	Nominal group	Preposition group

Table 1. John 4:23b

Of course, this sort of analysis, in and of itself, does not tell the full story, since each class of group serves different functions in the clause, depending upon which sort of structure one is looking at under the microscope. If, on the one hand, one is looking at modal structure, then nominal groups may serve as either Subject or Complement, the verbal group as Predicator, and both adverbial groups and preposition groups serve as Adjuncts.[42] If, on the other hand, one is looking into transitivity or experiential structure, then nominal groups serve in participant roles (e.g., Actor, Recipient, or Goal in material clauses), verbal groups as Process, and adverbial and prepositional groups as various types of Circumstance (e.g., Location, Extent, Manner).[43]

Focusing now on word groups, as I mentioned earlier, these are realized by complexes of words. Just as word groups have classes, so also do words; and just as different classes of word groups contribute in different ways to the semantics of clauses, so do different classes of words contribute in different ways to the semantics of word groups. Let

---

39. Halliday, IFG4, 362.
40. Fawcett, *Theory of Syntax*, 204–6; Porter, "Greek Prepositions," 21.
41. Porter, "Greek Prepositions," 21–22.
42. Halliday, IFG4, 362.
43. Halliday, IFG4, 362.

us focus our attention on the nominal group and its component parts.⁴⁴ Consider the first nominal group in John 4:23b (οἱ ἀληθινοὶ προσκυνηταί, "the true worshipers"). There are three classes of words in this group: an article, an adjective, and a noun. In the OpenText model, these classes of words are given the functional labels *specifier*, *definer*, and *head term* respectively, where *specifier* labels modifiers that classify or identify; *definer* labels modifiers that attribute features or that further define (inclusive of attributive and predicate adjectives as well as appositives); and *head term* is the label given to the main word in the group in relation to which all of the other words in the group are subordinate.⁴⁵ In Halliday's model, the article would be labeled as Deictic, the adjective would, in this particular instance, be labeled Classifier, and the noun would be labeled as Thing.

Now, it is not my intention to bring OpenText and Halliday into strict alignment; Halliday's model was developed primarily for English and OpenText for Greek. However, in making a few comparisons between the two models, we may be able to bring greater clarity and delicacy to the OpenText model. OpenText's *head term* and Halliday's Thing both refer to the semantic core of the nominal group. There are greater differences between OpenText's *specifier* and Halliday's Deictic, and these are generally the result of differences between Greek and English, especially regarding the particular ways that articles work in each language. Nevertheless, both models recognize that articles (among other classes of words, such as the possessive pronoun/adjective in Greek [i.e., ἐμός, σός, ἡμέτερος, and ὑμέτερος])⁴⁶ are a type of modifier that may identify a particular Thing specifically or may identify a type or category of Thing.

For the current discussion, I am most interested in the differences between what OpenText labels a *definer* but what Halliday's model would label Epithet. I will return to these labels more below, but I first need to put some boundaries on our discussion. I am most interested here in definers that appear in attributive structures. I exclude from this discussion definers in predicate structures because it seems to me that, with some exceptions,⁴⁷ predication occurs at the clause level and not at the

---

44. I am aware that definition also occurs in other classes of groups (e.g., in prepositional groups, as in εἰς τὸ πῦρ τὸ αἰώνιον [Matt 18:8]).

45. See "Word Group." See also Porter, "Greek Prepositions," 19n8.

46. Porter, *Idioms*, 131.

47. For example, as Porter (*Idioms*, 118–19) notes, some words, such as demonstra-

word group level—that is, it may be more helpful to consider predication as, in presentational terms, either attributive or identifying relational clauses, or, in orientational terms, as (monoglossic) propositions or claims[48] or explicit appraisals that are made about a given Subject.[49] At a certain level of abstraction, it makes complete sense to call modifiers in predicate structures *definers*, because they do, indeed, "add more definition to the qualities or characteristics of a substantive."[50] Yet, doing so *at the word group level*, has created an inconsistency in OpenText analysis and annotation. Herein lies the rub: such modifiers are called *definers* in the Word Group Model Specifications documentation, but they are never actually annotated as such in the word group annotation. They are usually simply annotated as nominal groups with no indication that they are definers. The OpenText annotation of Matt 9:37bc exemplifies this, which can be viewed in Figure 1.

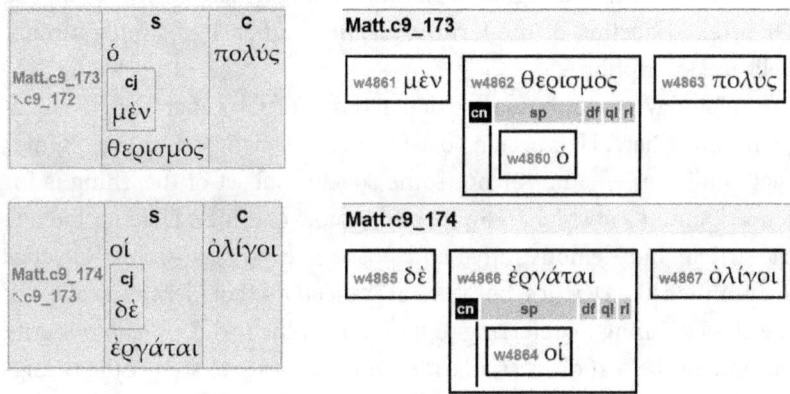

Figure 1. Matt 9:37bc

---

tives, always appear in predicate structure in relation to a substantive, yet still have an attributive force.

48. Dana and Mantey, *Manual Grammar*, 118, who write, "An adjective is in the predicate relation when it *makes an assertion* concerning the noun which it modifies."

49. An example of a predicate structure realized as an identifying relational clause may be found at Luke 19:2b (καὶ αὐτὸς ἦν ἀρχιτελώνης), where Zacchaeus is identified as a chief tax collector. An example of a predicate structure realized as an attributive relational clause may be found at Col 1:7 (ὅς ἐστιν πιστὸς ὑπὲρ ὑμῶν διάκονος τοῦ Χριστοῦ), where Paul calls Epaphras a faithful/reliable minister on behalf of the Colossians.

50. Porter, *Idioms*, 118.

This is a topic that begs further discussion or, at least, clearer definition in the OpenText Word Group Specification documentation, but let us return to modifiers in attributive structures.

Classifiers

Despite Moule's apparent position to the contrary, it seems to me that there is heuristic benefit in describing attributive *definers* with a greater level of precision or delicacy. Let us first consider Classifiers. According to Halliday, a Classifier indicates a particular subclass of the Thing that is being defined.[51] Consider as a simple example οἶνον νέον ("new wine") from Matt 9:17. Here, the Thing (or head term) οἶνον ("wine") is sub-classed as νέον ("new") which stands over against παλαιόν "old" wine. Hence, νέον in this instance functions as a Classifier. It is important to point out that this designation is not intended necessarily to oppose OpenText's labeling of the term as *definer*; rather, it is simply a more delicate description.

Halliday recognizes a particular kind of Classifier that is worth mentioning here. He calls it a post-Deictic. A Deictic is a kind of pointer that "indicates whether or not some specific subset of the Thing is intended, and if so, which."[52] Some of the most common Deictics include the article and demonstrative and possessive pronouns. Post-Deictics are pointers like Deictics, but these are adjectives that identify a subset of the class of Thing by referring to its status in the text (i.e., its familiarity or fame in the text or its similarity or dissimilarity to some other designated subset).[53] It is not uncommon in the Greek of the New Testament to place a non-adjective into an attributive structure in order to fill this post-Deictic role. The indefinite pronoun τις is often used this way, as in τινῶν ἀνθρώπων αἱ ἁμαρτίαι ("The sins of *certain* people," 1 Tim 5:24).[54] The intensive pronoun is also used this way, as in τὸν αὐτὸν ἀγῶνα ἔχοντες ("having the *same* struggle," Phil 1:30).[55] In terms of adjectives, λοιπός gets put to use in this way. In Acts 2:37, for example, upon hearing Peter's message, the people respond by asking "What shall we do?"

---

51. Halliday, IFG4, 377.
52. Halliday, IFG4, 365.
53. Halliday, IFG4, 373.
54. Interestingly, AGNT tags τις as an indefinite adjective.
55. Interestingly, AGNT tags αὐτός here as an adjective.

This question, the narrator informs the reader, is directed to Peter and τοὺς λοιποὺς ἀποστόλους ("the other/remaining apostles"), where λοιποὺς identifies a subset of the Thing ἀποστόλους.

Epithets

Closely related to Classifiers are Epithets,[56] which, according to Halliday, indicate some quality of the Thing that is being defined in the nominal group.[57] A simple example occurs in Mark 4:32 (κλάδους μεγάλους, "large branches") where the adjective μεγάλους indicates the largeness of the mustard plant's branches. Over in Mark 6:39, one finds τῷ χλωρῷ χόρτῳ ("[on] the green grass"), where the adjective χλωρῷ indicates the color of the grass. One may ask further how the language user construes the quality: Is it depicted as an objective quality of the Thing itself, or is it more of an expression of the language user's attitude/stance toward the Thing? The two examples I have provided exemplify the former and would be further designated *experiential* Epithets, because in each case the Epithets identify (potentially) defining characteristics of the Things they describe. However, Epithets that are an expression of one's attitude/stance, which are called *attitudinal* Epithets, do not identify any (potentially) defining characteristics of the Things they modify.[58] Consider the following portion of Rev 14:8 (ἔπεσεν Βαβυλὼν ἡ μεγάλη, "the great Babylon has fallen"). The adjective μεγάλη may be taken to mean "great" in the sense of "large in size" (an experiential Epithet), but context points us in a different direction. Most scholars believe that Babylon, likely an intertextual reference to ancient Babylon (see Daniel 1–6), was used by the writer of Revelation (and his Jewish contemporaries) as a cipher for Rome based in large part on the fact that "both were centers for world empires and both captured Jerusalem and destroyed the temple."[59] This likely being the case, it is more plausible to read μεγάλη in the sense of "eminent," which is an attitudinal Epithet—and an ironic one at that, since Babylon is depicted as having fallen.

---

56. They are so closely related, in fact, that Halliday notes that "sometimes the same word may function either as Epithet or as Classifier" (Halliday, IFG4, 377).

57. Halliday, IFG4, 376. See also Martin and Rose, *Working with Discourse*, 96.

58. Halliday, IFG4, 376.

59. Aune, *Revelation 6–16*, 829–31. See also Beale, *Book of Revelation*, 18–19, 755.

Numeratives

Another kind of definition is accomplished with numeratives. A numerative element "indicates some numerical feature of the particular subset of the Thing: either quantity or order, either definite or inexact."[60] Matthew 14:17 provides a straightforward example of quantifying numeratives that specify an exact number: οἱ δὲ λέγουσιν αὐτῷ· οὐκ ἔχομεν ὧδε εἰ μὴ πέντε ἄρτους καὶ δύο ἰχθύας ("They were saying to him, "We do not have [anything] here except five loaves and two fish"). Here, the cardinal numerals πέντε and δύο define a quantity of each Thing, i.e., loaves and fish, respectively. Another example is διπλῆς τιμῆς ("double honor") found at 1 Tim 5:17. Quantifying is not always exact, as in καὶ πολλοὶ ψευδοπροφῆται ἐγερθήσονται ("and many false prophets will arise," Matt 24:11). Here the adjective πολλοί is quantitative, but it does not specify exactly how many false prophets will arise. The adjective πᾶς, when used attributively as in τὸν πάντα χρόνον ("the whole/entire time," Acts 20:18), also fits into this category. It should also be noted that sometimes exact quantifying numeratives may in certain contexts be intended to express inexactitude, as in μυρίους παιδαγωγούς ("a myriad/ten thousand guardians/tutors") at 1 Cor 4:15. As always, context must be consulted in each case.

Ordering numeratives specify an exact place in a sequence, typically through the use of ordinals (e.g., πρῶτος, δεύτερος, or τρίτος). One example of this is located at Matt 16:21, where Matthew recounts that Jesus had begun to teach his disciples that it was necessary for him to go to Jerusalem and to suffer and to die at the hands of the elders and chief priests, yet τῇ τρίτῃ ἡμέρᾳ ἐγερθῆναι ("to be raised on the third day")—presumably the third successive day after being put to death. Inexact ordering (e.g., former, subsequent) tends to be expressed in Greek adverbially, but as part of a preposition group at Eph 4:22 Paul reminds the readers that they were taught in Christ Jesus to lay aside the old person in reference to τὴν προτέραν ἀναστροφὴν ("the former way of life"). In this case, although in a preposition group and not necessarily in a nominal group, πρότερον occurs as an attributive adjective.

---

60. Halliday, IFG4, 374.

Summary

I will now summarize the possible more delicate options related to definition, particularly for adjectives in attributive relations with a substantive. In nominal groups and, really, any group where substantives may receive further definition by means of adjectives in attributive position, we may identify the following more delicate types of definers:

1. Classifiers (including so-called post-Deictics): these define the Thing/head term as belonging to a particular subclass.
2. Epithets: these define some quality of the Thing/head term.
   - Experiential Epithets: the quality that is identified is a potentially defining characteristic of the Thing/head term.
   - Attitudinal Epithets: the quality that is identified is the language user's subjective attitude or stance toward the Thing/head term.
3. Numeratives: these indicate some numerical feature of the particular subset of the Thing.
   - Quantifying Numeratives: indicates the quantity of a Thing/head term, whether exact or inexact.
   - Ordering Numeratives: specifies the place of the Thing/head term in a sequence, whether exact or inexact.

BRINGING IT FULL CIRCLE

I, like Halliday, have tended to describe these functional/semantic options primarily from a presentational (or ideational) perspective, due in large part to the fact that adjectives and the nouns they modify are heavy lifters in the portrayal of the natural and social worlds. They depict and describe participants, and it is not out of the ordinary even to find them at work in the expression of circumstances. Yet adjectives also play an important role in construing orientational meanings, and this cannot be overlooked. Let us consider Matt 12:35 to help us bring this discussion full circle, connecting it back to where we began. The verse contains two ranking clauses. Both are primary clauses, and they stand in a coordinate relationship (see Table 2).

ὁ ἀγαθὸς ἄνθρωπος ἐκ τοῦ ἀγαθοῦ θησαυροῦ ἐκβάλλει ἀγαθά	The good person, out of good treasure, brings about good [things].
καὶ ὁ πονηρὸς ἄνθρωπος ἐκ τοῦ πονηροῦ θησαυροῦ ἐκβάλλει πονηρά	And the evil person, out of evil treasure, brings about evil [things].

Table 2. Matt 12:35 (A)

The clauses mirror one another structurally. Each one consists of four word groups (not counting the conjunction in the second clause): nominal group ^ preposition group ^ verbal group ^ nominal group. Presentationally, because the process (identical in each clause) is a material process (ἐκβάλλω in this co-text means something like "brings forth" or "brings about"), both clauses are identified as material clauses. The initial nominal group in each clause functions as Actor, and in each case the Thing is ἄνθρωπος ("person"). Also, in both instances the Thing receives further definition by adjectives that are in an attributive relationship (first position) with the head term.

ὁ ἀγαθὸς ἄνθρωπος	ἐκ τοῦ ἀγαθοῦ θησαυροῦ	ἐκβάλλει	ἀγαθά
"The good person"	"out of good treasure"	"brings about"	"good [things]"
Nominal group	Preposition group	Verbal group	Nominal group
Actor	Circumstance: Place	Process: Material	Goal
Subject	Adjunct	Predicator	Complement
MOOD...	RESIDUE...	...MOOD	...RESIDUE
PRIME	SUBSEQUENT		

καὶ	ὁ πονηρὸς ἄνθρωπος	ἐκ τοῦ πονηροῦ θησαυροῦ	ἐκβάλλει	πονηρά
"and"	"the evil person"	"out of evil treasure"	"brings about"	"evil [things]"
	Nominal group	Preposition group	Verbal group	Nominal group

	Actor	Circumstance: Place	Process: Material	Goal
	Subject	Adjunct	Predicator	Complement
	MOOD...	RESIDUE...	...MOOD	...RESIDUE
	PRIME	SUBSEQUENT		

Table 3. Matt 12:35 (B)

It is at this level that we begin to note a presentational difference between the clauses, because Jesus chooses a different Epithet to identify a different—and in this case opposing—quality that defines the Thing: in the first clause, ἄνθρωπος is defined with the Epithet ἀγαθός ("good"); and in the second, ἄνθρωπος is defined with the Epithet πονηρός ("evil," or "bad"). I have tagged each of these as Epithets rather than Classifiers (although the two are very close) because the actual classification is given on the basis of what each person produces or brings about. That is, one's behavior (contextually, their *verbal* behavior, and specifically what one says regarding the Son of Man and/or the Holy Spirit [v. 32]) is that by which people will be measured and classified. Thus, terms ἀγαθός and πονηρός are attitudinal Epithets rather than experiential Epithets.

Here is where we need to return to where we started. These Epithets not only contribute to the presentational meanings of the clauses in which they appear; they also contribute to the orientational meaning of the clauses (and beyond). They do so because they express two appraisals/evaluations from Jesus. What is asserted on the one hand is that the person whom Jesus considers "good" (honorable) is one who produces what is good (behaves honorably), but on the other hand, the person whom Jesus considers "evil/bad" (shameless) is one who produces what is evil/bad (behaves shamelessly). The assumption is that the hearers would desire to be considered good or honorable and would want to eschew what is considered to be shameless, so with these two opposing assertions of reality, the hearers are positioned to align with the first. Here, then, we see how the Epithets contribute to both the presentational and orientational meanings of the clauses and, really, to the Theme of the entire unit (which appears to run from at least from 12:31–37).[61]

---

61. On Appraisal Theory, see Dvorak, *Interpersonal Metafunction* and "To Incline Another's Heart."

CONCLUSION

In conclusion, it is important to reiterate a few points. First, my intent has not been to suggest that the OpenText model (or any other SFL modeling of Greek) needs to come into strict alignment with Halliday's model. After all, as we know, the editions of IFG contain Halliday's development of a Functional Grammar of English—and it is not even the only SFL model of English! That being said, Halliday does provide a solid example of what it means to think about a language and its grammar from a functional perspective, and we ought to allow his modeling even of English to provoke more and deeper thinking in terms of modeling Hellenistic Greek.

Secondly, the offerings of this essay are intended to be exploratory; therefore, they should be taken as tentative and subject to change. Much more modeling needs to be done with regard to definition, especially with regard to non-adjectives in attributive relations to substantives and, thus, functioning as definers (e.g., various pronouns, rank-shifted participial clauses, and the like). We also need better modeling of predication. In this vein, I hope to have reignited an interest in continued development of the OpenText.org functional model. Much of the documentation is incomplete, and what has been published stands in need of revision. For example, Porter's modeling of the preposition group in his *BAGL* article should be brought to bear on these documents,[62] as should work on orientational/interpersonal aspects of the language.[63] At the very least, I hope what I have put forward here will, in some way, provide some motivation to this end.

Finally, we who are engaged in the investigation, analysis, and modeling of Hellenistic Greek must never forget that our work with the grammar of the language—from morpheme to text—must always be done *in light of the broader notion that language is a social semiotic*. The people who spoke and wrote in Greek did so (in conjunction with other semiotic systems) as a means of acting or behaving socially with and towards others. Moreover, every instance of their linguistic behaviors both construed and *re*-construed both reality and relationships in order to mark out and maintain social boundaries (i.e., solidarity and difference).

---

62. Porter, "Greek Prepositions."
63. E.g., Dawson, "Language as Negotiation"; "Rules of 'Engagement.'"

BIBLIOGRAPHY

Aune, David E. *Revelation 6–16*. WBC 52b. Nashville: Thomas Nelson, 1998.

Bakhtin, M. M. "The Problem of Speech Genres." In *Speech Genres and Other Late Essays*, edited by Caryl Emerson and Michael Holquist, 60–102. Translated by Vern W. McGee. Austin: University of Texas Press, 1986.

Beale, G. K. *The Book of Revelation*. NIGTC. Grand Rapids: Eerdmans, 1999.

"Clause Level Annotation Specification." *OpenText.org*. No pages. Online: http://www.opentext.org/model/guidelines/clause/0-2.html.

Dana, H. E., and Julius R. Mantey. *A Manual Grammar of the Greek New Testament*. New York: Macmillan, 1927.

Dawson, Zachary K. "Language as Negotiation: Toward a Systemic Functional Model for Ideological Criticism with Application to James 2:1–13." In *Modeling Biblical Language: Selected Papers from the McMaster Divinity College Linguistics Circle*, edited by Stanley E. Porter et al., 362–90. LBS 13. Leiden: Brill, 2016.

———. "The Rules of 'Engagement': Assessing the Function of the Diatribe in James 2:14–26 Using Critical Discourse Analysis." In *The Epistle of James: Linguistic Exegesis of an Early Christian Letter*, edited by James D. Dvorak and Zachary K. Dawson. LENT 1. Eugene, OR: Pickwick, 2019.

deSilva, David A. *Honor, Patronage, Kinship and Purity: Unlocking New Testament Culture*. Downers Grove, IL: IVP, 2000.

Dvorak, James D. *The Interpersonal Metafunction in 1 Corinthians 1–4: The Tenor of Toughness*. LBS 19. Leiden: Brill, 2021.

———. "'Not Like Cain': Marking Moral Boundaries through Vilification of the Other in 1 John 3:1–18." *Dialogismos* 1 (2017) 1–19.

———. "Thematization, Topic, and Information Flow." *JLIABG* 1 (2008) 17–37.

———. "To Incline Another's Heart: The Role of Attitude in Reader Positioning." In *The Language and Literature of the New Testament: Essays in Honor of Stanley E. Porter's 60th Birthday*, edited by Lois K. Fuller Dow et al., 599–624. BINS 150. Leiden: Brill, 2017.

Dvorak, James D., and Ryder Dale Walton. "Clause as Message: Theme, Topic, and Information Flow in Mark 2:1–12 and Jude." *BAGL* 3 (2014) 31–85.

Elliott, John H. *What Is Social-Scientific Criticism?* GBS: New Testament Series. Minneapolis: Fortress, 1993.

Esler, Philip F., ed. *Modelling Early Christianity: Social-Scientific Studies of the New Testament in its Context*. London: Routledge, 1995.

Fairclough, Norman. *Analysing Discourse: Textual Analysis for Social Research*. New York: Routledge, 2003.

———. *Critical Discourse Analysis: The Critical Study of Language*. 2nd ed. Harlow, UK: Pearson, 2010.

———. *Discourse and Social Change*. Cambridge: Polity, 1992.

———. *Language and Power*. 2nd ed. Language in Social Life. London: Longman, 2001.

Fawcett, Robin P. *A Theory of Syntax for Systemic Functional Linguistics*. Amsterdam Studies in the Theory and History of Linguistic Science 206. Amsterdam: Benjamins, 2000.

Friberg, Barbara, and Timothy Friberg, eds. *Analytical Greek New Testament*. Baker's Greek New Testament Library. Grand Rapids: Baker, 1981. (AGNT)

Gee, James Paul. *An Introduction to Discourse Analysis: Theory and Method*. 4th ed. London: Routledge, 2014.

Halliday, M. A. K. "Categories of the Theory of Grammar." In *On Grammar*, edited by Jonathan J. Webster, 37–94. Collected Works of M. A. K. Halliday 1. London: Continuum, 2002.

———. *Explorations in the Functions of Language*. Explorations in Language Study. London: Arnold, 1973.

Halliday, M. A. K. *Halliday's Introduction to Functional Grammar*. Revised by Christian M. I. M. Matthiessen. 4th ed. London: Routledge, 2014. (IFG4)

———. *An Introduction to Functional Grammar*. London: Arnold, 1985. (IFG1)

———. *An Introduction to Functional Grammar*. 2nd ed. London: Arnold, 1994. (IFG2).

———. *An Introduction to Functional Grammar*. 3rd ed. Revised by Christian M. I. M. Matthiessen. London: Arnold, 2004. (IFG3)

———. *Language as Social Semiotic: The Social Interpretation of Language and Meaning*. London: Arnold, 1978.

Hart, Christopher. *Discourse, Grammar and Ideology: Functional and Cognitive Perspectives*. London: Bloomsbury, 2014.

Hodge, Robert, and Gunther Kress. *Social Semiotics*. Ithaca, NY: Cornell University Press, 1988.

Lemke, Jay L. *Textual Politics: Discourse and Social Dynamics*. Critical Perspectives on Literacy and Education. Abingdon: Taylor & Francis, 1995.

Malina, Bruce J. *Christian Origins and Cultural Anthropology: Practical Models for Biblical Interpretation*. 1986. Reprint, Eugene, OR: Wipf and Stock, 2010.

Martin, James R. *English Text: System and Structure*. Amsterdam: Benjamins, 1992.

Martin, J. R., and David Rose. *Working with Discourse: Meaning Beyond the Clause*. Open Linguistics Series. 2nd ed. New York: Continuum, 2007.

Martin, J. R., and P. R. R. White. *The Language of Evaluation: Appraisal in English*. New York: Palgrave Macmillan, 2005.

Meeks, Wayne. *The Origins of Christian Morality: The First Two Centuries*. New Haven: Yale University Press, 1993.

Moule, C. F. D. *An Idiom Book of New Testament Greek*. 2nd ed. New York: Cambridge University Press, 1959.

Neufeld, Dietmar, and Richard E. DeMaris. *Understanding the Social World of the New Testament*. London: Routledge, 2010.

Pilch, John J., ed. *Social Scientific Models for Interpreting the Bible*. BINS 53. Atlanta: SBL, 2001.

Pilch, John J., and Bruce J. Malina, eds. *Handbook of Biblical Social Values*. 3rd ed. Matrix: The Bible in Mediterranean Context 10. Eugene, OR: Cascade, 2016.

Porter, Stanley E. "Greek Prepositions in a Systemic Functional Linguistic Framework." *BAGL* 6 (2017) 17–43.

———. *Idioms of the Greek New Testament*. 2nd ed. BLG 2. Sheffield: Sheffield Academic, 1994.

———. "Systemic Functional Linguistics and the Greek Language: The Need for Further Modeling." In *Modeling Biblical Language: Selected Papers from the McMaster Divinity College Linguistics Circle*, edited by Stanley E. Porter et al., 9–47. LBS 13. Leiden: Brill, 2016.

Simpson, Paul. *Language, Ideology and Point of View*. Interface. London: Routledge, 1993.

Stubbs, Michael. "'A Matter of Prolonged Field Work': Notes Towards a Modal Grammar of English." *Applied Linguistics* 7 (1987) 1–25.

"Word Group Annotation." *OpenText.org*. No pages. Online: http://www.opentext.org/model/guidelines/wordgroup/0-2.html.

7

A Method for Identifying Speech Functions in Koine Greek

Galatians 2:11–21 as a Test Case[1]

David I. Yoon

INTRODUCTION

Discourse analysis in biblical studies has largely focused on textual meaning, analyzing textual features such as cohesion, prominence, and taxis. While these are certainly useful in applying discourse analysis to a text, the ideational and interpersonal meanings are largely ignored. This paper seeks to identify the resources in Hellenistic Greek to identify interpersonal meanings in a text. While there may be a variety of ways in which interpersonal meaning can be determined, including extra-linguistic or social roles between participants in the discourse, this paper focuses on interpersonal meaning through the examination of speech roles or speech functions. Starting with Michael Halliday, I further develop Stanley Porter's application of Halliday's speech functions to Greek, and then apply my framework to Gal 2:11–21, focusing on Paul's speech to Peter and the others with him in Antioch.[2]

---

1. This paper was incorporated into my now published dissertation. See Yoon, *Discourse Analysis of Galatians*.

2. Although there are differences of opinion as to whether Gal 2:15–21 was spoken by Paul at Antioch or whether it resumes Paul's direct discourse to the Galatians, it

SPEECH FUNCTIONS

Halliday proposed a taxonomy of speech roles, or speech functions, that the speaker/writer may have in a given discourse, largely based on the English mood system.[3] He states that the two fundamental types of speech functions are either (1) giving or (2) demanding; either the writer is giving something to his audience or demanding something (although the terms "inviting" or "requesting" are probably better, since "demanding" carries too much freight).[4] This can be seen in a simple directional picture: *writer → audience* = giving, or *writer ← audience* = demanding. Another fundamental category Halliday noted relates to the nature of the "commodity" being exchanged: (1) goods-and-services, or (2) information. Thus, Halliday identifies four primary speech functions: *offer*, *command*, *statement*, and *question*, as shown in the table below.

	Goods-and-Services	Information
Giving	offer	statement
Demanding	command	question

Table 1. Halliday's Major Speech Functions

Halliday proposed this system of speech functions along with possible responses to each of these functions, and Reed, as one of the first to implement this for biblical studies, took the model and applied it to Koine Greek for his discourse analysis of Philippians.[5] There have been, however, some identifiable difficulties with this system of speech functions, in both English and Greek. Porter notes at least six problems with this taxonomy, one of which includes the fact that the resources in English do not exactly transfer over to Greek, especially considering that Greek has a much more morphologically complex mood system than

---

seems that there is greater evidence that Paul said these words to Peter and others with him in Antioch (see Yoon, "Identifying the End of Paul's Speech").

3. Halliday, IFG1, 68–100; Matthiessen, "'Architecture' of Language," 523; cf. Porter, "Systemic Functional Linguistics," 20–32 for a detailed discussion on speech functions.

4. "Demand" has a forceful meaning, while "invite" or "request" has less force.

5. Reed, *Discourse Analysis*, 80–87. See also Lamb, *Text, Context, and the Johannine Community*, 95–100, who also strictly follows Halliday and Reed.

English does, and mood in Greek is realized at a different rank than in English (at the word rank in Greek rather than at the word group rank in English)—a crucial point not to be ignored.[6] But another important objection to Halliday's speech functions, according to Porter, is that the function of "so-called indirect speech acts" is not explained.[7] He uses the example of the statement *It's hot in here* to illustrate that Halliday's system only allows for this to be examined as a statement, rather than perhaps a command or a request at a semantic level. But admittedly, I am not sure any system that is strictly formally based can account for these types of semantic realizations, except for explaining it on the basis of a somewhat intuitive, or perhaps better, contextual, reading of the text. Or perhaps, though the intended outcome of the statement is the same as a command (i.e., to direct someone to turn on the air conditioner or open a window), perhaps it is not useful or even accurate to say that this statement *functions*, even semantically, as a command. Land, in that vein, notes that a breakdown of the resources available in Greek for a speaker/writer's "tone" may not be as helpful as compared to identifying *what* participants are doing in the discourse, suggesting that it is probably preferable to utilize Halliday's speech functions based on a semantic and (perhaps) an intuitive way than on a strict analysis of the lexicogrammar of Greek.[8] But Halliday even admits elsewhere that "a discourse analysis that is not based on the grammar is not an analysis at all, but simply a running commentary on a text . . ."[9] Considering both sides, then, it seems that both top-down and bottom-up approaches are necessary as a check-and-balance for each other, but even then, one has to begin *somewhere*. I agree that the advantage of a bottom-up approach is that it takes seriously the lexicogrammatical features and resources of the language for its interpersonal metafunction, and so I adopt such an approach in this study, that is, to start bottom-up, but to check it with a top-down view as well.[10]

6. Porter, "Systemic Functional Linguistics," 24–26.
7. Porter, "Systemic Functional Linguistics," 25.
8. Land, *Integrity of 2 Corinthians*, 61.
9. Halliday, IFG1, xvii.

10. In a previous article, however, I took a top-down approach, consisting of a slight amendment to Halliday by leaving out *offer*. While I think it might work in general, a more refined system of speech functions might be preferable, so I attempt to come up with a system from a bottom-up approach. Cf. Yoon, "Identifying the End of Paul's Speech."

Working with Halliday's four speech functions, Suzanne Eggins observes that discourse is a continuous exchange that warrants more than the four that Halliday identifies.[11] Thus she identifies eight speech functions: statement, question, command, offer, answer, acknowledgment, accept, and compliance—based on and corresponding to the anticipated responses that Halliday himself has proffered.[12] But there is not much of a significant difference between Eggins and Halliday. On the other hand, J. R. Martin and David Rose also offer a modification to Halliday's speech function system, including not only Eggins's (and essentially Halliday's) eight speech functions, which are categorized into a broader category of *negotiation*, but four more: *greeting, response to greeting, call*, and *response to call*, within the broader category of *attending* (in binary opposition and corresponding to *negotiation*).[13] But these are not necessarily an improvement upon Halliday's speech functions, as the above mentioned difficulties are not solved, and it is still basically Halliday's system, except maybe expanded to include responses and the category of attending. For instance, if Person A says, "Can you turn off the heat?" and Person B does not respond verbally, but goes and *complies*, is Person B's response properly called a *speech* function? And is Person A's speech a question or a command? Additionally, for purposes of studying the New Testament letters (in particular), we have little knowledge of what any of the responses actually were. In my estimation, expected or anticipated responses are irrelevant for this study, so they will not be included—although the Greek system for questions does have distinctions for expected (or directed) negative or positive answers (i.e., the difference of using οὐ or μή in questions), but this still does not mean the intended hearers (or readers) responded in the expected manner.

It is necessary, then, in beginning from the bottom-up, to start with the lexicogrammatical resources in Greek that realize the various speech functions, which are predominantly through verbal attitude as conveyed by the mood-forms.[14] Koine Greek has a total of four attitudes (mood-

11. Eggins, *Introduction*, 145.
12. Eggins, *Introduction*, 147.
13. Martin and Rose, *Working with Discourse*, 226.
14. I follow Porter in using the terminology of "attitude" instead of "mood," while calling the forms "mood-forms" (see Porter, *Idioms*, 50). It seems to be a more accurate label to label the semantic category as attitude and the lexicogrammatical category as mood-form.

forms): indicative, imperative, subjunctive, and optative, and several other related forms, such as the future form (which has traditionally been categorized as tense or *Aktionsart*), participles, and infinitives, as well as a "non-form," the verbless clause (or the predicative adjectival clause).[15] Porter has posited the idea that the future form is related morphologically to mood and that it grammaticalizes the semantic feature of expectation.[16] But since these other forms (participle, infinitive, future, and verbless clause[17]) are not actually mood-forms in the attitudinal system, only the four mentioned above should be included (see below for more discussion on the future form). The following list describes the four mood-forms along with their various functions:[18]

- Indicative: assertion (simple), question
- Imperative: command (simple)
- Subjunctive: assertion (projection), command (projection), question (projection)
- Optative: assertion (contingent, more remote than projection), command (contingent)

If one were to take a bottom-up approach in determining the speech functions in Greek, identifying the various forms and their corresponding functions is where one would begin.

Recently, Porter has posited a taxonomy of speech functions from a bottom-up approach, based on his proposed system network of Greek verbal attitude (i.e., mood-forms).[19] He exemplifies a bottom-up approach to determining the speech functions, beginning with the Greek lexicogrammar. What he has done differently from previous attempts to identify the various speech functions in Greek, however, is to identify not just the word and mood-form but the clause for identifying speech function, as well as lay out a system network for attitude.[20] This is admittedly a step forward for identifying speech functions at the level of discourse, as a more robust and rigorous way of identifying the speech

---

15. The functions of the mood-forms are based on descriptions in Porter, *Verbal Aspect*, 109, 163–77; and Porter, *Idioms*, 50–61.
16. Porter, *Verbal Aspect*, 403–39; Porter, *Idioms*, 43–44.
17. See Porter, *Idioms*, 287, for a brief discussion.
18. See Porter, *Idioms*, 50–61.
19. Porter, "Systemic Functional Linguistics," 27–28.
20. Porter, "Systemic Functional Linguistics," 26–29.

functions. He proposes the attitudinal system network for Greek as depicted in Figure 1.[21]

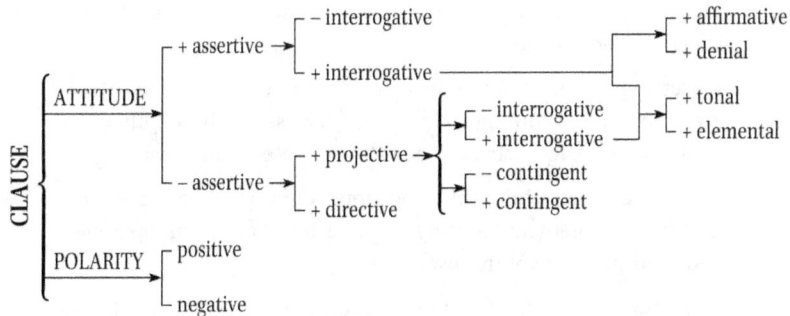

Figure 1. Porter's System Network of Attitude (Mood) for Greek

Based on his system network of attitude, he identifies twelve different clause types in Greek: declarative statement, positive question, negative question, open question, τ-question, projected statement, projected contingent statement, projected question, projected τ-question, projected contingent question, projected contingent τ-question, and command.[22] It should be noted that *primary* clauses are relevant for speech functions in discourse, not secondary clauses, such as dependent, relative, or embedded, since they supplement the primary clauses to which they are connected. Below is a more detailed list of the (primary) clause types and the forms they take in parentheses below each clause type:

> +assertion: -interrogation >> declarative statement (assertive clause with indicative mood form)
>
> +assertion: +interrogation: +affirmation >> positive question (assertive clause question formulated so as to expect a positive answer, with indicative mood form)
>
> +assertion: +interrogation: +denial >> negative question (assertive clause question formulated so as to expect a negative answer, with indicative mood form)

21. Porter, "Systemic Functional Linguistics," 27. This is based on his previous work in Porter, *Verbal Aspect*, 109; and Porter and O'Donnell, "Greek Verbal Network." See also Butler, *Systemic Linguistics*, 40–57; Porter, *Verbal Aspect*, 9–11; and Halliday, *System and Function*, 3–6, for brief descriptions of system networks (the Halliday article was originally published in 1969 and is found in a number of other places).

22. Porter, "Systemic Functional Linguistics," 28; see also Porter, *Letter to the Romans*, 33, for a condensed summary of this.

+assertion: +interrogation: +tonal >> open question (assertive clause, with question tonally indicated)

+assertion: +interrogation: +elemental >> τ-question (assertive clause, with question with one of the question words, with indicative mood form)

-assertion: +projection: -interrogation: -contingent >> projected statement (non-contingent projected clause, with subjunctive mood form, as in hortatory or prohibitive use when negated)

-assertion: +projection: -interrogation: +contingent >> projected contingent statement (contingent projected clause, with optative mood form, as in volitive use)

-assertion: +projection: +interrogation: -contingent: +tonal >> projected question (non-contingent projected clause, with subjunctive mood form, as in deliberative use)

-assertion: +projection: +interrogation: -contingent: +elemental >> projected τ-question (noncontingent projected clause, with question with one of the question words, with subjunctive mood form)

-assertion: +projection: +interrogation: +contingent: +tonal >> projected contingent question (contingent projected clause, with optative mood form, as in deliberative use)

-assertion: +projection: +interrogation: +contingent: +elemental >> projected contingent τ-question (contingent projected clause, with question with one of the question words, with optative mood form)

-assertion: +directive >> command (imperative mood form)[23]

As a result, he offers the following tentative speech function system for Greek, based on all of the primary clause types found in the language.[24]

Exchange Role	Goods and Services	Information
Giving	open question	declaration
Projecting	projective question	projective statement

23. Porter, "Systemic Functional Linguistics," 28.
24. Porter, "Systemic Functional Linguistics," 29.

Wishing	projective contingent statement	positive/negative question
Demanding	command	τ-question
Enquiring	projective contingent question (?)	projective (cont.) τ-question (?)

Table 2. Porter's Major (Greek) Speech Functions

While this is no doubt an improvement of Halliday's speech functions, especially as it relates to Greek, Porter himself admits that his speech functions are tentative and posited for the sake of further discussion; he is still unsatisfied with the precise functions and would like further development on this.[25] He also notes that a fuller system network should include interaction with the number and person systems, although I am not sure this is necessary for purposes of this study.[26] Taking his suggestion, then, I offer a reconsideration of the speech functions, specifically regarding the distinction between *goods and services* and *information*, a critique I would marshal against Halliday's original speech functions and the part Porter seems to find unsatisfactory.[27] The problem with this distinction is that the differences are quite opaque between these two categories when applied to the speech functions, and they should probably be undifferentiated. For example, an act of giving goods (offer), like *Here is my pen*, can still be understood in terms of giving information (statement): it is a statement that the speaker is giving a pen to the recipient; the actual act of giving the pen might be the offer. Or *Let me open the door for you*, presumably an offer (giving of a service), is probably more accurately understood in terms of a command (formally at least), if *Let me* is a command.

An explanation of the roles of the future form and verbless clause in the speech functions is appropriate here. Porter elsewhere includes the future form as grammaticalizing [+expectancy] in a cursory list of speech functions.[28] But despite the future form having shared morphological characteristics with the subjunctive, such as the sigma and similar vowel

25. Porter, "Systemic Functional Linguistics," 30.
26. Porter, "Systemic Functional Linguistics," 30–31.
27. See Porter, "Systemic Functional Linguistics," 24–25.
28. Porter, *Letter to the Romans*, 33.

configurations,[29] and despite it having only one set of forms (related to the indicative form) as compared to other tense-forms (which exists in all of the mood-forms), it is not fully attitudinal nor is it fully aspectual.[30] Thus, while some may wish to include the future form in a system network of attitude, even for those who take the future as grammaticalizing the semantics of expectancy,[31] I follow Porter's list of speech functions which does not include the future form; it is better left out of any attitudinal system network (except for when it appears in the "indicative," in which case the future form is still a type of statement), since it does not fit anywhere in the system network legitimately and is not strictly a mood-form. Regarding the verbless clause as a primary clause type, it probably best reflects a statement or question, depending on co-textual factors, but without the directness of the indicative mood-form. In this case, the terms *simple statement* or *simple question*, in distinction from *direct statement/question* that is labeled from the indicative, may be appropriate to describe the speech function of the verbless clause.

Having identified a system network of attitude in Greek (bottom-up) laid out by Porter, and having decided that the distinction between goods-and-services and information is illegitimate, it is appropriate to pause and see the bigger picture (top-down). The major question for tenor and the speech functions is: What is the speaker/writer *trying to do or accomplish*? And specific to this discussion: What are the various linguistic resources for doing so in Koine Greek? Looking back at Halliday's speech functions, I identified not only the problem of the strict division between goods-and-services and information, but also the problem with the term *demanding*, which to me seems too forceful in meaning. But the two directional words, giving (something) or requesting (something) seems to be the two broad functions of language; either the writer is giving something (information) for a more specific purpose, or requesting something (information, an action, a

---

29. Porter, *Idioms*, 43.

30. Porter, *Verbal Aspect*, 409–10. Some argue that the future is more or less aspectual and temporal (e.g., Campbell, *Verbal Aspect*, 159, who contends it encodes perfective aspects and future temporality) or just temporal (e.g., Fanning, *Verbal Aspect*, 123–24, argues that its primary meaning is temporal). While it is not appropriate to lay out a lengthy treatise on the future form and its aspectual (or non-aspectual) value, I would argue that [+expectancy] is the most convincing, and that it does not warrant inclusion in the attitude system network.

31. E.g., Dawson, "Language as Negotiation," 379–80.

response—a much broader range of objects) from the message recipient. Furthermore, the difference between *question* and *command* is not in the commodity being exchanged, since a question can very well request goods-and-services or information (such as *Are you available Tuesday to help me move?*) and a command can request information (such as *Tell me your name*), but the difference can be stated in terms of a difference in form, where a command in Greek has a different form than a question. But with the exception of the *offer* category, the other three Hallidayan speech functions of *statement*, *question*, and *command* can apply to Koine Greek. It contains lexicogrammatical resources for doing all three things—as seen in the system network above.

But on the other spectrum of Halliday's speech functions, instead of applying the category of type of commodity being given or demanded, the Greek attitude system seems to be characterized largely by the cline of assertion, projection, and contingency—which almost defines the attitude system—so this cline should be considered in identifying the speech functions in Greek. There are a variety of ways to make a statement, depending on the writer's attitude of the statement. The indicative mood-form is used to make a simple or assertive statement, while the subjunctive is used to make a projective statement. The optative, in turn, is used to make a projective-contingent statement. Typical grammars identify a variety of ways of commanding, through the imperative, subjunctive, and future forms. I would contend, however, that only the imperative mood-form actually *commands* and that the future and subjunctive forms only convey expectation and projection (respectively). I would also argue that sometimes the future and subjunctive forms can be used to have a *commanding* or directive use, or sometimes called the pragmatic effect, based on the context in which it appears (more on this below).

So, beginning with a bottom-up approach by laying out a system network of attitude based on the Greek lexicogrammar, and then viewing a potential system of speech functions from a top-down view, I propose the following framework for speech functions in Greek based on the clause types Porter identifies:

	Statement	Question	Command
Verbless	simple statement	simple question	—
Direct	declarative statement	negative/positive question; open question; τ-question	command
Probable	projective statement	projective question; projective τ-question	—
Possible	projective-contingent statement	projective-contingent question; projective-contingent τ-question	—

Table 3. Speech Functions for Hellenistic Greek

This system acknowledges the various forms and their respective functions at a basic, semantic level and also incorporates the feature of the cline of certainty that characterizes the attitude system of Greek. For those forms that are included in a single category—e.g., a probable question is asked in a variety of ways—the differences simply amount to the type of question the writer is asking (based on either the syntax, the content of the question, or social function in the discourse), but the certainty of the attitude and function is the same.

Now that I have laid out a system of speech functions based on Porter's system network of attitude in Greek, it is necessary to conclude with addressing the issue of how one gets from the speech function of a particular form to its social function or use, sometimes called *pragmatics*.[32] This deals with how the function of a clause (e.g., direct statement) based on the lexicogrammar (e.g., assertive clause with indicative mood-form) relates to the various ways in which speakers and writers are able to *do* different things with these forms, identified above as indirect or implicit speech acts. I have provided some examples already, but to give another example, a speaker might have the intended goal of convincing her child to clean his room. There are a variety of ways in

---

32. Porter, "Systemic Functional Linguistics," 32–47, who is unsympathetic to the semantics/pragmatics divide. SFL is known to include in the semantic stratum what some would call pragmatics. For example, see Halliday, *Explorations*, 64–94, where Halliday describes semantics but what others may call pragmatics. Cf. Levinson, *Pragmatics*.

which she could accomplish that in English: command (*Go clean your room*), question (*Would you clean your room?*), statement (*Your room is dirty*), and so on. That the speaker intends the child to respond with a particular action does not mean all of these are *commands*, although all of these examples desire the same effect. They are grammatically and semantically different from each other, and these distinctions are important to maintain. Especially for an ancient language without native speakers, maintaining a (strict) relationship between form and function can help prevent interpreters from reading their own biases into the text. Similarly, Butler has echoed an objection to what Sinclair and Coulthard have done with identifying the set of situational categories (statement, question, and command) and attempts to bridge the gap between syntax and discourse.[33] In Sinclair and Coulthard's attempt to identify an interrogative clause as a command, for example, they set forth the following criteria: (1) it contains one of the modals *can, could, will, would*, and (sometimes) *going to*; (2) the subject of the clause is also the addressee; and (3) the predicate describes an action that is physically possible at the time of utterance. But Butler rightly observes that "their rule provides no explanation for why the particular modals . . . can signal that an utterance is to be interpreted as a command [or, better, request]. To do this, we must examine the meanings of the modals concerned."[34] Additionally, does the mere presence of these modals in an interrogative clause necessitate a command? The difficulty, or rather impossibility, of connecting a strict formal identification to these indirect speech acts should be palpable by now, and this illustrates the difficulty of coming up with any set of formal criteria for contextual usage.

So, the question remains: How do we get from the speech function (e.g., direct statement) to the indirect speech act (e.g., commanding or directing)? The solution to the question involves the notion of stratification and being able to identify at what stratum these speech functions and their *indirect speech acts* are located. There are various proposed models for delineating the various strata of language, with the basic strata being (from bottom to top) phonology/phonetics (expression), lexicogrammar (content), semantics (content), and context (with context being broken down into further sub-strata). After reviewing the several proposals, Porter states that adopting the two traditional content

---

33. Butler, *Systemic Linguistics*, 161–62.
34. Butler, *Systemic Linguistics*, 162.

strata of lexicogrammar and semantics (or discourse semantics) is most helpful in distinguishing between potential and actualization of speech functions.[35] One way of doing this is in distinguishing clearly between *function* and *use*—Porter laments that these terms are often used synonymously and interchangeably in SFL literature. He argues, however, that we should be able to model how language *functions* in context, but that it is impossible to model how language is *used* in context, since its *use* is almost limitless, and *function* is usually in reference to *intrinsic function*. He illustrates this point with the example of a piano: a piano's function is to be played and make music, but its use can be variable, such as to be used as furniture, a stand for flowers, a collectible, and so on.[36]

This is a significant observation and point to accept, and distinguishing *function* and *use*—in correlation with speech function and indirect speech act—is immensely helpful for clarity. I would argue, however, that the indirect speech act, or *use*, is located within the context stratum and that the speech function is located in the semantics stratum, since it is based on the lexicogrammar (at the lexicogrammar stratum). If the speech function is based on the lexicogrammar of the language, and it communicates the function or meaning in instantiation, and if the speech function is used in context to achieve other things (so use of a direct statement to *command* or to *direct*), it seems appropriate to place *use* in the context stratum. If that is accepted, then, the speech function can be called, in light of stratification, the *semantic function* and the indirect speech act the *contextual function*. To illustrate this in English, the previous example of *It's hot in here* functions at the semantic level as a statement, but its use as *commanding* is at the contextual function, since it can be interpreted that way based on the context. An example in Greek might be in John 19:28, where Jesus simply says διψῶ ("I thirst"). It functions at the semantic stratum as a direct statement (assertive clause with indicative), but at the context stratum it may be a request for a drink. This interpretation is supported when he is given something to drink. Interpreting the contextual function of a clause, then, depends on its usage and is much more open to interpretation than identifying its semantic function.

Thus, I conclude that speech functions operate on two separate levels: the semantic stratum, which is based on form, and the context stra-

---

35. Porter, "Systemic Functional Linguistics," 43.
36. Porter, "Systemic Functional Linguistics," 43–44.

tum, which is how the form is used, based on the information available in the co-text and context (as discussed above). As Porter notes (using slightly different terms), the potential for contextual functions (or *uses*) of speech functions is almost infinite, while at the same time, simply mirroring its semantic function. But interpreters should start with the semantic function (or *function*). So, when identifying the linguistic tenor of a discourse and speech functions, the interpreter can distinguish between the *semantic function* of the speech and the *contextual function* of the speech, although many times the contextual function may mirror the semantic function of the clause.

SPEECH FUNCTIONS IN GALATIANS 2:11–21

The Antioch Incident is an important event, reported by Paul, in understanding Christian and Jewish relations in the early church. While the social dynamics between Paul, Peter, and the Antiochians have been thoroughly discussed, a linguistic analysis examining the speech functions will help elucidate the interpersonal meaning here, or, put more plainly, what Paul is *doing* in this discourse.

The first part of this sub-section (2:11–14a) continues the narrative and describes what happened in Antioch, when Paul opposed Peter for his hypocrisy. The six primary clauses that make up this part of the sub-section all have the semantic function of direct statement. They function contextually as a narrative of the events that took place there.

Paul's speech in Antioch begins in 2:14b, where Paul uses a conditional construction, the protasis reflecting a first-class conditional and the apodosis reflecting a direct question: εἰ σὺ Ἰουδαῖος ὑπάρχων ἐθνικῶς καὶ οὐχὶ Ἰουδαϊκῶς ζῇς (protasis), πῶς τὰ ἔθνη ἀναγκάζεις ἰουδαΐζειν (apodosis). The apodosis is the primary clause in this clause complex (the protasis is subordinate to it), and its clause type is open question. While its semantic function is direct question, its contextual function is a rhetorical question,[37] to make the point that the ideas posed in the protasis and apodosis oppose each other. In other words, this first-class conditional construction (a simple condition made for the sake of argument)[38]

---

37. I use "rhetorical question" here, not as a reference to ancient rhetoric or in a technical sense, but as in common usage, referring to a question where the answer is either obvious, unanswerable, or to point out the absurdity of the implication of the question.

38. Porter, *Idioms*, 256–59.

points out the absurdity of their behavior: that while they are Jews who live like Gentiles, they make Gentiles live "Jewishly." How can this be? The implied answer is that it cannot. He resumes with a simple statement (the semantic function of ἡμεῖς φύσει Ἰουδαῖοι καὶ οὐκ ἐξ ἐθνῶν ἁμαρτωλοί), which functions contextually also as a statement: "We are Jews by nature and not Gentile sinners." The next primary clause, ἡμεῖς εἰς Χριστὸν Ἰησοῦν ἐπιστεύσαμεν, is a direct statement that informs them (Peter and those with him at Antioch) that "we" believe in Christ Jesus (2:16), given that they know that justification is by faith in Christ and not by works of the law (this is a secondary clause). While the semantic function of the primary clause is a direct statement, its contextual function is more than simply providing information. This statement should be obvious to Paul's audience—that they believe in Christ Jesus—so its contextual function is to remind them of what Paul had taught them before, since they know (εἰδότες) this already.

Paul continues his point with another conditional construction, εἰ δὲ ζητοῦντες δικαιωθῆναι ἐν Χριστῷ εὑρέθημεν καὶ αὐτοὶ ἁμαρτωλοί, ἆρα Χριστὸς ἁμαρτίας διάκονος (first-class conditional). The primary clause is the apodosis, Χριστὸς ἁμαρτίας διάκονος, having the semantic function of simple question. As in the direct question above, this simple question functions contextually as a rhetorical question, pointing out the absurdity of what is posed. If in seeking to be justified in Christ they are found to be sinners, Paul rhetorically asks if Christ is then a minister of sin. The obvious answer is in the negative, but in case his audience is confused, he answers, μὴ γένοιτο.

The rest of this sub-section (2:18–21) is a series of direct statements (semantic function). The first primary clause (2:18) is part of another conditional construction (first-class), where Paul poses the idea that if he rebuilds what he has torn down (presumably seeking justification by works of the law based on the previous co-text), he proves to be a transgressor. He makes a series of direct statements explaining that he died to the law so that he would live to God, that he has been crucified with Christ and thus no longer lives, that Christ lives in him, and he lives by faith, and that he does not nullify the grace of God. The final direct statement (semantic function) is the apodosis of another conditional construction (first-class), where Paul poses that if justification were through the law, then Christ died for no reason. All of these direct statements (including the conditional) have a contextual function of informing them of the content of the gospel that Peter and the others were violating. Paul would not have had to state these things if their behavior was congruent with them.

In this sub-section, then, Paul uses direct statements, direct questions, and a simple question (including a first-class conditional construction) to note how their behavior is absurd and contradictory to who they are and what they believe. He also states what he believes, essentially the gospel (that he presumably taught them earlier), and that their behavior is incongruent with this gospel.

CONCLUSION

I have outlined a method by which to determine interpersonal meaning of a discourse through developing a framework for analyzing speech functions in Greek. I suggest that there are two strata in which speech functions operate: (1) the semantic stratum, reflecting the semantic function, and (2) the context stratum, reflecting the contextual function. In analyzing Paul's speech to Peter and the others with him in Antioch, I noted that Paul uses direct statements, direct questions, and a simple question—these are the semantic functions of the primary clauses in this speech. The contextual function of this text, however, reveals that Paul does several things. He points out the absurdity and inconsistency of Peter's (and others') behavior of withdrawing from Gentile tablefellowship. Their behavior is absurd and hypocritical. He also reminds them of the gospel they should have known already (being justified by faith and not by works of the law).

APPENDIX: SPEECH FUNCTIONS IN GALATIANS 2:11–21

Verse	Greek text (primary clause)	Process	Semantic Function
2:11	κατὰ πρόσωπον αὐτῷ ἀντέστην	ἀντέστην	DS
2:12	μετὰ τῶν ἐθνῶν συνήσθιεν	συνήσθιεν	DS
	ὑπέστελλεν	ὑπέστελλεν	DS
	ἀφώριζεν ἑαυτόν	ἀφώριζεν	DS
2:13	συνυπεκρίθησαν αὐτῷ [καὶ] οἱ λοιποὶ Ἰουδαῖοι	συνυπεκρίθησαν	DS

2:14	εἶπον τῷ Κηφᾷ ἔμπροσθεν πάντων	εἶπον	DS
	πῶς τὰ ἔθνη ἀναγκάζεις ἰουδαΐζειν;	ἀναγκάζεις ἰουδαΐζειν	DQ
2:15	ἡμεῖς φύσει Ἰουδαῖοι καὶ οὐκ ἐξ ἐθνῶν ἁμαρτωλοί	—	SS
2:16	ἡμεῖς εἰς Χριστὸν Ἰησοῦν ἐπιστεύσαμεν	ἐπιστεύσαμεν	DS
2:17	Χριστὸς ἁμαρτίας διάκονος;	—	SQ
	μὴ γένοιτο	μὴ γένοιτο	PS
2:18	παραβάτην ἐμαυτὸν συνιστάνω	συνιστάνω	DS
2:19	ἐγὼ (γὰρ) διὰ νόμου νόμῳ ἀπέθανον	ἀπέθανον	DS
	Χριστῷ συνεσταύρωμαι	συνεσταύρωμαι	DS
2:20	ζῶ (δὲ) οὐκέτι ἐγώ	ζῶ	DS
	ζῇ (δὲ) ἐν ἐμοὶ Χριστός	ζῇ	DS
	ἐν πίστει ζῶ τῇ τοῦ υἱοῦ τοῦ θεοῦ	ζῶ	DS
2:21	οὐκ ἀθετῶ τὴν χάριν τοῦ θεοῦ	ἀθετῶ	DS
	Χριστὸς δωρεὰν ἀπέθανεν	ἀπέθανεν	DS

(DS = direct statement; DQ = direct question; SS = simple statement; SQ = simple question; PS = possible statement)

BIBLIOGRAPHY

Butler, Christopher S. *Systemic Linguistics: Theory and Applications*. London: Batsford, 1985.

Campbell, Constantine R. *Verbal Aspect, the Indicative Mood, and Narrative: Soundings in the Greek of the New Testament*. SBG 13. New York: Peter Lang, 2007.

Dawson, Zachary K. "Language as Negotiation: Toward a Systemic Functional Model for Ideological Criticism with Application to James 2:1–13." In *Modeling Biblical Language: Selected Papers from the McMaster Divinity College Linguistics Circle*, edited by Stanley E. Porter et al., 362–90. LBS 13. Leiden: Brill, 2016.

Eggins, Suzanne, *An Introduction to Systemic Functional Linguistics*. 2nd ed. London: Bloomsbury, 2004.

Fanning, Buist M. *Verbal Aspect in New Testament Greek*. Oxford Theological Monographs. Oxford: Clarendon, 1990.

Halliday, M. A. K. *Explorations in the Functions of Language*. Explorations in Language Study. London: Arnold, 1973.

———. *An Introduction to Functional Grammar*. London: Arnold, 1985. (IFG1)

———. *System and Function in Language: Selected Papers*, edited by Gunther Kress. London: Oxford University Press, 1976.

Lamb, David A. *Text, Context, and the Johannine Community: A Sociolinguistic Analysis of the Johannine Writings.* LNTS 477. London: T. & T. Clark, 2014.
Land, Christopher D. *The Integrity of 2 Corinthians and Paul's Aggravating Absence.* NTM 36. Sheffield: Sheffield Phoenix, 2015.
Levinson, Stephen C. *Pragmatics.* CTL. Cambridge: Cambridge University Press, 1983.
Martin, J. R., and David Rose. *Working with Discourse: Meaning Beyond the Clause.* Open Linguistics Series. 2nd ed. New York: Continuum, 2007.
Matthiessen, Christian M. I. M. "The 'Architecture' of Language according to Systemic Functional Theory: Developments since the 1970s." In *Continuing Discourse on Language: A Functional Perspective,* edited by Ruqaiya Hasan et al., 2:505–62. 2 vols. London: Equinox, 2007.
Porter, Stanley E. *Idioms of the Greek New Testament.* 2nd ed. BLG 2. Sheffield: Sheffield Academic, 1994.
———. *The Letter to the Romans: A Linguistic and Literary Commentary.* NTM 37. Sheffield: Sheffield Phoenix, 2016.
———. "Systemic Functional Linguistics and the Greek Language: The Need for Further Modeling." In *Modeling Biblical Language: Selected Papers from the McMaster Divinity College Linguistics Circle,* edited by Stanley E. Porter et al., 9–47. LBS 13. Leiden: Brill, 2016.
———. *Verbal Aspect in the Greek of the New Testament, with Reference to Tense and Mood.* SBG 1. New York: Peter Lang, 1989.
Porter, Stanley E., and Matthew Brook O'Donnell. "The Greek Verbal Network Viewed from a Probabilistic Standpoint: An Exercise in Hallidayan Linguistics." *FN* 14 (2001) 3–41.
Reed, Jeffrey T. *A Discourse Analysis of Philippians: Method and Rhetoric in the Debate over Literary Integrity.* JSNTSup 100. Sheffield: Sheffield Academic, 1997.
Yoon, David I. *A Discourse Analysis of Galatians and the New Perspective on Paul.* LBS 17. Leiden, Brill: 2019.
———. "Identifying the End of Paul's Speech to Peter in Galatians 2: Register Analysis as a Heuristic Tool." *FN* 28–29 (2015–2016) 57–79.

8

Information Structure in the Greek of the New Testament

Doosuk Kim

INTRODUCTION

THE PRESENT PAPER IS about information structure. To explain succinctly, information structure (IS) is the way a speaker or author constitutes a sentence to convey the theme of that sentence. Thus, constituents of the sentence and word order are important factors to IS. Traditionally, linguists have regarded IS as the division of a sentence into two information units—the subject and predicate.[1] Put differently,

---

1. However, in this case, a clear definition of subject and predicate is required. There is a difference in the concepts that linguists refer to as the grammatical subject and predicate, on the one hand, and the psychological subject and predicate on the other hand, and these do not always align with each other. For instance, in the sentence *Karl goes to Berlin tomorrow*, the grammatical subject of the sentence is *Karl*, but, if this sentence is an answer to the question *Where does Karl go tomorrow?* the psychological subject would be the place where Karl goes (see von Heusinger, "Information Structure," 282). Chafe also points out the same problem of the ambiguity between grammatical, psychological, as well as the logical subject of the sentence. Chafe provides three different sentences: (1) "Betty peeled the onions"; (2) "The onions were peeled by Betty"; and (3) "The onions, Betty peeled" ("Givenness," 27). In the first sentence, it is relatively clear that Betty functions grammatically, logically, and psychologically as the subject of the sentence. But, in the second and third sentence, it is not clear as in the first sentence. Though we may readily identify the grammatical subject, readers would rec-

IS deals with distribution of information at the sentence level and divides the sentence into two units, the less informational (i.e., subject) and the more informational unit (i.e., predicate).[2] With this division, one may identify the element that is called the theme of the sentence (more on this below). As for analysis, linguists typically investigate IS at the sentence level and pay attention to the constituents, word order, and a simple division of the sentence. Having this brief sketch of IS in mind, this essay will propose an IS theory for the Greek of the New Testament considering, in particular, three matters as follows.

First, IS should not be restricted to the sentence level. Rather, the analysis of IS ought to extend to the discourse level because a language user does not just put all information in disconnected sentences but organizes it in order to convey the message as the text unfolds. When one speaks or writes about a particular topic, the topic is already in the author's mind. Then, the author distributes information to articulate his/her topic. That is to say, the author is an architect, and s/he organizes each information unit, which is a constituent of the discourse, to construct the discourse. Furthermore, the author introduces information linearly and hierarchically. It is linear because the author should choose the language and place it sequentially, from words, to phrases, to clauses, to sentences, and to larger units. It is also hierarchical, since information is regimented in a discourse by structures of linguistic units.[3] Thus, depending on how the author uses different language repertoires, the information would be structured differently. Then, through the analysis of IS, the reader would be able to identify how information is introduced

---

ognize the subject of each sentence differently depending on the information known in the context.

2. This informational dichotomy has been expressed differently by terms such as Psychological Subject–Psychological Predicate (von der Gabelentz, "Ideen"; Paul, *Prinzipien*), Theme–Rheme (Halliday, "Notes"; Ammann, *Die menschliche Rede*; Mathesius, "Zur Satzperspektive"), Topic–Comment (Reinhart, "Pragmatics"), Topic–Focus (Sgall et al., *Topic*), Presupposition–Focus (Chomsky, "Deep Structure"; Jackendoff, *Semantic Interpretation*), Background–Focus (Chafe, "Givenness"), Given–New (Chomsky, "Deep Structure"; Chafe, "Givenness"), Open proposition–Focus (Prince, "On the Inferencing"), and Notional Subject–Notional Predicate (Kiss, "Introduction").

3. Porter and O'Donnell, *Discourse Analysis*, 97. Porter and O'Donnell assert that "it is necessary to move beyond the level (or rank) of the clause and/or sentence in order to analyze how a message is structured and to follow the flow of information" (*Discourse Analysis*, 97).

and elaborated upon by the latter elements, how the author encloses a linguistic chunk as an information unit, and how each information unit collaborates to build up a discourse. Analysts ought to probe all message-making levels, from the clause level to the discourse level, and to identify how the information in a smaller unit develops in larger units. In this regard, the present paper will make use of analytic tools for each level of language—the clause, clause complex (sentential/super-sentential level), and discourse.

Second, unlike other IS theories that have mostly studied and applied to English and Czech, this paper will propose an IS theory that is compatible with the Greek of the New Testament.[4] As Halliday explains, English is a type of language in which position determines the theme of the clause.[5] Greek is not as configurational as English, however, and the position does not always determine the theme in Greek. In addition to this, one should not apply English word order or sentence structure to the Greek of the New Testament, since Greek, unlike English, has greater flexibility in the sentence structure and word order. Runge also points out this problem, stating that "in its present form, SFL [Systemic Functional Linguistics] is ill-suited to tackle ordered languages such as Greek and Hebrew ... Unfortunately, most recent NT studies of word order have followed Halliday's Sydney school of SFL, without addressing the fundamental problems raised within the linguistic community."[6]

---

4. Though the Prague School of linguistics initiated schematizing IS into a grammatical system, and in spite of Halliday's contribution on IS theory, no universal theory of IS has been suggested yet. This is because linguists systemize IS through the exploration of different languages. Through investigating Slavic language, Mathesius cast doubt on the strict and formal dichotomy of subject–predicate by proposing the incongruence between the sequence of words and sequence of thoughts (see Heusinger, "Information Structure," 285). Thus, instead of the oppositional pair of Subject–Predicate, Mathesius proposed a new pair, Theme–Rheme. Mathesius asserts that the theme does not always correspond to the grammatical subject nor the rheme with the grammatical predicate. Rather, Theme is the first part of the sentence which provides the basis of utterance, and then comes the Rheme, which gives relatively new information (Mathesius, "Functional Linguistics," 126–27). That is to say, as Runge explains, "the Theme corresponds to the established material of the clause, while the Rheme corresponds to the newly asserted or focal information" (*Discourse Grammar*, 201).

5. Halliday states that "in English, the theme is indicated by position in the clause" (IFG1, 38).

6. Runge, *Discourse Grammar*, 203–4. SFL is devised by M. A. K. Halliday. By characterizing language as a social semiotic system, Halliday distinguishes his theory and perspectives on language from other views. Whereas Chomskyan generative grammar

However, this is not an insurmountable problem as Runge seemingly intimates, but simply requires adaptation of the SFL framework for the Greek of the New Testament, which is one of the main tasks this paper takes up.

Third, linguists have investigated IS as a communicative approach in the spoken register. For instance, Halliday is one of the most outstanding linguists who systemizes IS in a rigorous theory. Concerning IS, his main interest was the structure of intonation in English. Halliday established his theory of IS for the phonological system of modern English, particularly tonality and tonicity. Halliday suggests tonality is the essential parameter of the information unit (IU).[7] He explains, "English has five tones, and connected speech can be analyzed into an unbroken succession of tone groups each of which selects one or other of the five tones."[8] In other words, "one information unit is realized as one tone group."[9] Alongside this, to Halliday, tonicity is another important notion regarding what can be classified as Given and New information. To him, where tonicity lies determines the information focus, which is accented as New information.[10] In other words, depending on the pitch or accent "the speaker's decision of where the main burden of the mes-

---

explains that the form of the language determines the meaning of the language, by looking at the language as a social semiotic, Halliday understands that the language is an aspect of human experience in the social structure. Therefore, to Halliday, the meaning of the language is not only determined by form, structure, and lexical definition, but the meaning of the language is related to multiple aspects such as social context, situational context, and the semantic systems of the language.

7. According to Halliday's definition, tonality is the "distribution of utterance into tone groups," while tonicity is the "distribution of tone group into tonic and pretonic" (Halliday, IFG1, 53; see also 12–13, where he spells out English phonology as follows: "The tone group comprises two elements which are tonic and pretonic, and tonic and pretonic consist of one or more than one complete foot. Foot is a phonological unit that is the rhythm in English and has a structure of two elements: ictus and remiss. Each foot consists of one or more than one syllable").

8. Halliday, *Intonation and Grammar*, 9. The five types of tone of English include the following: (1) fall; (2) high-rise; (3) low-rise; (4) fall-rise; (5) and rise-fall. Also, there are compound tones such as fall+low-rise ([1]+[3]) and rise-fall+low-rise ([5]+[3]) (*Intonation and Grammar*, 16–17).

9. Halliday, "Notes," 200.

10. For instance, in the sentence *Mary always goes to town on Saturday*, if an utterer accents *town*, then where *Mary goes* would be the new information of the sentence. On the contrary, if an addresser puts focus on *Saturday*, then when *Mary goes to town* would be the new information (Halliday, "Notes," 204).

sage lies will be different."[11] Therefore, the tonic in a tone group is the determinative factor for the prominence and newness of information.

Despite the fact that Halliday's theory results in one of the most systemized IS models, it does not hold for written texts for English, let alone those of another language such as those of the Greek New Testament.[12] This is mainly the case because modern readers cannot fully reconstruct intonation, pitch, or accent through ancient written texts. In addition to this, given that no contemporary people are native speakers of ancient Greek, no one is able to identify the subtle difference according to tonality and tonicity, such as prominence, focus, and nuance. Hence, for the Greek New Testament, it is very difficult to identify focal accent (new information) and tonal unit (information unit).[13] Therefore, it is necessary to adapt the SFL model for the Greek of the New Testament so that it accounts for the structure of information according to structures of syntax.[14]

---

11. Halliday, "Notes," 204.

12. Halliday himself also agrees on the limitation that written language may not fully embody the intonation of spoken language, and vice versa, such that spoken language cannot completely represent the system of punctuation such as boundary markers, status markers, and relation markers (*Spoken and Written Language*, 35). For Halliday's IS theory, see Halliday, "Notes."

13. Reed also points this out, saying, "Because Halliday's discussion of given–new information concerns spoken language, it is less helpful than theme–rheme for a discourse analysis of New Testament texts, where phonological units cannot be identified (although a study of rhythm might be informative)" (*Discourse Analysis*, 104).

14. To suggest establishing an IS theory in accordance with written text, however, does not indicate a simple dichotomy between spoken and written language. Most modern linguists reject the naïve dichotomy that written language is more syntactically complex and more structural than spoken language. Chafe and Danielwicz warn of the simple generalization of differences between spoken and written language ("Properties," 122) because variables in terms of language use exist not only between language modes but also as "each of the two modes, speaking and writing, itself allows a multiple of styles ("Properties," 84)." Halliday also presents skepticism to the simple division of spoken and written language, saying that "For one thing, 'written' and 'spoken' do not form a simple dichotomy; there are all sorts of writing and all sorts of speech, many of which display features characteristic of the other medium. For another thing, different people vary, and the same person varies on different occasions, in the 'implication of utterance' that is given to writing" (*Spoken and Written Language*, 32). Many modern linguists agree with these statements. They allege that even in spoken language, there are different types/registers/genres in spoken language such as personal interviews, dinner conversations, lectures, public speeches, and so on. Also, in written language, there are various types/registers/genres such as letters, academic journals, novels, poems, and so on. Chafe and Danielwicz propose that in some areas, letters (a

A METHODOLOGICAL PROPOSAL

Having the considerations proposed above in mind, the remainder of this paper will attempt to provide an IS theory for the Greek of the New Testament. But the analysis of IS needs to take multiple aspects into account. Particularly, this paper argues that given and new information, prominence, and thematization are to be taken into account to analyze IS of the Greek of the New Testament. However, all of these elements stem from different theories in linguistics.[15] Thematization deals with what is being talked about at the sentence level, while information structure

---

written language) and lectures (a spoken language) present similarities ("Properties," 111). Tannen also claims that narrative registers have common features with registers of conversation ("Oral and Literate Strategies"). Through her study, Kroll argues that not only registers or genres but also the individual sophistication of language use affects the features of both spoken and written language ("Combining Ideas"). Leckie-Tarry also argues that "spoken and written text types are in fact constituted by many different registers, and these differences in contextual backgrounds must be considered in comparing the linguistic structures of the texts" (*Language and Context*, 101). Therefore, different features from language modes, speaking and writing, different types, registers, genres, goals, and purposes produce language variations (see Halliday, *Spoken and Written Language*, 44; Leckie-Tarry, *Language and Context*, 95–101). Nevertheless, many linguists, through their case studies, have proposed different features between the two types of language. Halliday explains that whereas spoken language involves the property of syntactic intricacy, written language could be categorized by lexical density. Here, lexical density corresponds with the concept that fewer words, such as non-finite clauses and nominalization, may contain more information. Thus, written language is more highly information-packed than spoken language (Halliday, *Spoken and Written Language*, 87). Leckie-Tarry also claims a structural difference between spoken and written language, saying, "spoken registers show a greater proportion of subordinated Finite structures, while written registers show a greater proportion of reduced clauses or subordinated non-Finite structures" (*Language and Context*, 102). Chafe pursues the theoretical position that written language is apt to be more structural and hierarchical while spoken language is more sequential. The result of his research suggests that written discourse tends more toward nominalization, participles, attributive adjectives, conjoined phrases, and relative clauses than spoken language ("Integration and Involvement"). By a comparison of conversations, lectures, letters, and academic papers, Chafe and Danielwicz propose a statistical consequence—that is, spoken and written language present different distributions in terms of various areas of language repertoire such as the variety of vocabulary, level of vocabulary (colloquial vs. literary), clause construction, sentence construction, involvement with the audience, use of the third person pronoun, adverbial expressions, abstract subjects, passive forms, and indications of probability ("Properties").

15. This is one of the criticisms that Reed raises against Halliday's theory. Reed states that Halliday attempts to conflate two different theories, thematization and information structure into one (*Discourse Analysis*, 103–5).

concerns the recoverability of a particular item. Prominence is about saliency/markedness/grounding in discourse. All these notions, however, need to be considered in order to analyze IS. Thematization tracks how themes are developed in discourse and how they build an encompassing topic. Given and new information is concerned with how the author uses information in order to establish or to elaborate a theme or topic of discourse. Prominence is not restricted to a certain level of language but occurs at all levels of discourse. Through exploring prominence, one may detect what the author emphasizes in discourse and which part of discourse sticks out, so to speak—which often hints at why the author so structures the discourse.

Given and New Information

One of the biggest sources of confusion regarding the problem of given and new information is its different definitions among linguists. Conventionally, linguists have been given to studying given–new information with respect to the spoken language and psychological perception between the speaker and hearer. In other words, the concept of given–new addresses the speaker's assumption that the hearer already knows the distributed information (i.e., the given) or that the information is new to the hearer (i.e., the new). However, as Prince points out, the notion of given information has not reached a consensus as linguists continue to present the definition of givenness differently.[16] Prince succinctly recapitulates three notions of givenness typically proposed by linguists as follows:[17]

- Givenness^p (Predictability): The speaker assumes that the hearer can predict or could have predicted that a particular linguistic item will or would occur in a particular position within a sentence.[18]

---

16. Prince points out that "this intuitive appealing notion has never received a satisfactory characterization that would enable a working linguist to not only invoke it but to actually put it to use. In fact, if one considers the definitions that have been presented, one discovers that there is not one notion involved but at least three" ("Toward a Taxonomy," 225).

17. Prince, "Toward a Taxonomy," 226–31.

18. Kuno's notion of old information could be categorized here ("Generative Discourse Analysis"). His notion of old and new information is textual. In other words, if a linguistic item is recoverable by the preceding co-text, it is old information. Otherwise, it is new information (see 282–83).

- Givenness[s] (Saliency): The speaker assumes that the hearer has or could appropriately have some particular thing/entity ... in his/her consciousness at the time of hearing the utterance.[19]
- Givenness[sk] (Shared knowledge): The speaker assumes that the hearer knows, assumes, or can infer a particular thing.[20]

Regardless of how one defines given–new information, these notions involve extra-linguistic factors, particularly the psychological perception of the audience. Only within the shared context is the speaker able to assume that the hearer can predict that particular items will appear in the particular locus of the sentence. On the other hand, as mentioned above, Halliday's definition of given and new information implies that the emphasis of a particular linguistic item should remain as the primary focus of our attention.[21]

This paper, however, defines given and new information as follows. Given information is comprised of evocable or recoverable linguistic items.[22] It is evocable because it already occurred in the text and connotes a shared component of knowledge between the author and the reader. New information is not evocable or recoverable because it never appears in the text before this point and implies no shared knowledge with its readers. For instance, a given information component in the

---

19. Chafe's idea of given–new information could be situated in this category. He expounds that "given information represents that knowledge which the speaker assumes to be in the consciousness of the addressee at the time of the utterance, and new information is what the speaker assumes he/she is introducing into the addressee's consciousness by what he says" ("Givenness," 30).

20. Clark and Haviland's notion represents this definition. According to them, "Given is information that the speaker believes the listener already knows and accepts as true and new is information that the speaker believes the listener does not yet know" ("Comprehension," 4).

21. Halliday, "Notes," 204.

22. The definition of given and new information in this paper is similar to Halliday's and Prince's. Halliday defines new information as that which "the speaker presents ... as not being recoverable from the preceding discourse, and given information is that which is presented as recoverable from the previous discourse" ("Notes," 204). Prince proposes three types of information, which are new, evocable, and inferable. According to her definition, a new piece of information is not pre-known by the audience and is explicitly introduced by a full noun phrase. Evocable information is what we might call a "used" linguistic item in the discourse and is referred to through referential devices such as pronouns. Inferable information is that through which the speaker expects the audience may be able to infer a particular entity, though the item is not referred to directly ("Toward a Taxonomy," 233–37).

dialogue between two people in a common situation would be new information to another person who was not in the same situation.[23] In this regard, both situational and textual contexts are critical aspects with which to identify given and new information.

Given and new information in the textual context is straightforward. In the textual context, grammatical and textual features take a significant role in identifying given and new information.[24] In this view, given information is recoverable, while a new piece of information is not. That is to say, if an element in a sentence referred to another element, it amounts to given information. On the contrary, a new piece of information is something that may never have been mentioned before. The given information would be identified by linguistic tools such as reference, personal pronouns, relative pronouns, demonstrative pronouns, lexical repetition, and semantic similarities.[25] In this regard, cohesive ties are useful tools to identify given and new information according to the textual function of language.[26] Cohesive ties refer to a language

---

23. For instance, in a dialogue between two New Testament scholars, some terms such as "Historical Jesus," "New Perspective on Paul," or "Apocalypticism" are not new information since they represent or contain shared knowledge. On the contrary, when they explain these terms to those who are outside of the scholarly world, these would be new information to them.

24. Leckie-Tarry also brings this point, asserting that "with minimal information available from the context of situation, the information structure must be explicitly built up within the text ... Spoken texts place a strong reliance on an element of the context of situation which is not available to written texts, which are forced to rely solely on the context of text for the realization of information structure" (*Language and Context*, 150–51).

25. The analysis of Given information could be examined by cohesive ties. Cohesive ties can apply to an individual linguistic item and the clause or sentence as a whole as well. The former instance is comprised of so-called componential ties, and the latter, so-called organic ties. Cohesive ties deal with how the elements or items of discourse, such as words, phrases, clauses, sentences, paragraphs, and discourses, connect systematically. Reed defines cohesive ties that "refer to the language system's ability to for relations between particular linguistic items." Reed, "Cohesive Ties," 134. Reed classifies semantic relationships between individual items as componential ties. The original idea of the cohesive ties is from Hasan. See Hasan in Halliday and Hasan, *Language, Context, and Text*, 70–85. For my analysis, however, I would not include the article because, as Porter and O'Donnell comment, it is untenable to take the Greek article into account since the Greek article does not function as a definite indicator as in English (see Porter and O'Donnell, *Discourse Analysis*, 180).

26. Though Halliday's IS theory is based on English phonology, he provides an important notion that one can apply to the written text in question here. Halliday suggests cohesiveness as one of the features of information units. Halliday explains that "given

system that links linguistic items together. That is, cohesive ties deal with how the linguistic items are semantically related to one another. The semantic relation would be signified by personal pronouns, demonstrative pronouns, and relative pronouns.[27] For instance, in 2 Cor 8:1–2, Paul introduces the Macedonian church's generosity to the Corinthians. Here, Paul uses the pronoun αὐτός to refer to the Macedonians. Thus, the Macedonians and αὐτός ("they") are in the same cohesive tie, and they are given information. Also, even though a linguistic item is not referred to by pronouns, if it indicates the same semantic of another item, the two are likewise linked in a cohesive tie. For example, in Rom 9:3–4, two participants occur, namely "my brothers" (ἀδελφῶν μου) and the "Israelites" (Ἰσραηλῖται). Though no pronouns are used here to denote that the two entities are related, they are semantically related, indicating the same people group. Therefore, if a piece of information is anaphoric, it would be a given information. But on the contrary, if a linguistic item is not recoverable or non-anaphoric, it would be new information.

In addition to textual context, situational context is another facet by which to canvass given and new information. Although the situational context is extra-linguistic context, it is denoted in the text through lexico-grammar.[28] A discourse is not produced in a vacuum. Every text is a product of its situation in the sense that a particular text is derived from a particular situation, and it is a process in the sense that the author selects semantic options from the network of meaning potential.[29] Put a little differently, the author has the meaning that s/he wants to express, and then the author makes selections from the language's lexico-gram-

---

information tends to be represented anaphorically by reference, substitution, or ellipsis ... Anaphoric items are inherently given in the sense that their interpretation depends on identification within the preceding text. Substitutes ... cannot be structurally new" ("Notes," 206).

27. Halliday and Hasan, *Language, Context, and Text*, 73.

28. This is similar to Halliday, for whom registers are "a configuration of meaning that are typically associated with a particular situational configuration of field, tenor, and mode" (Halliday in Halliday and Hasan, *Language, Context, and Text*, 38–39). Halliday explains that three features of context of situation (field, tenor, and mode) are realized by three semantic components, ideational, interpersonal, and textual. In other words, field, tenor, and mode are reflected in grammatical patterns that we could call ideational (transitivity and subject matter), interpersonal (mood system, modality, participants), and textual (cohesion) meaning respectively. See Halliday in Halliday and Hasan, *Language, Context, and Text*, 27.

29. Halliday in Halliday and Hasan, *Language, Context, and Text*, 10.

mar to efficiently present the meaning. Therefore, through scrutinizing lexico-grammar, one may construe the context of situation of the text. Within the construable situation, readers are able to propose and understand given and new information.

For instance, in First Corinthians, when Paul deals with issues of the Corinthians that are already known to the Corinthians themselves, Paul constantly uses a particular phrase, περὶ δέ, in the front position of the clause. By doing so, Paul draws the attention of the reader by opening up the given information and indicates that he will go on to cope with those issues. And the following clauses and sentences elaborate upon the given information Paul proposes.

- 1 Cor 7:1 Περὶ δὲ ὧν ἐγράψατε, καλὸν ἀνθρώπῳ γυναικὸς μὴ ἅπτεσθαι
- 1 Cor 7:25 Περὶ δὲ τῶν παρθένων ἐπιταγὴν κυρίου οὐκ ἔχω, γνώμην δὲ δίδωμι ὡς ἠλεημένος ὑπὸ κυρίου πιστὸς εἶναι.
- 1 Cor 8:1 Περὶ δὲ τῶν εἰδωλοθύτων, οἴδαμεν ὅτι πάντες γνῶσιν ἔχομεν. ἡ γνῶσις φυσιοῖ, ἡ δὲ ἀγάπη οἰκοδομεῖ

In the above examples, the prepositional phrase περὶ δέ is encoded to signify the subject that Paul wants to discuss. By looking at the signals, the reader would be able to speculate that a given piece of information (pre-known issue or shared knowledge) is going to be addressed. Also, in Rom 14:1–3, Paul repeatedly utilizes nominalized forms to recall something for his audience regarding the issue they have. Beginning a new section, in Rom 14:1, Paul does not explicitly explain what "the weak in faith" (τὸν ... ἀσθενοῦντα τῇ πίστει) and "the one who eats" (ὁ ἐσθίων) mean. Rather, by nominalization, Paul brings given information which consists of shared knowledge between Paul and his readers.

Alongside this, participants that are referred to by first- and second-person forms are mostly given information, since they are the direct communicators in discourse. When the third-person is expressed by pronouns, it too would be given information. Also, when a participant occurs with an explicit full noun or nominal group, it may be new or given information. For instance, a long list in the last chapter of Romans is given information, since its members are known to the Romans, although names are explicitly addressed. Another good example may be found in 2 Tim 3:8:

ὃν τρόπον δὲ Ἰάννης καὶ Ἰαμβρῆς ἀντέστησαν Μωϋσεῖ, οὕτως καὶ οὗτοι ἀνθίστανται τῇ ἀληθείᾳ, ἄνθρωποι κατεφθαρμένοι τὸν νοῦν, ἀδόκιμοι περὶ τὴν πίστιν.

As Jannes and Jambres opposed Moses, these men also oppose the truth, men of corrupt mind, rejected concerning the faith.

Here, the pronoun οὗτος is given information, since it refers to the previous entities of the immediate co-text of 2 Tim 3:2–7. Although Jannes and Jambres seem to be new information, since they are introduced here for the first time and explicitly expressed by names, they would be given information if Timothy is familiar with the story of Moses in the Old Testament.

Thematization

Theme is about what is being talked about. Conventionally, linguists define theme as the subject of the sentence. However, to identify the theme/subject only in the sentence is often insufficient grounds from which to determine the topic of the discourse. Though a text talks about a specific topic, the subject of each sentence would be different and may not be directly related to the topic. Besides, concerning IS of the discourse, to investigate the development of a theme throughout the discourse is more important than simply analyzing a theme of a sentence. This study will therefore make use of Stanley E. Porter and Matthew Brook O'Donnell's theory of thematization, which is modeled for analyzing discourse at various levels all the way up to the levels of paragraph and discourse itself.[30]

To identify theme and topic of discourse, Porter and O'Donnell provide an analytic system that runs the gamut from the clause to the discourse level. For the clause level, they propose a sequence of prime–subsequent.[31] The prime is the initial element of the clause, and the subsequent is comprised of the elements that follow the prime in the

---

30. Porter and O'Donnell, *Discourse Analysis*, 96–127.

31. Porter and O'Donnell, *Discourse Analysis*, 105–7. In Greek, the first-position element does not always have thematic significance. Thus, to use theme at the clause level may give rise to the confusion that, like English, Greek also has thematic formation at the beginning of the clause. Alongside this, some linguists conflate the concept of theme and topic at the sentence level. To avoid this confusion, Porter and O'Donnell utilize the terminology of prime–subsequent. The analysis of prime–subsequent is all about the position of linguistic items at the clause level. It does not imply that the initial positional element necessarily has thematic prominence.

clause. Whereas the prime is the point of departure, the subsequent is the completion of the message in the clause. Thus, the division of prime and subsequent in the clause level is locational. For instance, in Matt 5:3 μακάριοι οἱ πτωχοὶ τῷ πνεύματι, the first element μακάριοι is the prime and the rest of the clause (οἱ πτωχοὶ τῷ πνεύματι) is collectively the subsequent.[32] Also, when the preposition or article comes first in the clause, the prime includes the next content word. In this case, the prime can be a word group. Hence, the first content word or word group of the clause is the prime, and the rest of the clause is the subsequent. Porter and O'Donnell also explain that "the prime can be defined as *who or what the clause is focused upon*, realized by the first clausal component in the clause, whether subject (S), predicator (P), complement (C), or adjunct (A)."[33] For instance, in Luke 13:31, ἐν αὐτῇ τῇ ὥρᾳ προσῆλθάν τινες φαρισαῖοι λέγοντες αὐτῷ, the prepositional phrase ἐν αὐτῇ τῇ ὥρᾳ is the prime of the clause and the remainder is the subsequent.[34]

For the clause complex level, Porter and O'Donnell propose the categories of theme and rheme. According to their definition, theme is *"the fully grammaticalized participant as the actor in a process chain."* And they define rheme as *"additional process information for the current ac-*

---

32. Porter and O'Donnell, *Discourse Analysis*, 105–7. Porter and O'Donnell do not include conjunctions in prime–subsequent analysis. Omitting conjunctions in prime–subsequent analysis seems appropriate, for the conjunction takes a conjunctive function at the clause complex level. Put differently, the conjunction is a relator and thus links words between sentences or clauses. Therefore, in my analysis, when the conjunction of connecting words is located in prime position, I will include them with the other element(s) in the first position as prime but within parentheses. For instance, in the clause ἀλλὰ τοῦτο κρίνατε μᾶλλον, I mark (ἀλλὰ) τοῦτο as the prime of the clause. This indicates that the conjunction itself cannot be the prime, since it is a linking word between sentences rather than a thematic element of the clause. Nevertheless, for the analysis of the sentence level and information unit, I would leave the conjunction as part of the prime element (within parentheses) when it appears in the initial position of the clause. Another reason for leaving the conjunction in prime position is its structural prominence. Porter expounds that there are established word-order patterns in Greek and conjunctions are included in the patterns. Such patterns are postpositive words (ἄν, γάρ, δέ, γέ, μέν, οὖν, ποτέ, πώς, τέ) that normally do not occur at the first position of the clause but the second or later position. Also, some words do not typically come up at the end of the clause. Such words are ἀλλά, ἤ, καί, οὐδέ, μηδέ. Lastly, fronted elements are the words that are apt to appear at the beginning of the clause. Such words are πρῶτον, ἔπειτα, εἶτα and most pronouns (Porter, *Idioms*, 288–89). Thus, if some of the words are located where they typically are, they would be unmarked.

33. Porter and O'Donnell, *Discourse Analysis*, 105 (emphasis original).

34. The example is taken from Porter and O'Donnell, *Discourse Analysis*, 105.

tor." They also add, "The theme is an explicit subject of a clause complex in a process chain."[35] Thus, a theme will most likely be grammaticalized as a nominal group, occurring in the independent clause. For instance, according to their analysis, Luke 7:36–40 has four themes: (1) Pharisee in v. 36; (2) woman in vv. 37–38; (3) Pharisee in v. 39; (4) and Jesus in v. 40. These are all explicit subjects which are actors in process chains.

Here at the clause complex level, this paper utilizes the term "thematic unit" (ThU) to indicate the smallest linguistic cluster that holds the same theme.[36] Thus, ThU may be defined across multiple clauses. How, then, can one demarcate a ThU? A new theme in the prime position would be the most explicit case for signaling a new ThU, as Porter and O'Donnell state, "The language user must start their message from some point and thus must select a beginning theme from which they will develop the message."[37] Also, Porter explains as follows:

> The expressed subject is often used as a form of topic marker or shifter (in a topic and comment sequence) and is appropriately placed first to signal this semantic function. What this means is that when the subject is expressed it is often used either to draw attention to the subject of discussion or to mark a shift in the topic, perhaps signaling that a new person or event is the center of focus.[38]

Therefore, if a new participant comes as new information in the first position of the clause (prime), it would be marked as a new ThU. However, theme does not always appear in the prime position of a clause, because the structure of Greek syntax does not rigidly restrict the position of explicit subjects in the clause, even in the case of a change of participant in a process chain. Sometimes, a theme of a thematic unit occurs in the middle of the unit. For instance, given that Rom 14:1–2 is a thematic unit, the theme of the unit is ὁ ἀσθενῶν ("the one who is weak in faith") since it is an explicit subject and a new participant. However, the theme itself does not appear until the last clause of the unit. Therefore, if a theme is proposed in either prime or subsequent position and is re-

---

35. Porter and O'Donnell, *Discourse Analysis*, 110 (emphasis original).

36. The thematic unit does not necessarily determine the topic of the entire text. It is just a sub-unit within the central topic that encompasses the whole discourse. Thus, a thematic unit could be just a sentence, or multiple sentences.

37. Porter and O'Donnell, *Discourse Analysis*, 98.

38. Porter, *Idioms*, 295–96.

ferred to by other linguistic elements, one may group it as a thematic unit. In other words, when a new participant occurs, it would signify a change of direction. Then, if the participant is recurring by a simple repetition or by semantic ties, it is a thematic unit. Thematic elements are often repeated. Therefore, though a new theme occurs, in a ThU it becomes given information eventually, as it is repeated and referred to by other linguistic items. Another thematic unit begins with another piece of new information and its own lexical and semantic recurrence.

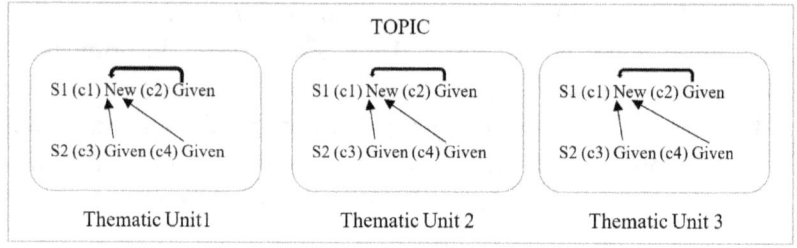

Figure 1. The Thematic Unit

The semantic and logical relation between primary and secondary/embedded clauses provide a clue toward the determination of ThU. That is, when the secondary or embedded clause elaborates upon the information given by the primary clause, it could be said to be a ThU because of the logico-semantic relation between the two clauses.[39] For instance, in John 11:27 (ἐγὼ πεπίστευκα ὅτι σὺ εἶ ὁ Χριστὸς ὁ υἱὸς τοῦ θεοῦ, "I have believed that you are Christ, the Son of God"), there are two independent clauses: ἐγὼ πεπίστευκα and σὺ εἶ ὁ Χριστὸς ὁ υἱὸς τοῦ θεοῦ, with two different subjects, "I" and "you." Though there is a subject shift, the second clause is projected through the primary clause, and the second clause is the content of the first clause. Thus, one may identify ThUs by examining the relationship between primary and secondary clauses and between independent clauses.[40] Pickering states that "one

---

39. Reed categorizes the logico-semantic relation between clauses and sentences as organic ties (see Reed, "Cohesive Ties").

40. For this reason, the present paper will use OpenText.org for the relation between the clauses. As the introduction for the model of opentext.org notes, "Clauses are divided into two levels: (1) primary clauses; and (2) secondary clauses. The primary and secondary distinction has to do with the two possible types of logical dependency, dependence (hypotaxis) or equality (parataxis). Primary clauses are connected to each other, while secondary clauses are connected to the primary clause to which [they are] dependent. The majority of primary clauses consist of clauses with a finite verb.

independent clause in a discourse should be described as subordinate to another independent clause in descriptions of discourse."[41] Therefore, by analyzing the sentence, one may assess how information, given by the primary clause, is built up and elaborated by the secondary clause. Also, at this level, one may identify the hierarchical structure of the text by examining how information components in clause complexes and sentences are structured—and how a succeeding sentence modifies the information given by the preceding sentence.

For the discourse level, finally, this paper uses the terminology of topic–comment. Though theme and rheme at the sentence/clause complex level would be able to suggest the boundary of a ThU by grammatical and semantical criteria, a *single* ThU does not determine the central topic of a discourse as a whole. Rather, the assembly of *each* ThU establishes the topic of the discourse. For instance, if the same theme appears in ThU1 and again in ThU3, and another theme occurs in between them, we should not promptly make a decision that they are different discourses. The topic is determined by the extent of semantic unity. As Lee explains, "a discourse unit beyond the sentence level is basically a unit of a semantic unity of theme which can be called a topical unity."[42] Porter and O'Donnell also have the same view. They claim that "we define topic as the *establishment of a new semantic environment for the text*, and comment as *supporting information for the current topic*. Topic and comment are the thematization functions at the paragraph and textual level, realized through semantic shifts or semantic boundaries."[43]

Then, how do we examine the semantic congruence between thematic units? As Lee suggests, two determinative factors ought to be considered: internal and external factors. Internally, conjunctions, lexical cohesion, and grammatical cohesion would be decisive factors for semantic unity.[44] In a similar vein, Porter and O'Donnell propose

---

Secondary clauses are typically distinguished by means of a subordinating conjunction. A second type of secondary clause, the embedded clause, involves the phenomenon of rank-shifting—a linguistic element is embedded to a level of grammar lower than the typical level at which it functions. The majority of secondary embedded clauses in Greek are participial and infinitival clauses" (see "Introduction").

41. Pickering, *Framework*, 20.
42. Lee, *Paul's Gospel*, 33.
43. Porter and O'Donnell, *Discourse Analysis*, 116.
44. The conjunction is one of the important factors to identify cohesion of a text, and cohesion is a useful tool with which to examine the information flow. Moreover,

a semantic cohesiveness that would be realized by semantic domains, semantic ties, changes of participants, and "changes in paradigmatic factors such as changes in tense-form, voice, and mood."[45] External factors would be spatio-temporal markers, which are indicators for the change of a situation,[46] the change of genre or the point of view,[47] and the change of participants or topical entities.[48] For example, in John 7:1, the narrator of the Gospel states, καὶ μετὰ ταῦτα περιεπάτει ὁ Ἰησοῦς ἐν τῇ Γαλιλαίᾳ ("and after this, Jesus went around Galilee"). Here a tempo-

---

how the speaker/author uses conjunctions may contribute to the analysis of IS. As Lee delineates, regarding the sequentiality (linearity) of the text, "cohesion is related to the linkage of textual components such as word, phrase, clause, sentence, etc., and focuses on how one textual component links to another" (*Paul's Gospel*, 31). Furthermore, some conjunctions may function as a sign, indicating a topical shift in the paragraph level. In this regard, including conjunctions and connecting words would be likely to contribute to IS analysis. Therefore, in my analysis, I would include conjunctions and connecting words in the position of Prime with other elements, but the conjunction itself cannot be Prime. By doing this, I would be able to identify the linear connectivity and would obtain plausible signs for any topical shift. Though conjunctions function as a relator between sentences, they also connect different information units and imply that two different information units are in the same topic. For instance, Luke 13:10–21 consists of two different information units. Luke 13:10 provides a new setting of the discourse by spatio–temporal markers ἐν μιᾷ τῶν συναγωγῶν ἐν τοῖς σάββασιν ("in a synagogue in the day of Sabbath") which is also an indicator of new information. Luke 13:18–21 is another information unit because v. 18 introduces new information, which is ἡ βασιλεία τοῦ θεοῦ ("the kingdom of God"). Though the two units seem to be a different topic, by the conjunction in v. 18 (οὖν), Luke connects the two units. In addition to this, some conjunctions function as boundary markers of a discourse. Also, Louw and Nida's semantic lexicon assigns domain 91 as discourse markers (see Louw and Nida, *Greek–English Lexicon*, 2:811–13).

45. Porter and O'Donnell, *Discourse Analysis*, 119.

46. Lee, *Paul's Gospel*, 35.

47. Reed, *Discourse Analysis*, 119. Acts 15:23–29, for example, is a different genre compared to its context. Whereas Acts 15:23–29 is epistolary in style, its context is narrative.

48. One may criticize that the proposed parameters are overlapped with those of the sentence level. However, this is unavoidable. Porter and O'Donnell also admit these concurring parameters throughout all levels of the discourse. They state, "It would seem to follow that those things thematized at the levels beneath the paragraph, that is, at the clause-complex and clause levels, would in some way reflect thematization at the paragraph level" (*Discourse Analysis*, 119). These overlapped criteria are inevitable since the smaller level belongs to the larger level. The discourse has sub-units, and each unit has sentences, and each sentence consists of one or more than one clause. The clause is the smallest unit that bears the author's message, and even structurally, the clause is always the beginning point.

ral marker (μετὰ ταῦτα) appears that distinguishes from the previous event. Also, a spatial marker (ἐν τῇ Γαλιλαίᾳ) occurs, differentiating the location from the preceding context, not unlike the way we might use a break between paragraphs on a typewritten page.

Prominence

Reed defines prominence "as those semantic and grammatical elements of discourse that serve to set aside certain subjects, ideas, or motifs of the author as more or less semantically and pragmatically significant than others."[49] That is, prominence is those salient linguistic features that the author employs in order to draw the reader's attention to highlight significant topics and motifs of the discourse.[50] That is to say, prominence may contribute in identifying the message and focus of the thematic unit.[51]

First, the syntactical variant is germane to prominence/markedness, and the prominence results in subtle semantic differences. In other words, prominence/markedness draws the attention of the reader, and it affects the meaning of the text. As Halliday defines it, prominence is "the phenomenon of linguistic highlighting, whereby some feature of the language of a text stands out in some way."[52] If the author just enumerates information without any highlighting or emphasis, the reader would be more likely to miss the point regarding the topic/theme of the text. By identifying prominence, one may be able to "set aside certain subjects, ideas or motifs of the author as more or less semantically and pragmatically significant than others."[53] Therefore, IS analysis needs to take both semantics and syntax into account, and some measurements for the significance of syntactical features would be required.[54]

49. Reed, *Discourse Analysis*, 106.

50. Reed, *Discourse Analysis*, 106.

51. Reed, *Discourse Analysis*, 108. As Reed rightly point out, not all prominences have sematic weight. Nevertheless, it is worthwhile to pay attention because prominence spotlights a specific linguistic element or participants in a thematic unit and contributes to identifying the message of the thematic unit.

52. Halliday, *Explorations*, 113. Hasan also states, "each utterance has a thesis: what it is talking about uniquely and instantially; and in addition to this, each utterance has a function in the internal organization of the text; in combination with other utterances of the text it realizes the theme, structure and other aspect" ("Linguistics," 109–10).

53. Reed, *Discourse Analysis*, 106.

54. Porter and O'Donnell, *Discourse Analysis*, 123.

Though Greek is a (mostly) non-configurational language, this does not mean that Greek has no prominence in terms of word order.[55] Porter states that "at the level of word order there is much more regularity in several NT Greek writers than many grammarians have been willing to recognize, even though individual authors may reflect differing patterns."[56] In *Idioms*, Porter provides a statistical result regarding the Greek word order:

> In the Greek of the NT, the adjectival modifier follows its noun approximately 75% of the time in Luke and Mark . . . [To the contrary,] it precedes its noun approximately 65% of the time in Paul . . . In the Greek of the NT, the demonstrative follows its noun far more frequently than it precedes it, approximately 85% in Paul and 78% in Luke . . . In the Greek of the NT, the genitival modifier follows its noun in Paul in 96% and in Luke in 99% of all instances . . . In the Greek of the NT, the object of the preposition virtually always follows its preposition, except for the use of such words as χάριν, χωρίς, and ἕνεκα . . . In the Greek of the NT, the relative clause follows its referent in Paul in approximately 93% and in Luke in approximately 96% of instances.[57]

Also, in terms of the clause structure, Porter elucidates that the simplest Greek clause structure is the predicate as a minimal unit. He continues, noting that there are three common clause structures: predicate–complement, complement–predicate, and subject–predicate structure.[58] According to the above statistical results, Porter concludes that "it is plausible to assert that the Greek New Testament is best described as a linear language, certainly for word order, but also probably for

---

55. Greek has significant flexibility in word order. The clause does not necessarily consist of subject and predicate. The finite verb itself contains the subject of the verb, so it is not necessary to syntactically divide subject and predicate. Thus, a verb itself could be a clause.

56. Porter, *Idioms*, 290. Porter delineates that "many of the standard reference grammars of the Greek New Testament [such as Winer, Robertson, BDF, and Moule] are convinced that standard New Testament Greek word order is VSO (verb–subject–object)." Porter, *Idioms*, 293. Porter states that "the majority of Greek clauses do not express all of the elements used in the formulation, and to base one's formulation of standard order on instances where all three elements are present mispresents the evidence and the result" (*Idioms*, 293). Porter proposes an alternative, that the most plausible pattern of the clause structure is verb–complement. When the subject exists in the clause, it would be subject–verb–complement (*Idioms*, 295).

57. Porter, *Idioms*, 290–92.

58. Porter, *Idioms*, 293–94.

sentence structure."⁵⁹ This discovery is very significant since it would contribute to the analysis of Information Structure in the sense that the proposed theme should be modified by subsequent linguistic elements. Alongside this, even in the sentence structure, this tendency means that the following clause should elaborate the preceding clause. Therefore, the compositional variant and idiosyncratic syntactic features in Greek would make semantic differences, and some word orders and positions would be marked or prominent.⁶⁰

Secondly, verbal aspect may function to determine prominence. "One of the discourse functions of verbal aspect," asserts Reed, "is to indicate the prominence of clauses in relationship to the larger paragraph or discourse."⁶¹ The theory of verbal aspect was initiated by McKay, flourished with Porter and Fanning, and was further developed by Decker, Campbell, and Huffman.⁶² For them, the Greek verb tense denotes a verbal aspect that shows the author's subjective perspectives on the process of the verb.⁶³ As the notion of verbal aspect itself indicates, verbal aspect is a systemic choice on the part of the author to present his/her point of view on events and activities. Thus, it is conceivable that when the author uses particular verbal aspects with particular words and sets them apart from other aspects and words in the same linguistic context, the result would have prominence. Also, speakers/authors may

---

59. Porter, *Idioms*, 292.

60. The relation between clause or sentence structure and prominence is also an important realm for Levinsohn. In his book, *Discourse Features*, after expounding the point of departure (the first element of the sentence), in the third chapter, Levinsohn explores the sentence structure. He provides the default structure of the Greek New Testament sentence and proposes marked orderings which are outside of the normal patterns (see *Discourse Features*, 29–47).

61. Reed, *Discourse Analysis*, 113.

62. McKay, *New Syntax*; Porter, *Verbal Aspect*; Fanning, *Verbal Aspect*; Decker, *Temporal Deixis*; Campbell, *Verbal Aspect*; Campbell, *Verbal Aspect and Non-Indicative Verbs*; Huffman, *Verbal Aspect Theory*.

63. As McKay defines it, "Aspect in ancient Greek is that category of the verb system by means of which an author (or speaker) shows how he views each event or activity he mentions in relation to its context" (*New Syntax*, 27). Fanning explains the Greek verbal aspect as "that category in the grammar of the verb which reflects the focus or viewpoint of the speaker in regard to the verb" (*Verbal Aspect*, 84). Porter defines Greek verbal aspect as "a synthetic semantic category (realized in the forms of verbs) used of meaningful oppositions in a network of tense systems to grammaticalize the author's reasoned subjective choice of conception of a process" (*Verbal Aspect*, 88).

alternate tense-forms to communicate information status.⁶⁴ Reed also maintains the following:

> In non-narrative, background prominence (*unmarked*) may be signalled by clauses using the aorist tense-form (perfective aspect). It is not so much that aorist tense-forms are thematically unimportant (nor are they always background material) but that they may be used in discourse to set apart some events from those signalled by the imperfective aspect (present and imperfect tense-forms). Thematic prominence may be signalled by the present and imperfect tense-forms (imperfective aspect) as well as future tense-form ... Focal prominence may be signalled by the perfect and pluperfect tense-form ... The perfective aspect lends itself to general descriptions of an event, whereas the imperfective aspect suggests the author is focusing on the particulars of an event. The stative aspect is even more accentuated, since the attention is placed upon an event that has resulted from other circumstances.⁶⁵

Thirdly, the Greek mood system may contribute to identifying prominence. Since the Greek mood system is formulated around a set of binary choices, it has prominence depending on the choice of the author, and it presents the attitude of the author.⁶⁶ Assertive statements, expressed by the indicative mood, are more salient than non-assertive statements that are purported to happen. Regarding the prominence of the Greek mood system, Reed explains:

> The subjunctive and optative moods, because their function is essentially that of non-assertion or projection, are often used to express background material. This partly explains their frequent use in subordinate clauses (e.g., purpose clauses), which typically play a rhetorically supportive role in discourse. In non-narrative, the imperative mood is also used in thematic material, due to its semantic attribute of "direction" (i.e., the speaker directs or commands others to do something).⁶⁷

For instance, in Rom 14:1 (τὸν δὲ ἀσθενοῦντα τῇ πίστει προσλαμβάνεσθε, "you should accept those who are weak in faith"),

---

64. Reed, *Discourse Analysis*, 115.
65. Reed, *Discourse Analysis*, 114–5 (emphasis mine).
66. For a complete and systematized explanation of the Greek mood system, see Porter, "Systemic Functional Linguistics," 26–32.
67. Reed, *Discourse Analysis*, 115.

Paul opens up the subject that he wants to deal with by proposing given information through nominalization ("those who are weak in faith"). Then, in the subsequent position, Paul uses an imperative mood. Thus, Paul brings an existing issue of what Paul and his audience share (given information), then he reveals his thoughts on the issue by using the imperative mood (new information and prominence)

CONCLUSION

This paper has attempted to offer a basic notion of IS and to propose a theory corresponding to the Greek New Testament. There are common features of IS throughout the history of linguistic research. First, IS is related to word order and the division of linguistic elements at the sentence level. Second, IS is associated with the shared context between speakers and hearers. However, as we have seen, there are reasons that one needs to amend the theory to identify the IS of the Greek of the New Testament. First, Greek has unique features compared to other languages. Greek is an inflected language and does not have a strong word order or pattern like that of English. Particularly, the Greek New Testament is a written language, and no contemporary people are native in that form of Greek. Thus, based on the linguistic situation we have, we ought to develop an IS theory accordingly. Secondly, IS should not be restricted to the sentence level. In other words, IS in the Greek of the New Testament should take the larger linguistics units into consideration, including that of the paragraph and even the discourse. The theme of each sentence is incomplete unless it is reviewed in light of the topic of the discourse. That is to say, a linguistic unit per se is like a piece of the puzzle that does not provide sufficient understanding unless it is located in the full picture. Besides, one needs to examine how individual pieces of given and new information develop throughout the discourse. Given and new information contributes to building a thematic unit and prominence in the thematic unit. This is a feature that is more prominent in Paul's correspondence. Though Paul's letter has communicative functions, Paul is the one who structures the entire letter. Thus, every letter (or even sub-units of the letter) has a certain message that Paul wants to convey. To convey the message, Paul, as a communicational architect, organizes and structures information.

In this regard, the present study has argued that IS of the Greek New Testament needs to take multiple aspects into consideration. Analysts should investigate situational and textual context in order to find given and new information. Also, they need to scrutinize more closely how the information develops and builds up the bigger levels of language which we know as the thematic unit and discourse. Then, finally, it is necessary that analysts examine which linguistic items and information stand out in the discourse. Taking these multiple facets together may explain what the central information is, how the information is construed in the bigger language levels, and which information is most salient to build up the discourse. By doing so, the analysis of information structure is not confined to the sentence level. Rather, to explore information structure is syntactic, in the sense that one may construe what information the speaker/author wants to convey through syntactical analyses; semantic, in the sense that different choices of information structure yield subtly different meanings; and pragmatic, in the sense that a speaker/author chooses the arrangement of the information.

BIBLIOGRAPHY

Ammann, Hermann. *Die menschliche Rede: Sprach-philosophische Untersuchungen, II: Der Satz*. Lahr: Schauenburg, 1928.

Campbell, Constantine R. *Verbal Aspect and Non-Indicative Verbs: Further Soundings in the Greek of the New Testament*. SBG 15. New York: Peter Lang, 2008.

———. *Verbal Aspect, the Indicative Mood, and Narrative: Soundings in the Greek of the New Testament*. SBG 13. New York: Peter Lang, 2007.

Chafe, Wallace. "Givenness, Contrastiveness, Definiteness, Subjects, Topics, and Point of View." In *Subject and Topic: Papers*, edited by Charles N. Li, 25–55. New York: Academic, 1976.

———. "Integration and Involvement in Speaking, Writing and Oral Literature." In *Spoken and Written Language: Exploring Orality and Literacy*, edited by Deborah Tannen, 35–54. Advances in Discourse Processes 9. Norwood, NJ: Ablex, 1982.

Chafe, Wallace, and Jane Danielwicz. "Properties of Spoken and Written Language." In *Comprehending Oral and Written Language*, edited by Rosalind Horowitz and S. Jay Samuels, 87–110. San Diego: Academic, 1987.

Chomsky, Noam. "Deep Structure, Surface Structure, and Semantic Representation." In *Semantics: An Interdisciplinary Reader in Philosophy, Linguistics and Psychology*, edited by Danny D. Steinberg and Leon A. Jakobovits, 193–217. Cambridge: Cambridge University Press, 1971.

Clark, H., and S. Haviland. "Comprehension and the Given–New Contract." In *Discourse Production and Comprehension*, edited by Roy O. Freedle, 1–40. Discourse Processes, Advances in Research and Theory 1. Norwood, NJ: Ablex, 1977.

Decker, Rodney J. *Temporal Deixis of the Greek Verb in the Gospel of Mark with Reference to Verbal Aspect*. SBG 10. New York: Peter Lang, 2001.

Fanning, Buist M. *Verbal Aspect in New Testament Greek*. Oxford Theological Monographs. Oxford: Clarendon, 1990.

Gabelentz, G. von der. "Ideen zu einer vergleichenden Syntax: Wort und Satzstellung." *Zeitschrift für Völkerpsychologie und Sprachwissenschaft* 6 (1869) 376–84.
Halliday, M. A. K. *Explorations in the Functions of Language*. Explorations in Language Study. London: Arnold, 1973.
———. *Intonation and Grammar in British English*. The Hague: Mouton, 1967.
———. *An Introduction to Functional Grammar*. London: Arnold, 1985. (IFG1)
———. "Notes on Transitivity and Theme in English: Part 2." *JL* 3 (1967) 199–244.
———. *Spoken and Written Language*. Oxford: Oxford University Press, 1985.
Halliday, M. A. K., and Ruqaiya Hasan. *Language, Context, and Text: Aspects of Language in a Social-Semiotic Perspective*. 2nd ed. Oxford: Oxford University Press, 1989.
Hasan, Ruqaiya. "Linguistics and the Study of Literary Texts." *Etudes de Linguistique Appliquée* 5 (1967) 106–21.
Heusinger, Klaus von. "Information Structure and the Partition of Sentence Meaning." In *Prague Linguistic Circle Papers: Volume 4*, edited by Eva Hajicová et al., 275–305. Amsterdam: Benjamins, 2002.
Huffman, Douglas S. *Verbal Aspect Theory and the Prohibitions in the Greek New Testament*. SBG 16. New York: Peter Lang, 2014.
"Introduction to the Annotation Model." *OpenText.org*. No pages. Online: http://opentext.org/model/introduction.html.
Jackendoff, Ray S. *Semantic Interpretation in Generative Grammar*. Studies in Linguistics Series 2. Cambridge, MA: MIT Press, 1972.
Kiss, É. Katalin. "Introduction." In *Discourse Configurational Languages*, edited by Katalin É. Kiss, 3–27. Oxford Studies in Comparative Syntax. New York: Oxford University Press, 1995.
Kroll, Barbara. "Combining Ideas in Written and Spoken English: A Look at Subordination and Co-ordination." In *Discourse Across Time and Space*, edited by Elinor Ochs Keenan and Tina Bennett-Kastor, 69–108. Los Angeles: University of Southern California Press, 1977.
Kuno, S. "Generative Discourse Analysis in America." In *Current Trends in Textlinguistics*, edited by Wolfgang U. Dressler, 275–94. Research in Text Theory 2. Berlin: de Gruyter, 1978.
Leckie-Tarry, Helen. *Language and Context: A Functional Linguistic Theory of Register*, edited by David Birch. Pinter: New York, 1995.
Lee, Jae Hyun. *Paul's Gospel in Romans: A Discourse Analysis of Rom 1:16—8:39*. LBS 3. Leiden: Brill, 2010.
Levinsohn, Stephen H. *Discourse Features of New Testament Greek: A Coursebook on the Information Structure of New Testament Greek*. 2nd ed. Dallas: SIL International, 2000.
Louw, Johannes P., and Eugene A. Nida. *Greek-English Lexicon of the New Testament Based on Semantic Domains*. 2 vols. 2nd ed. New York: United Bible Societies, 1989.
Mathesius, Vilém. "Functional Linguistics." In *Praguiana: Some Basic and Less Known Aspects of the Prague Linguistic School*, edited by Josef Vachek and Libuše Dušková, 121–42. Linguistic & Literary Studies in Eastern Europe 12. Amsterdam: Benjamins, 1983.
———. "Zur Satzperspektive im modernen Englisch." *Archiv für das Studium der modernen Sprachen und Literaturen* 155 (1929) 200–210.
McKay, K. L. *A New Syntax of the Verb in New Testament Greek: An Aspectual Approach*. SBG 5. New York: Peter Lang, 1994.

Paul, Hermann. *Prinzipien der Sprachgeschichte*. Konzepte der Sprache und Literaturwissenschaft 6. Tübingen: Niemeyer, 1880.

Pickering, Wilbur N. *A Framework for Discourse Analysis*. Dallas: Summer Institute of Linguistics, 1980.

Porter, Stanley E. *Idioms of the Greek New Testament*. 2nd ed. BLG 2. Sheffield: Sheffield Academic, 1994.

———. "Systemic Functional Linguistics and the Greek Language: The Need for Further Modeling." In *Modeling Biblical Language: Selected Papers from the McMaster Divinity College Linguistics Circle*, edited by Stanley E. Porter et al., 9–47. LBS 13. Leiden: Brill, 2016.

———. *Verbal Aspect in the Greek of the New Testament, with Reference to Tense and Mood*. SBG 1. New York: Peter Lang, 1989.

Porter, Stanley E., and Matthew Brook O'Donnell. *Discourse Analysis and the Greek New Testament: Text-Generating Resources*. T&T Clark Library of New Testament Greek 2. London: T. & T. Clark, 2024.

Prince, E. F. "On the Inferencing of Indefinite-This NPs." In *Elements of Discourse Understanding*, edited by Aravind K. Joshi et al., 231–50. Cambridge: Cambridge University Press, 1981.

———. "Toward a Taxonomy of Given-New Information." In *Radical Pragmatics*, edited by Peter Cole, 223–55. New York: Academic, 1981.

Reed, Jeffrey T. "Cohesive Ties in 1 Timothy: In Defense of the Epistle's Unity." *Neot* (1992) 131–47.

———. *A Discourse Analysis of Philippians: Method and Rhetoric in the Debate over Literary Integrity*. JSNTSup 100. Sheffield: Sheffield Academic, 1997.

Reinhart, Tanya. "Pragmatics and Linguistics: An Analysis of Sentence Topics." *Philosophica* 27 (1981) 53–94.

Runge, Steven E. *Discourse Grammar of the Greek New Testament: A Practical Introduction for Teaching and Exegesis*. Peabody, MA: Hendrickson, 2010.

Sgall, Petr, et al. *Topic, Focus and Generative Semantics*. Kronberg im Taunus: Scriptor, 1973.

Tannen, Deborah. "Oral and Literate Strategies in Spoken and Written Narratives." *Language* 58 (1982) 1–21.

9

Cohesive Harmony in Acts 15:1–35

WILLIAM CRAIG PRICE

ACTS 15 OCCUPIES THE physical center of the book and functions as a pivotal chapter for Luke's narrative structure in Acts.[1] Luke features participants from major social groups with divergent ideologies and social statuses in a context of situational conflict. The literary structure of Acts 15 combines narrative, participant speeches, and a letter woven into an account of conflict resolution in the early church. Linguistically, the text offers a significant sample of speech for observing interpersonal interaction (tenor) in Acts 15. Interpersonal participant structure concerns the interaction and relationships between participants in written or spoken text.[2]

---

1. Fitzmyer describes the Jerusalem decision as the "definitive break of the Christian church from its Jewish matrix." He resolves the double attestation issue with Gal 2 by contending that Luke has "sutured" data from two sources to bring two critical decisions together depicting the major turning point in the history of the early church, and this motivated Luke's placing of the story in the physical center-point of the book (see Fitzmyer, *Acts*, 538–40). Witherington states, "It is no exaggeration to say that Acts 15 is the most crucial chapter in the whole book" (*Acts*, 439). Marshall argues, "Luke's account of the discussion regarding the relation of the Gentiles to the law of Moses forms the centre of Acts both structurally and theologically" (*Acts*, 249).

2. The interpersonal metafunction is one of Halliday's three metafunctions in his theory of Systemic Functional Linguistics (SFL). The other two metafunctions are the ideational and textual metafunctions. See the discussion below for basic characteristics of each metafunction. Acts 15 offers an excellent sample of text for analyzing cohesive harmony in the interpersonal metafunction.

Consensus in mainstream scholarship today is that Luke did not have verbatim accounts of the speeches in Acts but faithfully presented his sources' narrative content and speeches.[3] Fitzmyer proposes that Acts 13:1—14:28 is from a Pauline source and that Acts 15:3–33 is from an Antiochene source. Luke then "sutured" these texts with his composition of 15:1–2.[4] Separating Lucan material from Pauline, Antiochian, or Jerusalem sources is challenging. However, the linguistic elements that create cohesive harmony in the discourse are measurable. Acts 15:1–35 offers a large sample of speech text for analyzing cohesive elements related to register. In light of this textual history, this paper investigates aspects of lexical cohesion in Acts 15:1–35 by performing a cohesion analysis of the linguistic features to determine the degree of cohesive harmony of the written text. The paper will also examine paragraph segmentation for two major codices—Codex Sinaiticus and Codex Vaticanus—to determine the extent of cohesion provided by paragraph segmentation using the Acts 15 passage. The combined effect of cohesive harmony with the cohesive features of paragraph segmentation will demonstrate cohesive harmony that results in coherence for the text of Acts 15:1–35.[5]

---

3. The debate over Luke's total invention of the speeches on one extreme (Dibelius) to the use of verbatim speech material on the other (Ramsay) has moderated over eight decades of discussion. Dibelius states, "These speeches, without doubt, are as they stand inventions of the author for they are too short to have been actually given in this form; they are too similar to one another to have come from different persons; and in their content they occasionally reproduce a later standpoint" (*Fresh Approach*, 262). On the other extreme, Ramsay says, "... a dispassionate consideration of the speeches in Acts must convince every reader that they are not composed by the author but taken *verbatim* from other authorities" (*St. Paul*, 27). While the purpose of this study is not to research the range and authorities holding to a given view, these views do impinge upon the question considered. Mainstream academic circles today widely agree that Luke did not have verbatim accounts of the speeches. This is not to say Luke was not faithful in his reporting from his sources. The speeches are Lucan compositions, and they preserve the "essential substance" as Luke relays their details (Keener, *Acts*, 1:258, 309–10). Bruce contends that Luke preserves the accounts from the speeches only in a condensed fashion ("Speeches in Acts," 53).

4. Fitzmyer, *Acts*, 540–41.

5. Ruqaiya Hasan theorizes that the greater the cohesive harmony of a given text, the greater the coherence of that text ("Coherence and Cohesive Harmony," 216).

METHODOLOGY

The notion of linguistic cohesion refers to conveying meaningful content in text, co-text, and context.[6] Halliday and Hasan used SFL to analyze cohesion for English text.[7] Hasan later demonstrated that simple lexical cohesion alone is not enough to determine cohesion in a text, so she proposed her theory of cohesive harmony based on the interaction of lexical cohesive ties within the text.[8] While her notion of cohesive harmony advanced our understanding of cohesion in English text, her method required modification to compute the results for cohesion in ancient Greek.[9] I use Halliday and Hasan's functional system as my primary methodology, but I compute and analyze the data utilizing Lee's modified version of Hasan's formula which is more suited for the morphologically rich text of Greek.[10]

The first task is to isolate the identity chains (IC) to discover the co-referent relationships in the text. Next, I will isolate the similarity chains (SC) that represent the co-classification and co-extension relationships in the text. Tokens represent each lexical item of a given chain and provide an empirical way to calculate these relationships. Hasan classified lexical items that form chains as relevant tokens (RT). The most substantial cohesion occurs when relevant tokens intersect two chains, which Hasan refers to as central tokens (CT). I will identify these central tokens, chart their distribution, and calculate a cohesive harmony index (CHI) percentage. After calculating the chains and tokens, I will examine the paragraph segmentation of Acts 15:1–35 using Porter's composite model for pericope markers.[11] Porter demonstrates cohesion from scribal segmentation in ancient manuscripts. I will examine the segmentation breaks for two early codices containing Acts 15:1–35—Codex Sinaiticus and Codex Vaticanus. Finally, I will compare the segmentation breaks with the data from the chain interactions and offer a composite view of cohesive harmony in the larger discourse of

---

6. Reed, "Cohesiveness of Discourse," 30.
7. Halliday and Hasan, *Cohesion in English*.
8. Hasan, "Coherence and Cohesive Harmony," 184–85.
9. Lee, "Cohesive Harmony Analysis," 92.
10. Lee, "Cohesive Harmony Analysis," 105.
11. Porter, "Pericope Markers."

Acts 15:1–35. The degree of cohesion in text is in direct proportion to the degree of coherency one might expect in a text.[12]

Cohesion and Register: Aspects of Field, Tenor, and Mode

Halliday's functional model of SFL provides the model for conducting the register analysis of Acts 15. The semiotic variables of field, tenor, and mode comprise three dimensions of register that relate to the context of situation and impact a speaker's linguistic choices. Field refers to the events or the "what-ness" of the semiotic act realized by the ideational metafunction.[13] Tenor concerns the "who-ness"[14] of the text within the social relationships in the context of situation realized by the interpersonal metafunction.[15] Mode concerns the "how-ness" of a text realized by the textual metafunction.[16] Mode involves elements of cohesion (how the text "hangs together"), its setting, and informational structure.[17]

Cohesion relates to register through these three metafunctions grammaticalized in field, tenor, and mode. Specifically, cohesion relates to field through the ideational characteristics of semantic domains as they form ties in similarity chains. The interpersonal metafunction (tenor) comprises the identity chains that form cohesiveness in the system of reference.[18] The textual metafunction (corresponding to mode) con-

---

12. Hasan, "Coherence and Cohesive Harmony," 216.

13. Porter, *Letter to the Romans*, 27. Field is the contextual variable that is realized in language by the experiential and logical metafunctions. Important semantic components of the experiential metafunctions, in particular, include semantic domains, transitivity structure, and verbal aspectual patterns.

14. Porter, *Letter to the Romans*, 30.

15. Porter, *Letter to the Romans*, 30–31. See also Porter, "Dialect and Register," 204–5.

16. Porter, *Letter to the Romans*, 34–35. Halliday states that mode "refers to what part the language is playing, what it is that the participants are expecting the language to do for them in that [context of] situation" (in Halliday and Hasan, *Language, Context, and Text*, 12).

17. For additional details on cohesion, see Porter, *Letter to the Romans*, 34–35; "Register," 216–22.

18. Halliday and Hasan's system of reference in English is classified into three types: personal, demonstrative, and comparative. The system of reference in Greek extends also to verbals and in particular finite verbs where person and number are grammaticalized. Since Greek clauses do not require explicit subjects, we did not consider grammatical person in the identity chains. We examined the system of reference with particular reference to pronominals (see Halliday and Hasan, *Cohesion in English*, 31–87).

tributes cohesiveness from the lower rank of clausal elements through the ranks to the larger discourse. Mode contributes to cohesion in discourse through conjunctions in the text. I utilized OpenText.org with its clausal annotations because it provides a ready-made, public source for examining these features of Acts 15:1–35.[19]

Cohesive Harmony: "Two-ness in the Text"

From Halliday and Hasan's original theory of cohesion in *Cohesion in English*, Hasan later revised their theory by introducing the concept of chain formation (identity chains and similarity chains) and reformulated portions of their theory.[20] Hasan proposed the notion of coherence and cohesive harmony where two text elements are "tied" or "hang together." By "hanging together," she means that semantic bonds exist in language as a "resource for meaning."[21] Any category of reference, substitution/ellipsis, lexical element, or conjunction is a potential resource for creating cohesive harmony. Cohesion occurs when any member bonds semantically with another member within the textual environment.[22] This bonding process is central to Hasan's "two-ness" notion. Cohesion as a semantic concept refers to "relations of meaning that exist within the text, and that define it as a text."[23]

Westfall notes that cohesion "involves some element in the text depending upon another element."[24] Cohesion occurs when two text elements bond into a "cohesive tie" through two broad cohesive devices: (1) grammatical cohesive devices and (2) lexical cohesive devices. These two categories of cohesive devices work together in mutual support despite being separate in systemic functionality.[25] These resources bond

---

19. I am indebted to Ji Hoe Kim and his work on cohesion in James. He demonstrates a way forward for mapping identity and similarity chains and their interaction in the Greek text (see "Beyond Paragraph").

20. In her explanation of her expanded and updated theory, Hasan regretted the exclusion of collocation as a category in the new system, but some collocations are subsumed under other categories as antonyms, like "go" and "come" (Hasan's example). For Hasan's revised categories, see Hasan, "Coherence and Cohesive Harmony," 201–3.

21. Hasan, "Coherence and Cohesive Harmony," 181–83.

22. Hasan, "Coherence and Cohesive Harmony," 185.

23. Halliday and Hasan, *Cohesion in English*, 4.

24. Westfall, *Discourse Analysis*, 31.

25. Hasan, "Coherence and Cohesive Harmony," 205. For a helpful chart depicting Hasan's summary of cohesive devices, see Hasan in Halliday and Hasan, *Language*,

semantically to form chains that relate to the system and the text simultaneously. These chains are semantically relevant paradigms that create coherence from a reader's or listener's perspective.

Individual lexical items or members within these chain types are countable, which Hasan refers to as tokens.[26] She identifies two kinds of tokens representing the components that create identity and similarity chains, resulting in textual cohesion. Relevant tokens are subsumed in chains and relate to each other through cohesion and topic development in the text. Peripheral tokens (PT) are not subsumed in chains and are not crucial to the "organization of experiential and textual meanings."[27] Hasan subdivides relevant tokens into central tokens that interact with tokens in other chains. That is, central tokens are relevant in that they are part of one chain *and* interact with another chain. She hypothesizes that the higher the ratio of CT to PT, the more coherent the text is.[28] Thus, central tokens "are directly relevant to the coherent development of the *topic* in the text."[29] Identity chains must contain a minimum of two central tokens each to create chain interaction and count as a chain.[30] The idea of two-ness is central to the notion of cohesion in a text.[31] Lee adds a category called facilitating tokens (FT) that represent lexical items that occur only once in the text but provide additional cohesion for the text.[32] Total tokens (TT) refer to the lexical words, and Token Index (TI) refers to the modified token values to distinguish between token numbers and token values.[33]

Context, and Text, 82.

26. Hasan, "Coherence and Cohesive Harmony," 214.
27. Hasan, "Coherence and Cohesive Harmony," 211.
28. Hasan, "Coherence and Cohesive Harmony," 217–18.
29. Hasan, "Coherence and Cohesive Harmony," 216.
30. Halliday and Hasan, *Language, Context, and Text*, 82.
31. Hasan, "Coherence and Cohesive Harmony," 184, 214, 219.
32. Lee, "Cohesive Harmony Analysis," 89–90.
33. Lee, "Cohesive Harmony Analysis," 88.

ISOLATION OF IDENTITY AND SIMILARITY CHAINS IN ACTS 15:1–35

Identity Chains

The participant structure generates identity chains that relate to the tenor of the text (interpersonal metafunction). Identity chain co-referents are pronominals, demonstrative pronouns, and comparative pronouns.[34] The context of situation gives rise to the interaction of the participants in the discourse. The verses in Acts 15:1–35 contain thirteen identity chains, as summarized in Table 1 below.[35] This semantic bond is realized through pronominal cohesion, simple equivalence, lexical repetition of generic entities, or a combination of grammatical and lexical cohesion.[36] Hasan notes, "The specifics of co-referentiality are situationally—and to that extent text-specifically—determined. In this sense, the identity chain is always textbound."[37] The participants are identified, and all co-referents for each participant are present in the text. The semantic bond of *co-referentiality* holds the resources together in the identity chains. Reed identifies additional cohesive features in Greek that Halliday and Hasan do not include in their research with the English language.

Organic ties include conjunctions, particles, prepositions, specific grammatical structures, and conventionalized lexical items that support the cohesion system in Greek. Particles, conjunctions, and prepositions receive a token value of one. Particles serve as transition markers in text and will be discussed in the segmentation portion at the end of the paper. Table 1 lists the Identity Chains with their RTs, PTs, and FTs. Hasan does not count the definite article in English, but the token counts include the Greek for this study. Lee demonstrated that Hasan's system requires modification with a morphologically rich language such

---

34. Halliday and Hasan include the definite article in English.

35. The data collected for all chain interaction is too large to present in this chapter. The results for the distributions are included for the discussion.

36. Hasan explains that identity chains are comprised of any of the following elements and are realized through: (1) pronominal cohesion as in *a ... girl* or *a ... boy*; (2) simple equivalence as in *sailor ... daddy*; (3) simple lexical repetition, *if* the entities in question are generic; (4) combined operation of grammatical and lexical cohesion as in *a ... girl, a ... boy, children*; and/or (5) through mediation of other intermediate pronominals (see Hasan, "Coherence and Cohesive Harmony," 205).

37. Hasan, "Coherence and Cohesive Harmony," 205.

as Greek.[38] This aspect of ancient Greek necessitates a modification in calculating the results. Each token refers to a lexical item (word) with a value count of one token. I follow Lee's calculation for Greek verbs where the grammatical subject for a finite verb is counted as 0.5, and the verb is also counted as 0.5. Thus, token counts are represented in both chains.[39] If the subject of the verb is stated in the text, then it receives a token of 1 and is included in the token tally. Table 1 below shows the tally for the thirteen identity chains.

IC Chains	Chain Name	Total Number of IC Chains	RT	PT	FT
IC1	Apostles and Elders	23	42		
IC2	Customs	1	2		
IC3	God	20	26		
IC4	James	5	4		
IC5	Judas (Barsabbas) and Silas	6	4.5		
IC6	Holy Spirit	2	8		
IC7	Lord, Jesus, or Christ	7	15.5		
IC8	Men/Mankind	8	10.5		
IC9	Paul & Barnabas	19	32		
IC10	Peter/Simeon	5	7		
IC11	Unspecified Third Party	12	15.5		
IC12	Persons and Places	15	27		
IC13	Moral and Ethical	3	6	1	0
Totals Identity Chains		126 chains	200 RT	1 PT	0 FT

Table 1. Summary of Identity Chains and Token Index Totals

The most significant number of tokens in an identity chain appears in IC1 (Apostles and Elders), the dominant IC for the passage in Acts. The chains IC3 (God) and IC9 (Paul and Barnabas) follow behind IC1

38. Lee, "Cohesive Harmony Analysis," 81–82.

39. See Lee's detailed explanation for modifying this token count in "Cohesive Harmony Analysis," 87–90.

and indicate the large number of co-referents as quantified by their RT calculations. These identity chains indicate the importance of leadership and the rise of Paul as a prominent primary participant in the remainder of the book of Acts. The purpose of the meeting was to decide whether Gentiles must follow the ritual of circumcision and observe the "customs of Moses" to be members of the group. The Unspecified Third Party (IC11) is exophoric in that it relates to unnamed participants in the text.

I separate Divine participants IC3 (God) and IC7 (Lord, Jesus, or Christ) for evaluative purposes, but together they span the entire chapter. Identity chain IC9 (Holy Spirit) spans twenty verses, even though it has only two tokens. This identity chain supports the claim of some commentators that Luke views the Holy Spirit as a dominant participant in the book. Thus, the identity chains demonstrate the prominence of the passage's interpersonal metafunction (tenor).

Similarity Chains

Like an identity chain, a similarity chain must have at least two lexical members. Hasan explains that members of similarity chains are not text-bound but bond semantically by (1) co-classification or (2) co-extension.[40] Substitutional cohesion, elliptical cohesion, or simple lexical repetition are examples of co-classification.[41] The lexical cohesive categories of synonymy, antonymy, hyponymy, and meronymy are all examples of co-extension. Similarity chains must contain at least two central tokens each to create chain interaction and count as a chain.[42] The greater the chain interaction in a text, the greater the cohesive harmony, resulting in greater coherency of the text.

The notion of identity chain refers to the "identity of reference," where every member or co-member of the IC refers to the "same thing or event."[43] On the other hand, the notion of similarity chain is "not

---

40. Hasan, "Coherence and Cohesive Harmony," 206.

41. Westfall, citing Halliday and Hasan notes, "The use of semantic repetition and associations between words is a primary factor in *cohesion*, which is the formal links within a passage or a discourse that make it 'hang together' internally with its immediate co-text" ("Blessed Be the Ties That Bind," 201). While repetitions are counted in this study, associational collocations have not been tabulated here. Hasan excluded them in her study on cohesive harmony and this study follows her methodology.

42. Hasan in Halliday and Hasan, *Language, Context, and Text*, 82.

43. Hasan, "Coherence and Cohesive Harmony," 84. For example, the "girl" and "she" form an identity chain in text.

identity of reference but similarity of reference, so that the referents lie within the same general field of meaning."[44] Louw and Nida's (LN) semantic domain theory helps determine the general field of meaning for every word in the Greek New Testament.[45] I mapped the semantic domains using the LN semantic domain categories.[46] For items listed in more than one domain, I follow O'Donnell's recommendation to disambiguate semantic domains by offering one category that covers the numerous semantic domains.[47] Despite this polysemic drawback of the lexicon, the semantic domain classification system still provides a helpful construct for analyzing the ideational metafunction (field). Table 2 displays the forty-two similarity chains in Acts 15:1–35.

---

44. Halliday and Hasan, *Language, Context, and Text*, 84–85. For example, "walking" and "going" form a similarity chain of meaning in text that might refer to "getting somewhere."

45. Louw and Nida (*Greek-English Lexicon*) provide a functional classification of New Testament lexis by grouping Greek words into semantic domains. The domains allow for examination of general semantic patterns in text. While these domain identifications are helpful, many words occur in several domains and, therefore, require disambiguation. In a previous study, I analyzed the elements of tenor and participant structure in Acts 15 using Porter's systemic network of attitude where he mapped potential realizations of speech functions (see Porter, "Systemic Functional Linguistics," 27). This analysis revealed that declarative statements by second order social participants (+assertive: –interrogative type clauses) characterize most clauses (see Price, "Register Discourse Analysis," 15, 22–23).

46. Porter critiques the use of semantic field theory as follows: First, semantic field theory is not a "theory-neutral framework, but a construct used to understand language." Secondly, one must decide "what the semantic fields are." He proposes deciding which fields "provide for the largest number of meaningful categories" and then organizing them into hierarchies. Thirdly, how does one quantify the relations? Porter contends that componential analysis theory offers help with our attempt to decide quantifiable degrees of similarity or difference between the domains (see Porter, *Studies*, 70–71). He offers several approaches to deal with this challenge. One can either present all the tags for the reader allowing her to select *or* decide which to use based upon the text and context.

47. O'Donnell notes the challenge of Louw and Nida's semantic domain categories where certain words occur in more than one domain. O'Donnell suggests two ways to disambiguate the multidomain issue: (1) include all domains that Louw and Nida offer and allow the user of the corpus to decide which domain is proper for the context; or (2) if one uses a manual annotation process, the annotator must select a domain based upon the text and context for a given, specific domain (see O'Donnell, "Use of Annotated Corpora," 86–87; *Corpus Linguistics*, 154). I have used his second option for purposes of this study. See Pitts for his discussion on the use of semantic domains at the OpenText.org website articles ("Semantic Domain Theory").

SC Chains	Chain Name	Total Number of SC Chains	RT	PT	FT
SC1	All	11	14		
SC2	Communication	37	55		
SC3	Socio-religious Groups	55	86		
SC4	Believe, Consider Decide	10	9		
SC5	Choose, Think	6	5		
SC6	Linear Movement	14	12		
SC7	Degree	2	3		
SC8	Do	4	2.5		
SC9	Duration	9	14		
SC10	Attitudes, Emotions	6	7.5		
SC11	Exchange	3	2		
SC12	Hear	4	2.5		
SC13	Strangled	2	3		
SC14	Restore	4	2.5		
SC15	Required	3	4.5		
SC16	Know: Revealed	4	3		
SC17	Saved	4	5		
SC18	Trouble/Relief	5	10		
SC19	Nature, Class, Example: same	1	2		
SC20	Seek Limit	3	1.5		
SC21	Body Parts	2	2		3
SC22	Physiological State	1	1		1
SC23	Comparison	2	2		
SC24	Case: agent	4	4		
SC25	Relations	70	78		
SC26	Religious Activity	9	10		
SC27	Able, Capable	3	2.5		

SC28	Be, Become	8	7.5		
SC29	Discourse Marker	3	4		
SC30	Association	1	.5		
SC31	Stances: stand	2	1.5		
SC32	Guide: obey	2	3		
SC33	Comparison	2	2		
SC34	Discourse Referential	9	12		
SC35	Psychological Faculties:	3	6		
SC36	Affirm/Negate	1	2		
SC37	First/Kinship	2	3		
SC38	Help	2	1.5		
SC39	Destroy	3	4		
SC40	Construction	2	4		
SC41	Exist in Space	3	3.5		
SC42	Artifacts: idols	3	5		
		Total # of Similarity Chains	Total # of Relevant Tokens	Total PT	Total FT
	Totals for the Similarity Chains	332 SC	404.5	0	4

Table 2. Summary of Similarity Chains and Token Index Totals

Linguistic cohesive ties are componential (meaningful) or organic (transitional). Similarity chain SC25 (Relations) is the tally for organic ties operating in the conjunctive system of Greek particles (e.g., γάρ, ἀλλά, δέ, τέ, καί, etc.), prepositions, grammatical structures, and other lexical items.[48] These organic ties factor into cohesion across the passage, and we expect a significant number of ties in thirty-five verses. We ob-

---

48. See Reed, "Cohesiveness of Discourse," 32–46 for a discussion of these linguistic features as they relate to cohesion in Greek. He maintains that organic cohesion in Greek is valuable for cohesion in Koine Greek. See also, Porter, *Idioms*, 103–14, 304–7, for his thorough treatment of the importance of the Greek article and other connectives that provide cohesion in the Greek text.

serve the componental nature of chains SC3 (Social-Religious Groups) and SC2 (Communication) dominate the number of similarity chains for the passage. These SCs demonstrate the social interaction and communication between the participants in the speeches, the narration, and the letter in the passage and operate in the tenor of the participants. This observation is consistent with what one would expect with a discourse composed of travel narratives and participant speeches. The second grouping of similarity chains is composed of SC6 (Linear Movement), SC1 (All), SC3 (Believe), SC26 (Religious Activity), and SC28 (Become), mark the movements of the travel narrative and the interaction of the participants in the groups (All) and decisions determined by the meeting of the leaders. The chain SC34 (Discourse Referentials) and SC29 (Discourse Markers) come into play in the paragraph segmentation.

Central Tokens and Chain Interaction

For cohesive harmony to occur, Hasan says that the formation of identity and similarity chains alone is insufficient.[49] There must be an "additional source of unity" provided by chain interaction.[50] The elements (tokens) of one similarity chain must interact with elements of another similarity chain to create greater cohesion. Lee's modified method for locating and calculating token indices provides a way to apply Hasan's cohesive harmony theory to ancient Greek texts.[51] There are 106 central tokens in Acts 15:1–35. Table 3 displays this interaction with each chain's verse location and Token Index. Note that several central tokens have multiple chain interactions.

Chains	Verse	TI	Chains	Verse	TI
SC2/IC11	1	1	IC1/SC4	28	1
SC26/SC3	1	2	SC3/SC8	29	1
SC27/SC3	1	2	SC3/SC22	29	1
SC2/SC3	1	1	SC6/IC9	30	3
IC9/SC6	3	3	IC9/SC11	30	1

49. Hasan says, "The degree of chain interaction is in direct correlation with the degree of coherence in a text so that it can be claimed that the greater the cohesive harmony in a text, the greater the text's coherence." See Hasan, "Coherence and Cohesive Harmony," 216.

50. Hasan, "Coherence and Cohesive Harmony," 216.

51. Lee, "Cohesive Harmony Analysis," 87–92.

IC9/SC8	3	1		SC10/SC3	31	1
SC30/IC9	4	1		IC5/SC25/SC10	32	5
SC2/IC9	4	1		SC25/IC5/SC27	32	2
IC3/SC8	4	3		IC5/SC6	33	1
IC11/SC31	5	2		IC9/SC25/SC41	35	5
SC26/SC15	5	2		IC3/SC5	9	2
SC6/IC1	6	2		SC20/IC1	10	1
IC10/SC2	7	2		SC37/IC1 SC36/SC27	10	6
SC3/SC16	7	2		SC3/SC4	11	1
IC3/SC5	7	3		SC1/SC3/SC2	12	4
IC3/SC2	8	4		IC1/SC12	12	1
IC8/SC20	17	3		IC3/SC8	12	3
SC1/SC3/SC20	17	4		IC4/SC2	13	1
IC7/SC2	17	2		SC3/IC8/SC12	13	3
IC4/SC4	19	2		IC10/SC16	14	2
SC2/SC11	21	2		IC3/SC38	14	3
IC11/SC4	22	1		SC2/SC4/SC3	15	3
IC1/SC12	24	1		IC3/SC6	16	1
IC11/SC10	24	2		IC3/SC14	16	1
IC1/SC4	25	2		IC3/SC14	16	1
IC1/SC6	27	1		IC3/SC14	16	1
				Total CTs		106

Table 3. Central Token Interaction between Chains

Calculating Cohesive Harmony

Hasan's calculation formula is straightforward for short English text samples. She divides the TT into the CT. I follow Lee's modified formula for large sections of Greek text (e.g., Acts 15:1–35). His formula works with the unique morphological characteristics of ancient Greek, and it functions well with long passages. Lee calculates the cohesive harmony index (CHI) by calculation using the following formula: $((CT + RT + FT) \div 2TT) \times 100 = CHI$.

For Acts 15:1–35, the TTs are 620. The number of CTs in Table 3 is 106. The combined RT for identity chains and similarity chains is

604.5. There are four FTs and only one PT. The PT is not figured into the formula. The numbers are as follows: $((106 \text{ [CT]} + 604.5 \text{ [RT]} + 4 \text{ [FT]}) \div (2 \times 620)) \times 100 = 57.62$ percent.

This high percentage suggests that Acts 15:1–35 is cohesive text, and we predict that the reader finds the text coherent. Paragraph segmentation is another source of cohesion at higher rank levels. Now that the ICs, SC, and CTs are identified and quantified through the Cohesion Similarity Index, I turn to the second part of my research question: "What is the relationship of the cohesive elements to paragraph segmentation in the text of Acts 15:1–35?"

PARAGRAPH SEGMENTATION OF ACTS 15:1–35 IN CODICES SINAITICUS AND VATICANUS

To answer this question, I will compare the interaction of similarity chains to the segmentation (paragraphs) in two of our earliest codices containing the entire New Testament—Codex Sinaiticus and Codex Vaticanus (hereafter Sinaiticus and Vaticanus). Sinaiticus and Vaticanus are significant exemplars of this purpose for several reasons. First, scholars consider them among the earliest extant manuscripts containing the entire New Testament. Secondly, Porter's study on ancient paragraphing in Sinaiticus provides a comparison of the results of this study by the same scribe.[52] I can examine the cohesion characteristics and segmentation breaks in Sinaiticus and compare them to a different scribal hand with Vaticanus.

To accomplish this task, I first examined digital photographs of each Codex for Acts 15:1–35.[53] Next, I compared the interaction chains described above to the segmentation breaks for Sinaiticus and Vaticanus. To evaluate these segmentations, I used Porter's composite classification of "common features" of ancient paragraphing to label the segmentation

---

52. In his work on ancient paragraphing using selected portions of Romans and Mark, Porter identifies seven characteristics for paragraph segmentation in the ancient world. By selecting Codex Sinaiticus, he was able to view characteristics of paragraphing for narrative and exposition by the same scribal hand. Porter admits that paragraphing in ancient documents is problematic and that more work needs to be conducted in this area ("Pericope Markers," 175–76).

53. I examined digital facsimiles to determine the segmentation for Codex Sinaiticus and Codex Vaticanus using the *Accordance* package of codex manuscripts that accompanies the Center for Textual Studies of New Testament Manuscripts critical textual apparatus for the New Testament.

features.[54] Thirdly, I plotted the segmentation breaks at the appropriate clauses for each codex. Lastly, I overlaid the interaction of similarity chains for Sinaiticus and Vaticanus. The results are charted in Table 4 below.

The scribes of both codices employed different techniques for segmenting the discourse. The scribe of Sinaiticus used *ekthesis* (a slight offset into the left margin) to mark the segmentations (paragraphs),[55] and the scribe of Vaticanus used a *paragraphos* line (a small line in the left side of the text columns) to mark the line where a space indicates the segmentation. Table 4 displays the segmentation results for each codex with the mode and marker identifiers for comparative purposes.

Reference in Codex Sinaiticus	Initial Conjunction / Particle Mode	Paragraph Marker	Reference in Codex Vaticanus	Initial Conjunction / Particle Mode	Paragraph Marker
Acts 15:1–2	καί	Conj/Part[56]	Acts 15:1–4	καί	Conj/Part
Acts 15:3	μὲν οὖν	Conj/Part	Acts 15:5–12	δέ	Conj/Part

54. Porter, "Pericope Markers," 176, 180–82. These features include the following: (1) conjunctions and particles (openings and closings); (2) cohesion and segmentation, participant structure, tense/aspect, lexical and referential chains, thematic structure, etc., which are used to segment units and establish breaks; (3) participants, full reference, pronouns, and anaphoric markers, about which Porter notes that "pronominalizing and anaphora need to be linked to participants and participants to word order and referential distance in order to indicate paragraph structure"; (4) word order and referential distance, where referential distance is the length in sentence numbers between references; (5) topic shifts, meaning that paragraphs are sometimes distinguished by topic shifts that are established by use of words from semantic domains, and usually, the topic is introduced at the first of the paragraph and decreases through the paragraph; (6) theme, which considers that the topic may not be the thematic focus of the paragraph, and so the introduction of theme in narrative involves a thematic participant usually through use of grammaticalized reference in the fronted position and is developed by rhematic material of individual clauses where topicality and thematization are distinct but linked; and (7) literary text types, which are features used to mark beginnings and endings that may vary within a given textual context. They may be distinct between various literary text types such as between narrative and exposition.

55. Textual critics use the term segmentation to refer to the paragraph breaks in manuscripts. I use the terms interchangeably here.

56. The abbreviations "Conj" and "Part" signify Conjunction and Particle, respectively.

Acts 15:4-5	δέ	Conj/Part	Acts 15:13-21	δέ	Conj/Part
Acts 15:6-11	δέ/τέ[57]	Conj/Part	Acts 15:22-23a	τότε	Conj/Part
Acts 15:12	δέ	Conj/Part	Acts 15:24-29	ἐπειδή	Conj/Part
Acts 15:13-23a[58]	δέ	Conj/Part	Acts 15:30-35	μὲν οὖν	Conj/Part
Acts 15:23b[59]	οἱ ἀπόστολοι καί	Participant	Acts 15:36	δέ	Conj/Part
Acts 15:24-29	ἐπειδή	Conj/Part			
Acts 15:30-33	μὲν οὖν	Conj/Part			
Omit verse 34					
Acts 15:35	δέ	Conj/Part			
Acts 15:36-38	δέ	Conj/Part			

Table 4. Summary of Segmentation of Acts 15:1–35 in Sinaiticus and Vaticanus

The two most frequently used segmentation markers for Acts 15:1–35 in both codices are conjunctions and particles.[60] Three SCs tallied in

---

57. The facsimile clearly uses δέ in this segmentation. The τέ is listed in the Alexandrian text of NA28 and UBS5 as a textual variant in P46. The editors chose τέ. I have analyzed the δέ here to remain consistent with the reading in Codex Sinaiticus.

58. Codex Sinaiticus starts the next segmentation at the words οἱ ἀπόστολοι in v. 23b. The words γράψαντες διὰ χειρός αὐτῶν are included in the section before this segmentation. This would be a logical segment for a scribe as the address of the letter written to the Gentiles starts with οἱ ἀπόστολοι καὶ οἱ πρεσβύτεροι.

59. This verse is the beginning of the letter to the Gentiles from the Jerusalem Council. No conjunction occurs in the opening of the letter. This segmentation is clear in the facsimile as *ekthesis* with οἱ ἀπόστολοι καὶ οἱ πρεσβύτεροι as Porter's fourth category of "participants" as a paragraph marking device.

60. Halliday and Hasan call conjunctions organic because they constitute a whole message rather than components. As meaning units they are not dependent upon any

Table 2 are helpful here: SC25 (Relations) has 70 RTs and spans almost every verse in Acts 15:1–35.[61] Three occurrences of SC29 (Discourse Markers) occur in vv. 1, 3, 9. Nine occurrences of SC34 (Discourse Referentials) occur in vv. 2, 6, 9, 10,2 16, 28,2 and 30. The heavy use of conjunctions in Acts 15:1–35 is consistent with Porter's findings in his study using Sinaiticus. The scribe of Sinaiticus uses ten segmentations compared to seven in Vaticanus. The most used conjunction/particle found in each codex is δέ.[62] I utilize Porter's definition of particles and conjunctions for this discussion.[63]

The conjunction δέ is one of the New Testament's most common segmentation markers.[64] As a conjunction, δέ has "adversative or connective or emphatic, or postpositive" uses.[65] Sinaiticus uses δέ in vv. 4, 6, 12, 13 as a connective for moving the discourse along. In the travel portion (v. 4), δέ connects the narrative as the group arrives in Jerusalem. We observe how δέ serves as a connector for the speeches of Peter, Paul

---

other element linguistically (*Language, Context, and Text*, 81).

61. The only verses that do not contain an RT for SC25 are: 14, 18, 24, 26, and 34. The majority of RTs for SC25 are καί.

62. Porter and O'Donnell make several comments regarding ancient Greek conjunctions. First, they constitute a functional system of discourse markers. Secondly, conjunctions are procedural or functional words, not content words. Thirdly, the semantic contribution of conjunctions is minimized by Halliday and Hasan, Schiffrin, Dik, and Stephanie Black while others maximize the semantics of all conjunctions. On this latter view, they are not meaningless (LN provide semantic categories for all conjunctions) and do provide functional guidance. The tendency in New Testament Greek studies is to maximize conjunctions. Fourthly, conjunctions can be weighed and determined to have markedness and prominence by viewing frequency of distribution, semantics, and context of use in heavily marked contexts. That is, they are placed on a cline determined by these categories and weighed for markedness (see Porter and O'Donnell, "Conjunctions," 5–8).

63. Porter (*Idioms*, 204–17) writes, "A particle is a word of set form (i.e., an indeclinable word) used for the purpose of introducing subjective semantic nuances (i.e., nuances of meaning) to a clause or to the relationship between clauses. Conjunctions are a subclass of particles used to join various grammatical units, such as phrases, clauses, and so on."

64. The discussion on δέ is long and complex. One of the best summaries for the discussion of δέ is Stephanie Black's extensive work on conjunctions in the Gospel of Matthew. She summarizes the history of the arguments and presents her findings for the Gospel (see Black, *Sentence Conjunctions*, 143–78). Space limitation does not allow for expansion of the conversation on conjunctives and particles.

65. Porter, *Idioms*, 208. Porter says that δέ rivals καί as the most common sentence conjunction in the New Testament.

and Barnabas, and James in vv. 4, 6, 12. Verse 35 is an adversative contrast between Silas's departure and Paul's and Barnabas's decision to remain in Antioch.

Vaticanus uses δέ in v. 5 as an adversative to segment the Pharisees' protest in v. 4. In v. 13, δέ is a connective for the speech of James. In v. 36, δέ connects the discourse flow between the Antioch visit (vv. 30–35) to the launch of Paul's subsequent travel narrative and his dispute with Barnabas over taking John Mark on the journey (vv. 37–39).

Καί is the most widely used conjunction and particle in the New Testament.[66] Porter says that καί, like δέ, may be connective, adversative, or emphatic.[67] Both Sinaiticus and Vaticanus use καί to link the narrative from ch. 14 to ch. 15. Sinaiticus uses the participants to mark a segmentation at Acts 15:23b. The facsimile clearly shows *ekthesis* with no use of a conjunction. This example fits Porter's "participant reference" classification as a segmentation break.

Both Sinaiticus and Vaticanus use the conjunctive adverb ἐπειδή to mark a segmentation in Acts 15:24. The causal adverb comes at the opening of the letter from "the apostles and elders" to the Gentiles. They expressed the reason or cause for the letter they prepared for delivery to the Gentiles. The conjunction functions causally for this purpose, posing a segmentation break in both codices. Bauer categorizes this conjunction as a "marker of cause or reason" for the letter.[68]

Vaticanus uses the adverb τότε to express segmentation in v. 22. This particle is temporal in meaning and functions to indicate a specific time.[69] This segmentation in Vaticanus functions as a break to initiate the reply to the Council's decision in favor of the Gentiles. Sinaiticus does not segment here.[70] Westfall notes that Luke uses μὲν οὖν throughout Acts to mark narrative, typically introducing a new stage in the discourse.[71] This observation is consistent for both Sinaiticus and

---

66. Porter, *Idioms*, 211. Καί serves as both a conjunction and particle.
67. Porter, *Idioms*, 211.
68. BDAG 360.
69. Porter, *Idioms*, 216.
70. For a different use of τότε, see Black, *Sentence Conjunctions*, 220–53. Black notes that Matthew's use of τότε may well have a Semitic background, but she is hesitant to pull it into the Aramaic Gospel debate. She argues that τότε is used by Matthew differently in the Greek text than for that of Aramaic.
71. Westfall, "Οὖν," 294.

Vaticanus. Sinaiticus uses μὲν οὖν in Acts 15:3 to segment the narrative as the envoys departed Antioch to go to Jerusalem. Both Sinaiticus and Vaticanus use μὲν οὖν in Acts 15:30 to segment the departure of the envoys to deliver the Council's letter to Antioch.

In summation, Luke's use of conjunctives and particles provides strong cohesion throughout the discourse in Acts 15, regardless of which type of segmentation the scribes used. The scribes of Sinaiticus and Vaticanus placed their segmentation breaks at different places for the same discourse material.

INTERACTION OF SIMILARITY CHAINS AND SEGMENTATION

The conclusion drawn from the interaction of the similarity chains is that there is strong cohesion in the early and latter segments of Acts 15:1–35—specifically in vv. 2–12 and vv. 27–34. The inner segments from vv. 13–26 show cohesion through the ties created by identity chains, similarity chains, and conjunctions. Acts 15 is "bookended" by the stronger similarity chain interactions that bind the segments together and provide cohesion and coherence to critical portions of the discourse. Sinaiticus appears to have the most substantial evidence of cohesive ties based on the placement of segmentation breaks in the manuscript, especially where the similarity chain interaction crosses these segmentation breaks.

CONCLUSION

In this study, I identified the chain interaction in Acts 15:1–35 and compared it to the segmentation breaks in Sinaiticus and Vaticanus. First, I isolated the identity chain elements of co-referents and the similarity chain elements of co-classification and co-extension. Next, I identified the central token interaction between the identity and similarity chains to calculate the cohesive harmony for the entire discourse. The cohesive harmony index (CHI) is 57.62 percent. Thirdly, I examined the segmentation breaks by the scribes of Sinaiticus and Vaticanus, making note of the organic conjunctions at the points of segmentation. Fourthly, I compared the interaction chains to the segmentation breaks for Codex Sinaiticus and Codex Vaticanus to observe cohesive relationships across the segmentation breaks.

Throughout the discourse, we observe cohesion from the elements of identity chains, similarity chains, and conjunctions. The stronger cohesion, however, is seen in the discourse where similarity chain interaction occurs where the central tokens interact between two or more chains. For Acts 15:1–35, this cohesion occurs in vv. 1–12 and vv. 27–35. Comparing the similarity chains with the segmentation breaks, Codex Sinaiticus exhibits greater cohesion than Codex Vaticanus for these verses. We base this conclusion upon the similarity chain interactions as they encompass (or cross) the segmentation breaks in the sections. This observation may simply be a factor of the larger number of segmentation breaks in Sinaiticus. Factoring all the observations with the empirical evidence, I conclude that the passage of Acts 15:1–35 contains strong cohesion and I predict that the probability of coherence in the passage is also very high. Further study is warranted to determine if there is a significant relationship between segmentation breaks and the interaction of similarity chains in other Greek manuscripts.

BIBLIOGRAPHY

Black, Stephanie L. *Sentence Conjunctions in the Gospel of Matthew: καί, δέ, τότε, γάρ, οὖν and Asyndeton in Narrative Discourse*. JSNTSup 216; SNTG 9. London: Sheffield Academic, 2002.

Bruce, F. F. "The Speeches in Acts—Thirty Years After." In *Reconciliation and Hope: New Testament Essays on Atonement and Eschatology Presented to L. L. Morris on His 60th Birthday*, edited by Robert Banks, 53–68. Carlisle, UK: Paternoster, 1974.

Dibelius, Martin. *A Fresh Approach to the New Testament and Early Christian Literature*. Westport, CT: Greenwood, 1979.

Fitzmyer, Joseph A. *The Acts of the Apostles: A New Translation with Introduction and Commentary*. AB 31. New Haven: Yale University Press, 2008.

Halliday, M. A. K., and Ruqaiya Hasan. *Cohesion in English*. English Language Series 9. London: Longman, 1976.

———. *Language, Context, and Text: Aspects of Language in a Social-Semiotic Perspective*. 2nd ed. Oxford: Oxford University Press, 1989.

Hasan, Ruqaiya. "Coherence and Cohesive Harmony." In *Understanding Reading Comprehension: Cognition, Language, and the Structure of Prose*, edited by James Flood, 181–219. Newark, DE: International Reading Association, 1984.

Keener, Craig S. *Acts: An Exegetical Commentary*. 4 vols. Grand Rapids: Baker Academic, 2014.

Kim, Ji Hoe. "Beyond the Paragraph: Using Cohesive Harmony for Grouping Paragraphs in James 1 as a Test Case." Paper presented at the Virtual Meeting of the Evangelical Theological Society, November 2020.

Lee, John J. H. "Cohesive Harmony Analysis for Ancient Greek: SelPal I:112 and PMich VIII:491 as a Test Case." *BAGL* 7 (2018) 81–106.

Louw, Johannes P., and Eugene A. Nida. *Greek-English Lexicon of the New Testament Based on Semantic Domains*. 2 vols. 2nd ed. New York: United Bible Societies, 1989.

Marshall, I. Howard. *The Acts of the Apostles*. London: Sheffield Academic, 2003.

O'Donnell, Matthew Brook. *Corpus Linguistics and the Greek of the New Testament*. NTM 6. Sheffield: Sheffield Phoenix, 2005.

———. "The Use of Annotated Corpora for New Testament Discourse Analysis: A Survey of Current Practice and Future Prospects." In *Discourse Analysis and the New Testament: Approaches and Results*, edited by Stanley E. Porter and Jeffrey T. Reed, 71–118. JSNTSup 170. Sheffield: Sheffield Academic, 1999.

Pitts, Andrew. "Semantic Domain Theory: An Introduction to the Use of the Louw-Nida Lexicon in the Opentext.Org Project." *OpenText.org*. No pages. Online: http://opentext.org/resources/articles/a10.html.

Porter, Stanley E. "Dialect and Register in the Greek of the New Testament: Theory." In *Rethinking Contexts, Rereading Texts: Contributions from the Social Sciences to Biblical Interpretation*, edited by M. Daniel Carroll R., 190–208. Sheffield: Sheffield Academic, 2000.

———. *Idioms of the Greek New Testament*. 2nd ed. BLG 2. Sheffield: Sheffield Academic, 1994.

———. *The Letter to the Romans: A Linguistic and Literary Commentary*. NTM 37. Sheffield: Sheffield Phoenix, 2016.

———. "Pericope Markers and the Paragraph: Textual and Linguistic Implications." In *The Impact of Unit Delimitation on Exegesis*, edited by Raymond de Hoop et al., 175–95. Pericope: Scripture as Written and Read in Antiquity 7. Leiden: Brill, 2009.

———. "Register in the Greek of the New Testament: Application with Reference to Mark's Gospel." In *Rethinking Contexts, Rereading Texts: Contributions from the Social Sciences to Biblical Interpretation*, edited by M. Daniel Carroll R., 209–29. Sheffield: Sheffield Academic, 2000.

———. *Studies in the Greek New Testament: Theory and Practice*. SBG 6. New York: Peter Lang, 1996.

———. "Systemic Functional Linguistics and the Greek Language: The Need for Further Modeling." In *Modeling Biblical Language: Selected Papers from the McMaster Divinity College Linguistics Circle*, edited by Stanley E. Porter et al., 9–47. LBS 13. Leiden: Brill, 2016.

Porter, Stanley E., and Matthew Brook O'Donnell. "Conjunctions, Clines and Levels of Discourse." *FN* 20 (2007) 3–14.

Price, William Craig. "Register Discourse Analysis of Acts 15: The Tenor of Participant Social Structure." Paper presented at the Annual Meeting of the Society of Biblical Literature, Boston, MA, November 21, 2017.

Ramsay, W. M. *St. Paul the Traveller and the Roman Citizen*. 15th ed. London: Hodder & Stoughton, 1971.

Reed, Jeffrey T. "The Cohesiveness of Discourse: Towards a Model of Linguistic Criteria for Analyzing New Testament Discourse." In *Discourse Analysis and the New Testament: Approaches and Results*, edited by Stanley E. Porter and Jeffrey T. Reed, 28–46. JSNTSup 170. SNTG 4. Sheffield: Sheffield Academic, 1999.

Westfall, Cynthia Long. "Blessed Be the Ties That Bind: Semantic Domains and Cohesive Chains in Hebrews 1.12.4 and 12.5–8." *JGRChJ* 6 (2009) 199–216.

———. *A Discourse Analysis of the Letter to the Hebrews: The Relationship between Form and Meaning*. LNTS 297. London: T. & T. Clark, 2005.

———. "Οὖν in the New Testament: The Minimal Semantic Contribution of a Discourse Marker." In *The Language and Literature of the New Testament: Essays in Honor of Stanley E. Porter's 60th Birthday*, edited by Lois K. Fuller Dow et al., 218–302. Boston: Brill, 2016.

Witherington, Ben, III. *The Acts of the Apostles: A Socio-Rhetorical Commentary*. Grand Rapids: Eerdmans, 2009.

10

A Proposal for Systemic Functional Linguistics Register Theory as a Septuagint Commentary Writing Tool

JOHN J. H. LEE

INTRODUCTION

In this paper, I will mount a case for the methodological potential and fecundity of register theory for analyzing LXX/OG texts and propose that this theory can serve as a productive tool for writing commentaries for the Greek Old Testament. To demonstrate the viability of this approach I will apply this methodology to the OG text of Jonah 1.

Currently, there are two major English-language commentary series for LXX/OG texts. One is the Society of Biblical Literature Commentary on the Septuagint (henceforth SBLCS) and the other the Brill Septuagint Commentary Series (henceforth SEPT). Just as there is no perfect commentary writing philosophy, both series are not without weaknesses. One of the outstanding frailties of the SBLCS would be that it is too rigidly interlinear. The SBLCS approach is also unhealthily fixated on the sentence-level, and therefore fails to pay due attention to units larger than the sentence. Another weakness of the SBLCS is that it normally places the Greek in a subservient position to the Hebrew without proper justification. While this study argues that the SEPT takes the preferable approach, it is not without room for improvement because it seems that none of the thirteen published volumes takes into consideration modern discourse theories. Lack of discourse-analytical approaches in the SEPT, of course, is not a serious weakness in itself. It is also true that there are some who deal with units larger than the sentence in their biblical studies without having recourse to discourse analysis. However, few would deny that modern discourse theories can advance LXX/OG studies because they are able to provide a comprehensive analytical framework. I therefore argue in the current study that LXX/OG commentary writing may benefit considerably from a type of discourse analysis called register analysis as conceived within a framework of Systemic Functional Linguistics (SFL).

Hence, this paper has been structured as follows: First, I offer a very brief sketch of the status quo of LXX/OG commentary writing in terms of the two competing philosophies of LXX/OG interpretation and commentary publishing (i.e., the SBLCS and the SEPT). In what follows, I discuss SFL register theory as fully as the scope of this paper permits. The penultimate section of the paper applies register theory to the Codex Vaticanus (B) text of Jonah 1 to conduct a register analysis on the Greek text as a test case. I conclude by summarizing my findings and suggesting some ideas for future research.

LXX/OG COMMENTARIES

That most of LXX/OG texts are Greek translations from Hebrew *Vorlagen* creates a substantially different *modus operandi* to write a commentary on the Greek texts. There are currently two major competing English-language approaches to this problem. These two views can conveniently be labeled "text-as-produced" and "text-as-received" (or the "text in its own right") approaches.[1] The former is advocated and defended by the SBLCS and the latter by the SEPT.[2]

The SBLCS is one of the two core projects of the International Organization for Septuagint and Cognate Studies (IOSCS). Its two major projects include the New English Translation of the Septuagint

---

1. Pietersma, "Society of Biblical Literature Commentary," 2.

2. To avoid confusion with the SBLCS, this study uses SEPT to refer to the Brill series (see Hess, "Setting Scholarship Back a Hundred Years?" 63).

(NETS)[3] and the commentary series (SBLCS).[4] The NETS and SBLCS are so closely related that we may speak of them as "two stages of a single interpretive effort."[5]

The most pervasive feature of the SBLCS approach is its strong belief in the *"interlinear paradigm."*[6] It seems to me that what underlies their adherence to the interlinear approach is their low view of Greek; they thus contend that LXX/OG texts, merely being a translation from the Hebrew, can only be properly understood by "mapping the Greek text onto the Hebrew (or Aramaic) source text."[7] To them, therefore, an interlinear framework, in a sense, refers to a "Hebrew-Greek diglot," which they claim is the only viable platform where the relationship of the Greek to its parent can properly be conceptualized.[8] Consequently, in their approach, the Greek text is always in a subservient position to the Hebrew. Pietersma uses strong language to argue for Greek's "inferiority." According to what he asserts, the primary character of LXX/OG texts is its "dependence" on the Hebrew text.[9] Pietersma and Wright also aver that the Hebrew is the *Sitz im Leben* of the Greek Septuagint.[10] It cannot be denied that LXX/OG texts are translated texts from their Hebrew *Vorlagen*. Thus, the interlinear paradigm does have a place and can advance our understanding of LXX/OG texts. Serious students or scholars of the Greek Old Testament, for instance, will surely find the interlinear approach illuminating and helpful in many possible ways. However, this rigid adherence to the interlinear paradigm in LXX/OG commentary writing seems to fail to recognize the fact that few read a translated text in such an interlinear way, comparing and contrasting the translation and the original text. As such, our commentary writing should take this fact into consideration.

What the interlinear approach of the SBLCS necessarily entails is its fixation on the sentence-level. As the SBLCS Prospectus makes clear, the core part of their commentary is produced by the "verse-by-verse"

3. "Electronic Editions."
4. "International Organization."
5. Pietersma, "Society of Biblical Literature Commentary," 2.
6. Pietersma, "New Paradigm," 338 (emphasis original).
7. Pietersma, "Society of Biblical Literature Commentary," 6.
8. Pietersma and Wright, eds., *New English Translation*, xiv.
9. Pietersma, "New English Translation," 179.
10. "General Introduction."

approach.¹¹ This often makes the commentator focus on even smaller units—it normally ends up in interlinear comparisons of the Greek word/phrase to the Hebrew—and, eventually, the reader loses track of the literary "force" of the text, i.e., they lose sight of what is really going on in the text. Again, I am not arguing that there is inherent inferiority in the sentence-level approach. What I take issue with, however, is that such atomistic sentence-level fixation causes the commentator to fail to grasp the role of context in the process of meaning making.¹² As will be clear in the following section, my contention is that an atomistic problem on a lexeme or phrase may be solved by having recourse to the context.

The other approach to LXX/OG commentary writing is represented by the text-as-received view of the Brill Septuagint Commentary Series (SEPT), which appreciates LXX/OG texts "as literary compositions in their own right."¹³ Glenny, for example, commenting on Amos, makes it clear that his analysis is concerned with the Greek text "in its own right and primarily for its own sake, not as a witness to the developing tradition of the Hebrew book of Amos."¹⁴ It thus appears that the SEPT strives to recognize the long-ignored aspect that LXX/OG translators were probably not just mechanically rendering word for word or sentence for sentence; it is plausible enough to think that they tried to understand and appropriate the Hebrew texts before them and studiously undertook to translate them into the best possible Greek knowing that they were translating a certain literary unit that is supposed to make sense and read as beautifully and naturally as possible.¹⁵ It is a mistake, however, to think that the SEPT entirely jettisons Hebrew texts because SEPT commentators do not hesitate to discuss the corresponding Hebrew whenever it deems necessary, because the SEPT does recognize that LXX/OG are, in essence, translations from the Hebrew.¹⁶ When

---

11. "Prospectus." See, e.g., Büchner, "Leuitikon 3.1–17."

12. The notion of context will be discussed in full detail in the following section.

13. Hess, "Setting Scholarship Back a Hundred Years?" 64. The SEPT websites too states that LXX/OG texts were a "set of primary texts used by Jewish and Christian religious communities in the Greco-Roman world" (see "Brill Septuagint Commentary Series").

14. Glenny, *Amos*, 1.

15. Hess, "Setting Scholarship Back a Hundred Years?" 67.

16. One of the numerous examples of this can be seen in Walser, *Jeremiah*, 271.

Hess writes, "the SEPT is more interested in the literary outline and structure of the argument as found in the LXX book than it is concerned how this or that word may have required an understanding of Hebrew to appreciate its full semantic range,"[17] what he means is that the text-as-received approach is concerned about raising awareness to the long-forgotten fact that LXX/OG texts were written as a well-functioning Greek literary unit. It should be highlighted again that the SEPT has nothing against the Hebrew texts.

While the SBLCS uses eclectic editions as its base text, the SEPT is written based on one of the three major codices (i.e., Vaticanus [B], Sinaiticus [א], and Alexandrianus [A]).[18] The primary rationale behind this stance lies in the irrefutable fact that the three main codices are the texts "that actually existed in a particular reading community."[19] Of course, there are challenges involved. For instance, the Old Testament portion of א suffered severely at St. Catherine's Monastery and no more than one-third of the Old Testament portion has survived.[20] Some defects notwithstanding, however, the recognition of the value of diplomatic texts in SEPT is also corroborated by the fact it is beneficial to consider all the para-textual traits of the codices, for example, marginal notes, paragraphing, *nomina sacra*, etc. In the application section that will follow later, I will therefore use the Vaticanus text of Jonah 1.

SEPT commentaries generally follow a similar structure. They first introduce the reader to the text, date of composition, provenance, author, genre, methodology, etc., which is normally followed by Greek texts and translations. The commentary proper is where there is a significant difference from SBLCS commentaries. SEPT commentators never attempt atomistic comments. They normally divide the text into meaningful subunits and comment on those units, e.g., deSilva provides a comprehensive

---

17. Hess, "Setting Scholarship Back a Hundred Years?" 65.

18. See, e.g., deSilva, *4 Maccabees*, 2006 (א); Brayford, *Genesis*, 2007 (A); Littman, *Tobit*, 2008 (א); Bird, *1 Esdras*, 2012 (B); Walser, *Jeremiah*, 2012 (B); Glenny, *Amos*, 2013 (B); Adams, *Baruch and the Epistle of Jeremiah*, 2014 (B).

19. Brayford, *Genesis*, 24.

20. Kenyon, *Text of the Greek Bible*, 47. Its Old Testament portions are housed in three places; forty-three leaves in Leipzig, Germany; fragments of three leaves in St. Petersburg, Russia; 199 leaves in London, UK; and twelve leaves and many fragments in St. Catharine's Monastery. There have been fragments discovered since Kenyon (see, e.g., Sarris, "Discovery").

comment on 4 Macc 9:26–32.[21] In doing so, some SEPT commentaries provide sub-section headings.[22] By contrast, however, SBLCS commentaries seem strictly adherent to their verse-by-verse approach, which normally results in word-by-word or phrase-by-phrase treatment.[23]

In what precedes, I have introduced and compared the two most representative approaches to LXX/OG interpretation and commentary writing. I am convinced that the SEPT approach is a more productive way forward for the reasons I have outlined. However, as I close this section, my nagging question is whether we can push the SEPT approach a bit further toward a full-fledged discourse analysis. As Muraoka rightly observes, LXX/OG texts are "full, running texts," not fragmentary,[24] which I believe champions the need for a more robust framework for text analysis.

In the following chapter, I present Systemic Functional Register Theory as a promising interpretive tool for LXX/OG commentary writing primarily because it helps the commentator secure a better grasp of the context of the text on which he or she is commenting

REGISTER THEORY

This section presents register theory within a SFL framework, which provides the model for which I propose commentaries on LXX/OG texts should be written. I, however, make no attempt to be exhaustive in the treatment of the prodigious theory. One of the primary reasons that I propose SFL as a LXX/OG commentary writing tool is because SFL is keenly attentive to how language functions in its situational context; it helps us model the language-context relationship in a systematic way.[25] It is emphasized within SFL that "language is not realized in the abstract: it is realized as the activity of people in situations."[26] This emphasis of SFL on language and the community (i.e., the people) where language is used shows the comprehensive and holistic nature of SFL.[27] It follows,

---

21. deSilva, *4 Maccabees*, 181–82.
22. See, e.g., Bird, *1 Esdras*, 109.
23. See, e.g., Smith, "God, Judges, Snakes, and Sinners."
24. Muraoka, *Syntax*, xxxvii.
25. Porter, *Letter to the Romans*, 24.
26. Halliday et al., *Linguistic Sciences*, 89.
27. Halliday, IFG4, 20.

therefore, that SFL may serve as a useful tool to treat LXX/OG texts in their entirety.

Hallidayan SFL postulates five theoretical strata in human language. A first is the context stratum. Halliday normally divides it into two, i.e., context of culture and context of situation.[28] A second is the stratum of semantics, and the next is the lexicogrammar stratum. The phonology stratum occupies the fourth stratum, and a fifth is phonetics/graphology stratum:

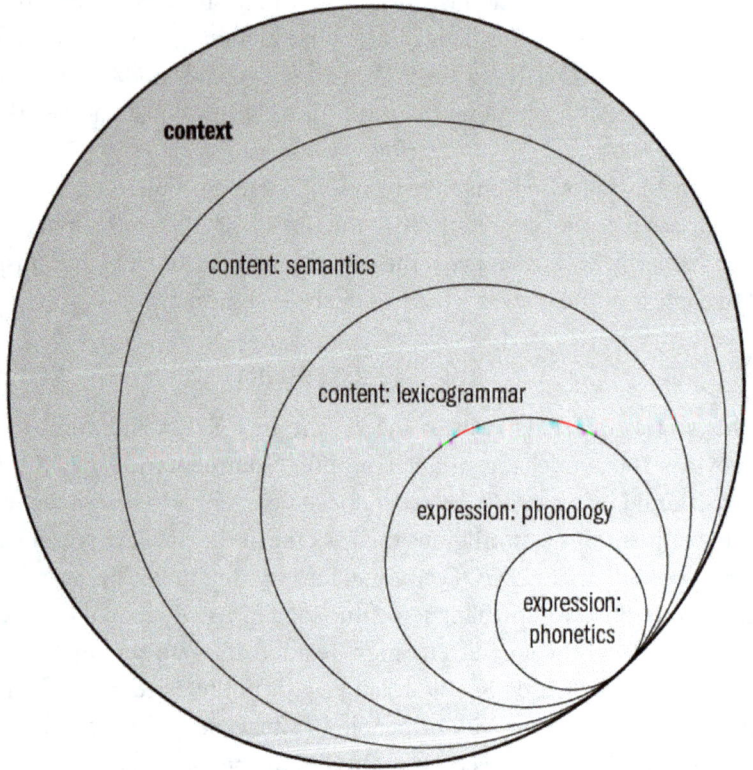

Figure 1. Strata in Human Language[29]

Some may legitimately ask what this notion of stratification will have to offer to LXX/OG commentary writing. Most of all, it helps the commentator begin to recognize that texts only exist in relation to the context. In other words, the idea that human language consists of these

---

28. These two strata are "non-linguistic" (see Porter, *Letter to the Romans*, 24).
29. Halliday, IFG4, 26.

strata urges LXX/OG commentators to remember that no LXX/OG texts exist in a contextual vacuum. However, the fact that LXX/OG texts are mostly translations complicates the matter because it means that we may need to consider multiple contexts—the original writer's own situation and the translator's situation—in using SFL register theory to write a commentary. I deal with this challenge later in more detail.

In SFL, there are two types of context: context of situation and context of culture. The context of culture is the system of which the context of situation is an instance. SFL thus holds that the relationship between the context of culture and the context of situation is that of instantiation. The same principle applies to language. In SFL, language is differentiated into "language as system" and "language as text," and it is posited that "the system of a language is 'instantiated' in the form of a text."[30] For example, in the Hellenistic world of the second to first centuries BC, according to SFL's understanding, we can say that the system of Hellenistic Greek is instantiated in LXX/OG texts. Any given text systematically betrays the traces of the situational context in which the text has been produced. This relationship between the context and the text is that of realization. Below is the diagrammatical display of both the relationship of instantiation and the relationship of realization.

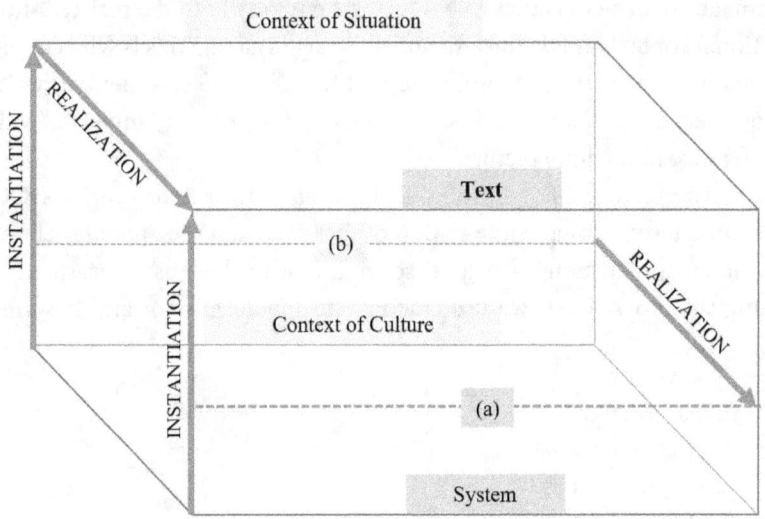

Figure 2. Instantiation and Realization

30. Halliday, IFG4, 27.

The system (see the System pole) refers to the meaning-making potentials of a language while a text (see the Text pole) is any type of "instance" of the underlying system of a language, e.g., coffee-ordering, inauguration speech, etc. In this sense, the text is "around us all the time."[31]

Halliday rightly notes that the instantiation relationship (see INSTANTIATION) is a cline. This means that, between the Text pole and the System pole, there are numerous "intermediate patterns," one of which, for example, is represented by pole (a) in Figure 2.[32] So, pole (a) is a text type if looked at from the Text pole. When we observe (a), we can also see that the situational context pole (b) has been realized in the text type (a). The diagram above therefore embodies one of SFL's tenets that different contextual variables generate different texts. Various text types are thus in fact "all ways of using language in different contexts."[33] In the case of the diagram above, text (a) embodies a way of language usage in context (b). But if pole (a) is viewed from the System pole of the cline of instantiation, it may be considered as a register.[34] Taking this all together, therefore, we can say that register (a) which is associated with the specific context (b) is realized by text type (a). Suffice it to say here that a register is an "instantiation pattern linked with a situation type."[35]

One of the things that the SFL diagram of instantiation and realization above evinces is that LXX/OG texts embody both the realized situational context and the instantiated language system. This is why I argue that SFL may serve as a profitable tool for LXX/OG commentary writing, because it always strives to understand aspects of language "with reference to the total picture."[36]

The final component of SFL that I claim is salutary in LXX/OG commentary writing is the notion of metafunction. The metafunctions of language make up a helpful schema that enables us to grasp what language does. First, we use language to make sense of and describe

---

31. Halliday, IFG4, 27.
32. Halliday, IFG4, 28.
33. Halliday, IFG4, 29.
34. Halliday, IFG4, 29.
35. Halliday, IFG4, 29. The notion of register is discussed in detail in the remainder of the present essay.
36. Halliday, IFG4, 20.

our experience of both the outside and inside worlds.[37] Second, we use language to interact with others, "to establish and maintain relations with them, to influence their behavior,"[38] and to act out "our social relationships."[39] Finally, language also contains a third function that enables us to "organize our messages in ways which indicate how they fit in with the other messages around them and with the wider context in which we are talking or writing."[40]

The first is called the ideational metafunction, whose core function in human language is to "construe" our experience.[41] We use language to understand, interpret, categorize, and remember our experiences of the world. In other words, we use language to transform our experience into meaning.[42] The second is called the interpersonal metafunction, which is primarily concerned about "enacting our personal and social relationships with the other people around us."[43] While the ideational metafunction presents language as "reflection" upon our experience of the world, the interpersonal metafunction shows language as "action" toward and among language users.[44] The final component of the grammar is called the textual metafunction. This meaning component concerns generating texts. It "embodies the specifically text-forming resources of the linguistic system."[45] The textual metafunction is somewhat unique in that it serves as an "enabling or facilitating function."[46] It is a facilitating function because the other two rely on the textual metafunction. The textual metafunction enables the language-user to "build up sequences of discourse," organize the "discursive flow," and create "cohesion and continuity as it moves along."[47]

37. Halliday, IFG4, 30. See also Thompson, *Introducing Functional Grammar*, 28.
38. Thompson, *Introducing Functional Grammar*, 28.
39. Halliday, IFG4, 30.
40. Thompson, *Introducing Functional Grammar*, 28.
41. Halliday, IFG4, 30. SFL, in fact, distinguishes the ideational metafunction into two components. For the experiential metafunction, see "Clause as Representation" (Halliday, IFG4, 211–358), and for the logical metafunction, see "Above the Clause: The Clause Complex" (Halliday, IFG4, 428–556).
42. Halliday, IFG4, 30.
43. Halliday, IFG4, 30. See "Clause as Exchange" (Halliday, IFG4, 134–210).
44. Halliday, IFG4, 30.
45. Halliday, *Language as Social Semiotic*, 133.
46. Halliday, IFG4, 30.
47. Halliday, IFG4, 31.

Systemic-functional register theory is a "form of discourse analysis"[48] and it can be a comprehensive text-analytical tool because it aims to hold both the text and the context together. Register analysis includes both the text and the context because it is convinced that there is a systematic connection between the two. This keen attention to the "reciprocal character" of language (text) and environment (context) is what I think makes systemic-functional register theory a promising tool for LXX/OG commentary writing. In other words, register analysis not only investigates the "textual evidence" but also attempts to recover the "original context of situation."[49] In what follows, therefore, I delineate the notion of register with special attention to its locus and function in relation to context and text.

Context

First, the context of culture refers to a set of "broad cultural features" that affects language use.[50] It is thus the environment of the language system.[51] As insuperable as the task may seem, SFL, however, does not dismiss the discussion of context of culture. Second, the context of situation is not only an instance within the context of culture but also an environment itself "in which a text is embedded."[52] Biber extends the definition of the context of situation to say it refers to the "circumstances of text production and reception."[53]

SFL uses three parameters to describe a context of situation: field, tenor, and mode. The field of discourse refers to "what is going on" in the language event.[54] Porter describes this concept by labeling it as "the 'what-ness' of the semiotic act."[55] Systemic-functional register theory claims that any language has the ideational metafunction and that the field of discourse of the context of situation activates the language's

---

48. Porter, *Letter to the Romans*, 24.
49. Porter, "Register," 210.
50. Porter, *Linguistic Analysis*, 125.
51. Halliday, IFG1, xxxii.
52. Halliday and Hasan, *Cohesion in English*, 21. Halliday too defines it as the environment of the text (see Halliday, IFG1, xxxii).
53. Biber, "Register and Discourse Analysis," 191.
54. Halliday et al., *Linguistic Sciences*, 90.
55. Porter, *Letter to the Romans*, 27.

ideational metafunction.[56] The tenor of discourse pertains to the "who-ness" of the language event,[57] and according to SFL, this "who-ness" of the situational context is reflected in the language of the given text.[58] It is the tenor of discourse that activates the interpersonal metafunction of language. The mode of discourse is concerned about "the 'how-ness' of a text."[59] The mode of discourse can also be described as the "shape" of the language of the discourse, or the "medium" of discourse. Put simply, the mode of discourse concerns answering this question: What kind of shape (i.e., mode) of the language is being required within the given field and tenor of discourse in the given context of situation? The mode of discourse, too, like the textual metafunction, is a facilitating component on which the field and tenor rely to move the language event forward. This is why Porter writes, "the mode of discourse is the linguistic or language-in-use means by which the field and tenor become a text."[60]

Register theory thus enables the LXX/OG commentator to address all the related communicative dimensions of the given text. In other words, register theory is a promising means by which the commentator could heed the text-external situation that would have engendered such a translated text. In the following section, I discuss the notion of register and show how it functions between context and text.

Register and Text

The simplest definition of register would be that a register is a certain kind of language variety in a certain kind of situation. Drawing from Halliday's most recent work, the register can be defined as "ways of using language in different contexts."[61] One of the most noteworthy characters of register, however, is that a register is a "semantic configuration."[62] To put it more precisely, a register is a clustering of semantic resources in a certain environment. When the semantic resources are generated to form a register, they are clustered in the register not randomly but sys-

---

56. Porter, *Letter to the Romans*, 27.
57. Porter, *Letter to the Romans*, 30.
58. Porter, *Letter to the Romans*, 30.
59. Porter, *Letter to the Romans*, 34.
60. Porter, *Letter to the Romans*, 34.
61. Halliday, IFG4, 29.
62. Halliday and Hasan, *Language, Context, and Text*, 39.

tematically, i.e., "according to situation type."⁶³ So it should be kept in mind that a register does not exist in a vacuum or as a standalone entity but is always connected to a particular situation type.

Register theory, however, does not claim that the given situation directly dictates the language usage;⁶⁴ instead, the theory posits that the environment summons a certain register that will then place "constraints on that usage."⁶⁵ Then, because of these constraints, there arise language varieties in the given situation. This is what Halliday et al. mean when they write, "when we observe language activity in the various contexts in which it takes place, we find differences in the type of language selected as appropriate to different types of situation."⁶⁶ How then would register be positioned in relation to the given situation type? Systemic-functional register theory proposes the three situational components—i.e., field, tenor, mode—as well as the central semantic components that form the register. We can then say the situational components "correlate" with the components of the register.⁶⁷

The register-text relationship is that of governing. When a register is called upon within a specific situation type, it means that the field, tenor, and mode of discourse of the given situation are invoking, respectively, the ideational, interpersonal, and textual metafunctions of the language. These semantic components clustered in the register according to the corresponding contextual parameters are then expressed in a form of text. We thus can say that the formal expression that we see in the text is "governed" by the semantic components. Based on this, we can argue, ultimately, that a specific situation type results in certain "linguistic features."⁶⁸ In other words, we can find the traces of the context of situation by examining the linguistic features of the text, because any given text is governed by the register that is correlated to a specific situation; the linguistic features that we observe in the text are therefore

---

63. Halliday, *Language as Social Semiotic*, 68. See also Halliday, *Learning How to Mean*, 126.

64. Porter, *Letter to the Romans*, 27.

65. Porter, *Letter to the Romans*, 27.

66. Halliday et al., *Linguistic Sciences*, 87.

67. Porter, "Dialect and Register," 199–200. Halliday et al., however, say the register can be best defined identified as the "product" of the situational components (see Halliday at al., *Linguistic Sciences*, 93).

68. Porter, "Register," 209.

the "formal properties" of the register.⁶⁹ In this sense, the register is the fountain of water from which the rivulet of the text flows.

However, as I have previously mentioned, most of LXX/OG texts are translations, which implies that we are dealing with multiple layers of situational contexts and registers. Hatim and Mason rightly observe the unique place of translators; the translator is a "special kind of text user" because he or she is both the reader (receiver) and the author (producer) at the same time.⁷⁰ The translator of OG Jonah, therefore, was both the reader of the Hebrew *Vorlage* and the author of OG Jonah texts. I thus propose that we take into consideration the following elements. First, we know that the translator read the Hebrew *Vorlage*. Secondly, the translator must have tried to make sense of his Hebrew Jonah. In a way, we can say that the translator tried—albeit unconsciously—to identify the Hebrew text's register because, according to Gregory, this normally is the preliminary process in translation.⁷¹ As a result, the translator was aware of the "register membership" of Hebrew Jonah.⁷² Thirdly, we know the translator himself was an author because he was generating a disparate text in Hellenistic Greek. So, we should also consider the translator's register that was governing the formation of OG Jonah. It thus follows that an OG Jonah commentary should at least aim, based on the textual data, to establish the register that had been identified by the translator and the register that was formed by the translator's own situation to govern the production of OG texts. One more layer of complication that should be reckoned with is the literary nature of OG Jonah; it is a narrative text that contains multiple situation types. To be a rigorous analysis, this phenomenon of narrative-internal fluctuations of register should also be addressed.⁷³

Therefore, a comprehensive description of the register of the given text should include these three aspects, and this should be a significant goal of LXX/OG commentary writing. Register theory is of course not a cure-all solution. But I agree with Porter that systemic-functional register analysis has much to offer to biblical studies.⁷⁴ In the following

---

69. Halliday et al., *Linguistic Sciences*, 90.
70. Hatim and Mason, *Discourse*, 33.
71. Gregory, "Perspectives," 466.
72. Hatim and Mason, *Discourse*, 55.
73. Halliday et al., *Linguistic Sciences*, 94.
74. Porter, *Linguistic Analysis*, 124–27.

chapter, I apply register theory to interpret the OG text of Jonah 1 and propose an alternative way of LXX/OG commentary writing.

JONAH 1: REGISTER ANALYSIS

This section is a sample register analysis of OG Jonah 1 based on the Old Greek text in Codex Vaticanus (B). The reader should note that our final goal of register analysis as a commentary writing tool is to describe the register of the OG text in terms of three layers: the register that the translator identified concerning his Hebrew *Vorlage*; the register that was formed by the translator's own situation to govern the production of the OG text; text-internal or sub-registers within the given narrative. It should perhaps be worth mentioning here that this chapter by no means purports to be exhaustive. Rather, the goal of the following analysis is to give the reader a basic idea of what an analysis of OG Jonah 1 would look like if systemic-functional register theory is applied. Due to the limited space of the paper, however, the present analysis does not discuss the mode element of discourse. The discussion of the field and tenor, however, will satisfactorily show both how a register analysis is done and how the contexts in which the target text was generated and read can be established and described.

Field of Discourse and Ideational Metafunction

A look at the participants in the text is a good starting point for describing the field of discourse in register analysis.[75] The text-internal participants—i.e., the participants that are linguistically observed in the text—include the Lord God (κύριος), Jonah (Ἰωνᾶς), and the people on the boat headed to Tarshish.[76] This observation, albeit cursory, should help the reader draw a preliminary picture regarding what this narrative pertains to; that is, the field of discourse of the text-internal situation includes an event where God, Jonah, and the people on the boat act toward and upon one another. We can also think of text-external participants. By text-external participants, I mean the participants who may have been involved in text production and reception. In this sense, both the OG translator of Jonah and his possible readers may be counted

---

75. Porter, *Letter to the Romans*, 31.

76. Note that this participant group of "people on the boat" subsume within it the sailors (οἱ ναυτικοί, v. 5) and the captain (ὁ πρωρεύς, v. 6) as well.

as the external participants of our text. While neither the translator nor the readers has been explicitly reflected in the text, the tenor concerning them is textually expressed, which will be dealt with in the next section.

Studying the lexical patterns too should help.[77] Jonah 1 in Codex Vaticanus has a total of 396 words.[78] Among these 396 words, the five most frequent lexemes are κύριος, θάλασσα, Ἰωνᾶς, μέγας, and λέγω. This observation may enable us to infer that the field of discourse of the text-internal situation connected to our narrative is concerned with the following: first, God and Jonah are the main actors in the situation; second, the narrative pertains to an event, attribute, or thing whose scale is huge (μέγας); third, the place of the event is the sea (θάλασσα); fourth, the narrative moves primarily by means of dialogic exchanges (λέγω).

It is worth noting that, regarding the register that was formed by the translator's own situation to govern the production of OG Jonah 1, we are unable to uncover much. It should also be noted that the translator's own register may have been influenced by his own understanding of the original register that had generated the Hebrew *Vorlage*. Since the five most frequent lexemes may be an indication of the traces in the text that point to the translator's own register, suffice it to say regarding the translator's contextual situation that he chose in his situation to use the five lexemes (κύριος, θάλασσα, Ἰωνᾶς, μέγας, and λέγω) with a relatively high frequency in his Greek translation.

Examining the semantic domains, too, is a critical tool of ideational metafunction analysis in register theory, because semantic domain theory is concerned about "how the senses of lexemes form meaningful clusters."[79] Following the domain number in Louw and Nida's lexicon, The semantic domains most represented by of the seventeen most frequently used words are "Supernatural Beings and Powers" (domain 12);[80] "Be, Become, Exist, Happen" (domain 13);[81] and "Artifacts" (domain 6).[82] Domains 12 and 13 are worth a further explanation because their

---

77. Porter, *Letter to the Romans*, 28.

78. Note that the Rahlfs-Hanhart edition's text of Jonah 1 has a total of 404 words because they include τίνος ἕνεκεν ἡ κακία αὕτη ἐστὶν ἐν ἡμῖν in v. 8 (see Rahlfs and Hanhart, *Septuaginta*, 526). But this clause is omitted in B.

79. Porter, *Letter to the Romans*, 28.

80. Louw and Nida, *Greek–English Lexicon*, 2:135.

81. Louw and Nida, *Greek–English Lexicon*, 2:148.

82. Louw and Nida, *Greek–English Lexicon*, 2:52.

frequency indicate the divine act described in the text. As is seen in, KC ἐξήγειρε ΠΝΑ ἐπὶ τὴν θάλασσαν "the Lord aroused a wind on the sea" (v. 4)[83], KC (LN 12) performs a divine and supernatural act of arousing a wind, ἐξήγειρε (LN 13). So, based on the information retrieved from the semantic domain pattern, we can infer one more component of the field of discourse of the text-internal context of situation of Jonah 1: that God (Supernatural being; domain 12) is performing a mighty act (domain 13).

Register theory also holds that the field of discourse of the situational context can be uncovered by examining the grammatical patterns of the text. In the simplest sense, studying grammatical patterns means attempting to find out "who does what to whom and how."[84] We can examine this transitivity in Jonah 1 by investigating the causality, agency, and aspectuality in the text.[85] Causality can be accounted for by studying the voice-forms of the verbal units. In our text, the active voice-form is predominant; among the sixty-eight finite verbs in the text, the active voice-form occupies 79 percent. This is an indication that in our text direct causality is prevalent. Next, agency is a notion that concerns the "level of participatory involvement in the event."[86] My analysis yields the following as the active agents in the text: first, Jonah is the active agent (i.e., actor of twenty processes; the people in the boat are the Actor of twenty-one processes; God is the Actor of five predicates; it is interesting that the sea is also given as the Actor of five predicates. This result looks akin to the findings of the lexical patterns study that I conducted above. By studying aspectuality, we can see the prominence structure of the text. My study has limited its scope to the finite verbs in the indicative mood-forms. Not surprisingly, our narrative text is teeming with the aorist tense-form, which is a proto-typical pattern of narrative texts. The aspectual analysis shows there are some salient places in the text that deserve our attention. For instance, in v. 4, the danger that the boat is facing is foregrounded by the imperfect tense-form (ἐκινδύνευε) against the backdrop of what God had done (ἐξήγειρεν, aorist tense-form). We could cautiously infer that the translator's understanding of the origi-

---

83. The Rahlfs-Hanhart text has κύριος ἐξήγειρεν πνεῦμα εἰς τὴν θάλασσαν (see Rahlfs and Hanhart, *Septuaginta*, 526).

84. Martin-Asensio, *Transitivity-Based Foregrounding*, 162.

85. Porter, *Letter to the Romans*, 29–30.

86. Porter, *Letter to the Romans*, 29.

nal register was that there had been the necessity to stress the relative salience of the "danger" that the boat had to face. This recognition then reflected one portion of the field of the translator's own situation, that is, the translator may have felt it was necessary to elevate its prominence for the readers of his translated text. There is an overwhelmingly turbulent area in the text (vv. 11–14) for there are numerous aspectual turns. The sea was coming (or becoming) (ἐπορεύετο, imperfect, v. 11), and finally, Jonah spoke (εἶπεν, aorist, v. 12). His speech shows a clear indication of prominence by using the perfect tense-form: ἔγνωκα ἐγώ "I now know myself" (v. 12); Jonah is at last in a state of realizing what is going on. But v. 13 shows the people's desperation to solve the problem without sacrificing Jonah; this desperation is well captured in the four consecutive uses of the imperfect tense-form: παρεβιάζοντο ("they were exerting themselves"), οὐκ ἠδύναντο ("they were not being able"), ἐπορεύετο ("the sea was coming [becoming]"), and ἐξηγείρετο ("the sea was stirring up"). And finally, in the deepest fear and despair, realizing that there is no other way, they cry out to God, completely overwhelmed by his might and power (πεποίηκας, perfect tense-form, v. 14). The aspectual fluctuations in vv. 11–14 may give us a clue to the understanding of the field of discourse of the translator's situation because he could have chosen the present tense-form if his aim was simply to render the corresponding Hebrew ידע. We could posit that the translator was convinced of the need to stress Jonah's realization, which in turn prompted him to express the verb in the stative aspect.

I have so far briefly discussed the field of discourse of the situations connected to OG Jonah 1. I will now move on to discuss the tenor of discourse in the next section

Tenor of Discourse and Interpersonal Metafunction

We can attempt to track the tenor of discourse first by closely observing the participants. The best step would be to study the fully lexicalized participants for social roles the realize.[87] The most significant and frequent participant who is fully lexicalized is κύριος (vv. 1, 3, 4, 6 [θεός], 9 [θεός], 10, 14, 16). Ἰωνᾶς, of course, is the second most frequently lexicalized participant in our text (vv. 1, 3, 5, 7, 12, 15). Although the people in the boat are expressed in a full lexeme (οἱ ἄνδρες, vv. 10, 13, 16), the text

---

87. Porter, *Letter to the Romans*, 31.

shows that there are two sub-groups of οἱ ἄνδρες: the sailors (οἱ ναυτικοί, v. 5) and the captain (ὁ πρωρεύς, v. 6). This observation of the fully lexicalized participants evinces the "who-ness" of the given text.[88] Again, the reader should note that the list of the fully lexicalized participants is not radically different from my previous study of participants. And the reader is expected to be attentive regarding how these participants' relationships unfold in the narrative.

It is perhaps helpful to direct our attention to the fully lexicalized participants which are followed by a form of elaboration (e.g., Παῦλος ἀπόστολος Χριστοῦ Ἰησοῦ, "Paul, an apostle of Christ Jesus" [Eph 1:1]), because, as Porter says, such a construction establishes a certain tenor.[89] What merits further discussion, then, is κύριος θεός in v. 9 where the word group τὸν κύριον θεόν is elaborated by the following word group τοῦ οὐρανοῦ. This is Jonah's own description of the Lord God, which indicates the tenor between him and God; Jonah elaboratively delineates κύριος θεός, which establishes the tenor. The Lord God is of the heaven, but Jonah himself is not. This tenor is even more solidified by another elaboration, the relative clause ὃς ἐποίησε τὴν θάλασσαν καὶ τὴν ξηράν, "who made the sea and the dry land" (v. 9).

It is also necessary to examine the participants who are expressed through pronouns because we indeed use grammatical person to indicate "a relationship among participants."[90] One of the most notable features is that God (κύριος or θεός) is never expressed via the third-person pronoun in the text. When God needs to be in the third-person, he is given full lexical specification, e.g., ΚΣ ἐξήγειρεν ΠΝΑ (v. 4). The participant that is most frequently expressed through the first- and second-person pronouns is Jonah. He refers to himself using the first-person ἐγώ twice in v. 9 to stress to the people that he himself is the one who has to reckon with the Lord God who is bringing this massive storm. It is noteworthy that in v. 12 the high frequency of the first-person pronouns (με 3x; ἐγώ 1x) is a device to bring the reader's attention to the centrality of Jonah as the primary cause of this calamity. Also, the fact that Jonah and the people on the boat address each other using the second-person pronoun (σύ, vv. 6, 8, 11, 12) is a clear indication of the tenor of this

---

88. Porter, *Letter to the Romans*, 30.
89. Porter, *Letter to the Romans*, 32.
90. Porter, *Letter to the Romans*, 32.

text-internal relationship between Jonah and the people that there is no sign of hierarchy.

Another crucial component of interpersonal metafunction analysis is attitudinal semantics. I have used the twelve clause types suggested by Porter based on the "attitudinal system of the Greek lexicogrammar."[91] The overwhelmingly predominant clause type in OG Jonah 1 is the declarative statement (+assertive and -interrogative). Every verse grammaticalizes clauses of this type. While this aligns well with the fact that the given text is a narrative, it may also reveal the tenor of discourse of the translator's own situational context. The translator predominantly uses declarative statements ([+assertive]) in his text, which, I think, shows something about the relationship between the translator and his readers. Studying the structure of the commands in the text shows an interesting pattern to note in the tenor among the text-internal participants. First, God only commands and none commands him. Second, Jonah and the others on the boat can command one another (vv. 6, 8, 12). As for questions, I observe that the people use τ-questions (+assertive; +interrogative; +elemental, vv. 8, 10, 11) when they ask Jonah a question.[92]

In this section, I have discussed the tenor of discourse as to the contextual situations related to our text. I should admit that this section has not been able to reveal much about the text-external participants' tenor. I, however, have demonstrated that register analysis is a helpful tool for analyzing who are involved and what their relationships are like in the given text.

CONCLUSION

I began the present study by introducing and comparing the two approaches to LXX/OG commentary writing and argued that the literary approach of the SEPT is a preferable method. I then proposed systemic functional register theory to supplement the SEPT, and I laid out the core components of SFL and register analysis. The analysis section of the current study then applied register theory to the text of OG Jonah 1 and attempted to explain the text with keen attention to the relevant registers and situational contexts in terms of the field and tenor of discourse. Register theory cannot of course solve all the problems. But this study

---

91. Porter, "Systemic Functional Linguistics," 27–28.
92. Porter, "Systemic Functional Linguistics," 28.

has demonstrated that it may be a helpful tool for LXX/OG interpretation and commentary writing by applying the framework to OG Jonah 1 to find several valuable points with respect to the context of situation of the text.

BIBLIOGRAPHY

Adams, Sean A. *Baruch and the Epistle of Jeremiah: A Commentary Based on the Texts in Codex Vaticanus*. Septuagint Commentary Series. Leiden: Brill, 2014.

Biber, Douglas. "Register and Discourse Analysis." In *The Routledge Handbook of Discourse Analysis*, edited by James Paul Gee and Michael Handford, 191–208. New York: Routledge, 2012.

Bird, Michael F. *1 Esdras: Introduction and Commentary on the Greek Text in Codex Vaticanus*. Septuagint Commentary Series. Leiden: Brill, 2012.

Brayford, Susan. *Genesis*. Septuagint Commentary Series. Leiden: Brill, 2007.

"Brill Septuagint Commentary Series." *Brill*. No pages. Online: https://brill.com/view/serial/SEPT.

Büchner, Dirk. "Leuitikon 3.1–17: The Sacrifice of Deliverance." In *The SBL Commentary on the Septuagint: An Introduction*, edited by Dirk Büchner, 95–122. SCS 67. Atlanta: SBL, 2017.

deSilva, David A. *4 Maccabees: Introduction and Commentary on the Greek Text in Codex Sinaiticus*. Septuagint Commentary Series. Leiden: Brill, 2006

"Electronic Editions of NETS." *New English Translation of the Septuagint*. No pages. Online: http://ccat.sas.upenn.edu/nets/edition.

"General Introduction: To the Reader of NETS." *New English Translation of the Septuagint*. No pages. Online: http://ccat.sas.upenn.edu/nets/intro/text.html.

Glenny, W. Edward. *Amos: A Commentary Based on Amos in Codex Vaticanus*. Septuagint Commentary Series. Leiden: Brill, 2013.

Gregory, M. J. "Perspectives on Translation from the Firthian Tradition." *Meta* 25 (1980) 455–66.

Halliday, M. A. K. *Halliday's Introduction to Functional Grammar*. Revised by Christian M. I. M. Matthiessen. 4th ed. London: Routledge, 2014. (IFG4)

———. *An Introduction to Functional Grammar*. London: Arnold, 1985. (IFG1)

———. *Language as Social Semiotic: The Social Interpretation of Language and Meaning*. London: Arnold, 1978.

———. *Learning How to Mean: Explorations in the Development of Language*. London: Arnold, 1975.

Halliday, M. A. K., et al. *The Linguistic Sciences and Language Teaching*. Longman Linguistics Library. London: Longmans, 1964.

Halliday, M. A. K., and Ruqaiya Hasan. *Cohesion in English*. English Language Series 9. London: Longman, 1976.

———. *Language, Context, and Text: Aspects of Language in a Social-Semiotic Perspective*. 2nd ed. Oxford: Oxford University Press, 1989.

Hatim, B., and I. Mason. *Discourse and the Translator*. Language in Social Life Series 2. London: Longman, 1990.

Hess, Richard S. "Setting Scholarship Back a Hundred Years? Method in the Septuagint Commentary Series." In *The Language and Literature of the New Testament: Essays* in Honor of Stanley E. Porter's 60th Birthday, edited by Lois K. Dow et al., 63–68. Leiden: Brill, 2017.

"The International Organization for Septuagint and Cognate Studies." *The International Organization for Septuagint and Cognate Studies*. No pages. Online: http://ccat.sas.upenn.edu/ioscs/commentary.

Kenyon, Frederick G. *The Text of the Greek Bible: A Student's Handbook*. 2nd ed. London: Gerald Duckworth, 1949.

Littman, Robert J. *Tobit: The Book of Tobit in Codex Sinaiticus*. Septuagint Commentary Series. Leiden: Brill, 2008.

Louw, Johannes P., and Eugene A. Nida. *Greek–English Lexicon of the New Testament Based on Semantic Domains*. 2 vols. 2nd ed. New York: United Bible Societies, 1989.

Martín-Asensio, Gustavo. *Transitivity-Based Foregrounding in the Acts of the Apostles: A Functional-Grammatical Approach to the Lukan Perspective*. JSNTSup 202. SNTG 8. Sheffield: Sheffield Academic, 2000.

Muraoka, Takamitsu. *A Syntax of Septuagint Greek*. Leuven: Peeters, 2016.

Pietersma, Albert. "A New English Translation of the Septuagint." In *LXX: IX Congress of the International Organization for Septuagint and Cognate Studies—Cambridge 1995*, edited by Bernard A. Taylor, 177–87. SCS 45. Atlanta: Scholars, 1995.

———. "A New Paradigm for Addressing Old Questions: The Relevance of the Interlinear Model for the Study of the Septuagint." In *Bible and Computer: The Stellenbosch AIBI-6 Conference*. Proceedings of the Association Internationale Bible et Informatique "From Alpha to Byte," edited by Johann Cook, 17–21. Leiden: Brill, 2002.

———. "The Society of Biblical Literature Commentary on the Septuagint: Basic Principles." In *The SBL Commentary on the Septuagint: An Introduction*, edited by Dirk Büchner, 1–16. SCS 67. Atlanta: SBL, 2017.

Pietersma, Albert, and Benjamin G. Wright, eds. *A New English Translation of the Septuagint: And the Other Greek Translations Traditionally Included under that Title*. Oxford: Oxford University Press, 2007.

Porter, Stanley E. "Dialect and Register in the Greek of the New Testament: Theory." In *Rethinking Contexts, Rereading Texts: Contributions from the Social Sciences to Biblical Interpretation*, edited by M. Daniel Carroll R., 190–208. Sheffield: Sheffield Academic, 2000.

———. *The Letter to the Romans: A Linguistic and Literary Commentary*. NTM 37. Sheffield: Sheffield Phoenix, 2016.

———. *Linguistic Analysis of the Greek New Testament: Studies in Tools, Methods, and Practice*. Grand Rapids: Baker Academic, 2015.

———. "Register in the Greek of the New Testament: Application with Reference to Mark's Gospel." In *Rethinking Contexts, Rereading Texts: Contributions from the Social Sciences to Biblical Interpretation*, edited by M. Daniel Carroll R., 209–29. Sheffield: Sheffield Academic, 2000.

———. "Systemic Functional Linguistics and the Greek Language: The Need for Further Modeling." In *Modeling Biblical Language: Selected Papers from the McMaster Divinity College Linguistics Circle*, edited by Stanley E. Porter et al., 9–47. LBS 13. Leiden: Brill, 2016.

"A Prospectus for A COMMENTARY ON THE SEPTUAGINT." *The International Organization for Septuagint and Cognate Studies*. No pages. Online: http://ccat.sas.upenn.edu/ioscs/commentary/prospectus.html.

Rahlfs, Alfred, and Robert Hanhart. *Septuaginta: Editio Altera*. Stuttgart: Deutsche Bibelgesellschaft, 2006.
Sarris, Nikolas. "The Discovery of a New Fragment from the Codex Sinaiticus." *Sinaiticus: The Bulletin of the Saint Catherine Foundation*, 13. London: Saint Catherine Foundation, 2010.
Smith, Jannes. "God, Judges, Snakes, and Sinners: A Commentary on the Old Greek Text of Psalm 57 (MT 58)." In *The SBL Commentary on the Septuagint: An Introduction*, edited by Dirk Büchner, 241–56. SCS 67. Atlanta: SBL, 2017.
Thompson, Geoff. *Introducing Functional Grammar*. New York: Arnold, 1996.
Walser, Georg A. *Jeremiah: A Commentary Based on Ieremias in Codex Vaticanus*. Septuagint Commentary Series. Leiden: Brill, 2012.

Modern Authors Index

Adams, Sean A., 218
Ammann, Hermann, 167
Arnauld, Antoine, 62
Althann, R., 43
Andersen, Francis, 11
Arnold, Bill .T, 44
Aubrey, Michael, 21
Aune, David E., 139

Bakhtin, Mikhail, 83, 130
Bandstra, Barry, 14, 15
Barr, James, 5, 43
Bazell, Charles E., 25
Bekins, Peter, 8
Biber, Douglas, 224
Bird, Michael F., 218, 219
Black, Stephanie, 27, 28, 72, 74, 208, 209
Black, Stephen, 129
Blass, Friedrich, 62, 64, 65
Blass, Regina, 113
Blomberg, Craig L., 118
Blomqvist, Jerker, 74
Bloomfield, Leonard, 20
Bompiani, Brian, 8
Boyer, James L., 107, 108, 110
Brayford, Susan, 218
Brook, James A., 105
Bruce, F. F., 192
Büchner, Dirk, 217
Bühler, Karl, 76–78
Burton, Ernest DeWitt, 105
Buth, Randall, 72, 107
Butler, Christopher S., 3, 28, 153, 159

Cairnie, Andrew, 11
Callahan, Scott, 9

Campbell, Constantine R., 156, 185
Chafe, Wallace, 166, 167, 170, 171, 173
Chamberlain, William Douglas, 105
Choi, John H., 44
Chomsky, Noam, 2, 3, 4, 10, 16, 19, 20, 167
Chomsky, William, 42
Cirafesi, Wally, 27, 28
Clark, H., 173
Conway, Mary, 15
Cook, John A., 6, 9, 11
Coulthard, R. M., 159
Croft, William, 2
Cruse, D. Alan, 2

Dahood, Michell Joseph, 42, 43
Dallaire, Hélène, 8, 14
Dana, H. E., 90, 104, 108, 137
Danielwicz, Jane, 170, 171
Danove, Paul, 21, 23, 24
Dawson, David, 12
Dawson, Zachary K., xx, 72, 76, 78, 83, 90, 144, 156
Decker, Rodney, 185
Denniston, J. D., 74, 104, 105, 112, 115
DeMaris, Richard E., 129
deSilva, Daivid, 129, 218, 219
Dibelius, Martin, 192
Dik, Simon, 4, 9, 14, 208
Dille, Sarah, 16
Disse, Andreas, 13
Dooley, Robert, 16
Driver, Samuel R., 6
Droste, Flip G., 4
Dvorak, James D., xx–xxi, 78, 130, 131, 133, 134, 143
Dyer, Bryan, 27, 28

Dyk, Janet W., 10

Eggins, Suzanne, 78–80, 151
Elliot, John H., 134
Eming, Elodie Ballantine, 108, 112
Endo, Yoshinobu, 9
Eskhult, Mats, 8
Esler, Philip F., 129
Evans, Vyvyan, 23
Ewald, Heinrich, 6
Exter Blokland, François den, 13

Fairclough, Norman, 76, 129, 131, 132
Fanning, Buist M., 156, 185
Fantin, Joseph, 22, 23
Fawcett, Robin P. A., 134, 135
Fewster, Gregory, 27, 47
Fillmore, Charles, 23
Fitzmyer, Joseph A., 191, 192
Follingstad, Carl Martin, 16
Frow, John, 83
Fuller, David, xix, 15, 39, 40
Funk, Robert, 20, 112
Futato, Mark D., 43

Gabelentz, G. von der, 167
Gee, James Paul, 129
Gell, Philip, 6
Gesenius, Wilhelm, 6, 44
Givón, Talmy, 3, 24
Gleason, Henry, 20
Glenny, W. Edward, 217, 218
Goldfajn, Tal, 9
Goodwin, William W., 109
Gordon, Cyrus, 42
Graffi, Giorgio, 63
Green, Joel B., 22
Green, Melanie, 23
Greenlee, J. Harold, 107
Gregory, M. J., 227
Gross, Walter, 8, 9
Gutt, Ernest-August, 22

Hacken, Pius ten, 4
Halliday, Michael A. K., xix, xx, 3, 25, 28, 40, 47, 48, 54, 62–64, 67, 74–82, 85–94, 97, 128, 130–36, 138–41, 148–51, 153, 155, 157, 158, 167–71, 173–75, 183, 191, 193–97, 199, 200, 207, 208, 219–226
Hanhart, Robert, 229
Harber, Esther, 44
Hardy, Humphrey Hill, 44
Hasan, Ruqaiya, xxii, 64, 74, 75, 82, 85, 87, 90, 92–94, 174, 175, 192–97, 199, 200, 203, 204, 207, 208
Hatim, B., 227
Haviland, S., 173
Hayes, Elizabeth, 16
Hecke, Pierre van, 17
Heckert, Jacob K., 116
Heim, Erin, 22
Heimerdinger, Jean-Marc, 13
Heller, Roy, 12
Hess, Richard S., 217, 218
Heusinger, Klaus von, 168
Hodge, Robert, 129–31
Hoftijizer, Jacob, 8
Holmstedt, Robert, 10, 11
Holquist, Michael, 83
Howe, Bonnie, 22
Huffman, Douglas, 185
Hunt, Benjamin B., 80, 87

Jackendoff, Ray, 3
Jenni, Ernst, 9, 43
Jindo, Job, 16
Johnson, Bruce, 21
Johnson, Mark, 16
Joosten, Jan, 9
Joseph, John E., 4
Joüon, P., 44, 45

Kamp, Albert, 16
Kautzsch, E., 6, 44
Kay, Paul, 23
Keener, Craig S., 192
Kenyon, Frederick G., 218
Khan, Geoffrey, 13
Kijine, J. J., 107
Kim, Doosuk, xxi, 166
Kim, Ji Hoe, 195
King, Philip, 16
Kiss, Katalin, 167
Kress, Gunther, 129–31
Kroll, Barbara, 171
Kuno, Susumu, 3, 172

Modern Authors Index

Kustár, Péter, 8
Kwong, Ivan, 27

Lakoff, George, 4, 16
Lambrecht, Knud, 13
Lancelot, Claude, 62
Land, Christopher, 27, 28, 150
Lanier, Gregory, 22
LaPolla, Randy, 2–5, 7, 10, 14, 16, 17, 19, 22, 29
Langacker, Ronald, 3, 4, 23
Leckie-Tarry, Hellen, 171, 174
Lee, Jae Hyun, 27, 181, 182
Lee, John J. H., xxii, 193, 196, 198, 203, 204, 214
Lemke, Jay L., 75, 78, 83, 129, 131, 132
Levinsohn, Stephen, 16, 21, 24, 25, 30, 73, 113, 158, 185
Levita, Elias, 6
Littman, Robert J., 218
Longacre, Robert., 11, 12, 14
Louw, J. P., 19, 20, 79, 83, 90, 91, 93, 94, 96–98, 182, 200, 229
Lunn, Nicholas, 9
Lyle, Kristopher, 46

Malina, Bruce J., 129, 130
Mann, William C., 14
Manson, I., 227
Mantey, Julius R., 90, 104, 108, 137
Marshall, I. Howard, 191
Martin, J. R., 75, 76, 78, 79, 81, 83–86, 88, 89, 92, 93, 98, 128, 130, 131, 151
Martín-Asensio, Gustavo, 27, 229
Mathesius, V., 167, 168
Matthewson, David L., 108, 112
Matthiessen, Christian M. I. M., 63, 77, 78, 87
McKay, K. L. A., 79, 80, 96, 185
McNeel, Jennifer, 22
Meeks, Wayne, 129
Mel'cuk, Igor, 4
Merwe, Christo van der, 6–8, 10, 14, 46
Metzger, Bruce M., 121
Michel, Andreas, 9
Miller-Naudé, Cynthia, 9
Moorehouse, A. C., 110

Morales, Nelson, 22
Moshavi, Adina, 9
Moule, C. F. D., 113, 128, 138, 184
Moulton, James Hope, 107, 109
Muraoka, Takamitsu, 8, 10, 44, 45, 219

Neufeld, Dietmar, 129
Niccacci, Alviero, 10
Nida, Eugene A., 79, 83, 90, 91, 93, 94, 96–98, 182, 200, 229

O'Connor, Michael P., 5, 45
O'Donnell, Matthew Brook, 27, 72–74, 79, 153, 167, 174, 177–79, 181–83, 193–94, 200, 202, 205, 206, 208, 209
Olsson, Birger, 21

Palmer, Micheal W., 19–21
Pardee, Dennis, 43
Pattemore, Stephen, 22
Paul, Hermann, 167
Peng, Kuo-Wei, 21
Peters, Ronald, 27, 28, 65
Pickering, Wilbur N., 181
Pietersma, Albert, 215, 216
Pike, Kenneth L., 11, 12
Pilch, John J., 129
Pitts, Andrew, 200
Porter, Stanley E., xix, 19, 27, 28, 46, 72–74, 76, 78, 79, 86, 87, 90, 93–98, 106, 110, 133–37, 144, 148–53, 155–61, 167, 174, 177–79, 181–85, 219, 220, 224–33
Prince, E. F., 3, 167, 172, 173, 200
Price, William Craig, xxi, 191
Proctor, Mark, xx, 104

Rahlfs, Alfred, 229
Ramsay, W. M., 192
Reed, Jeffrey, 27, 28, 40, 86–89, 92–95, 97, 149, 170, 171, 174, 180, 182, 183, 185, 186, 193, 202
Regt, Lénart de, 13
Reinhart, Tanya, 167
Revell, E. J., 13
Richter, Wolfgang, 9, 13
Robar, Elizabeth, 17

Robertson, A. T., 62, 64, 65, 104, 106, 107, 110, 112, 113, 115, 184
Robinson, William, 22
Rose, David, 75, 76, 79, 81, 83, 84, 86, 88, 89, 92, 93, 98, 128, 151
Rosenbaum, Michael, 14
Rundgren, Frithiof, 8
Runge, Steven, 24, 25, 30, 73, 112, 168, 169

Sarris, Nikolas, 218
Sarna, Nahum M., 42
Saussure, Ferdinand de, 6, 8, 10, 17, 18
Schiffrin, Deborah, 208
Schmidt, Daryl D., 19
Schroeder, N. W., 6
Sgall, Petr, 167
Shimasaki, Katsuomi, 13, 14
Silverstein, Michael, 3
Sim, Margaret, 22, 23
Sinclair, J. M., 159
Smith, Jannes, 219
Sperber, Dan, 22
Stern, Frank, 118
Stovell, Beth, 22, 27, 28

Talmy, Leonard, 3
Talstra, Eep, 13
Tannen, Deborah, 171
Tappenden, Frederick, 22
Tatu, Silviu, 15
Tene, David, 5
Tesnière, Lucien, 62, 66–68
Titrud, Kermit, 112
Toffelmire, Colin, 15, 40

Tompson, Geoff, 74, 75, 77, 80–84, 92, 223
Tompson, Sandra A., 3, 14
Turner, Nigel, 107

Van Neste, Ray, 27
Van Valin, Robert, 2–5, 7, 10, 14, 16, 17, 19, 22, 29

Wallace, Daniel B., 62, 65, 104, 108
Walser, Gerg A., 218
Waltke, Bruce, 5, 45
Walton, Ryder Dale, 133
Webster, Jonathan J., 76–78
Weinrich, Harald, 10
Westfall, Cynthia, 27, 28, 73, 195, 199, 209
White, P. R. R., 78, 83, 130, 131
Widder, Wendy, 17
Wierzbicka, Anna, 3, 22
Wilson, Deirdre, 22
Winbery, Carlton L., 105
Winer, G. B., 184
Winther-Nielsen, N., 14
Wishart, Ryder A., xix, 61
Witherington, Ben III., 191
Wolde, Ellen van, 17
Wong, Simon, 23
Wonneberger, Reinhard, 19
Wright, Benjamin G., 216

Young, Richard A., 111
Yoon, David I., xxi, 148–50

Zerwick, Maximilian, 106–8
Zevit, Ziony, 9

Ancient Sources Index

OLD TESTAMENT/ HEBREW BIBLE

Genesis
1–11	14

Leviticus
7:17	42
8:32	42

Joshua
3:16	42

2 Samuel
5:13	42

2 Kings
3	13
23:33	42

1 Chronicles
14:3	42

Job
4:21	42
5:21	42
12–14	17
20:20	42

Psalms
33:1	42

Isaiah
40–50	14

Jeremiah
1–24	16
1:22	42

Jonah (LXX)
1	214, 228–30, 233
1:1	231
1:3	231
1:4	230–32
1:5	231, 232
1:6	231–33
1:7	231
1:8	232, 233
1:9	232
1:10	231, 233
1:11–14	231
1:11	231–33
1:12	231–33
1:13	231
1:14	231
1:15	231
1:16	231

Habakkuk
1:5a	51
1:5c	51

Habakkuk (continued)

1:7b	51
1:8d	51
1:8e	50
1:10b	50
1:12c	49
1:12d	50
1:14a	51
1:16	50
1:16a–16b	50
1:16a	51
2:1a–1b	51
2:2d	51
2:3	50
2:4b	51
2:5	50
2:5e–5f	50
2:5e	50
2:6	50
2:6a	50
2:7c	50
2:8	50
2:10a	50
2:11a	51
2:13b	50
2:13c	50
2:16a	51
2:16e	51
2:17	50
2:20a	51
3:3a	51
3:4b	51
3:5b	51
3:8	51
3:8a–8c	50
3:11b–11c	52
3:13a	50
3:15a	51
3:16	50
3:16d	51
3:17b	51
3:17f	51
3:18a–18b	50
3:19c	51

PSEUDEPIGRAPHA

4 Maccabees

9:26–32	219

NEW TESTAMENT

Matthew

5:3	178
12:4	90
12:31–37	143
12:32	143
12:35	141–43
13:8	91
14:17	140
16:21	140
24:11	140
25:29	66
26:24	110

Mark

1:23	82
7:6	69
14:21	110

Luke

6:4	90
7:36–40	179
7:36	179
7:37–38	179
7:39	179
7:40	179
13:10–21	182
13:10	182
13:18–21	182
13:18	182
13:31	178
15:27	69
19:42	110

John

7:1	182
9:33	110
11:27	180

15:20c	110
15:22	110
15:24a	110
18:36	110
19:11	110
19:28	160

Acts

12:1	86
13:1–14:28	192
14–15	209
15	xxi, 191, 192, 194, 210
15:1–35	xxi, 191–95, 197, 200, 204, 205, 207, 208, 210, 211
15:1–12	211
15:1–4	206
15:1–2	192, 206
15:1	208
15:2	208
15:3–33	192
15:3	206, 208, 210
15:4–5	207
15:4	208, 209
15:5–12	206
15:6–11	207
15:6	208, 209
15:9	208
15:10	208
15:12	207–9
15:13–23a	207
15:13–21	207
15:13	208, 209
15:16	208
15:22–23a	207
15:22	209
15:23b	207, 209
15:23–29	182
15:24–29	207
15:24	209
15:27–35	211
15:28	208
15:30–35	207, 209
15:30–33	207
15:30	208, 210
15:35	207, 209
15:36–38	207
15:36	207, 209
15:37–39	209
20:18	140
26:32	110

Romans

1–8	27
6:1	94
8	27
9:3–4	175
10:9	68
12:1–15:1	21
14:1–3	176
14:1–2	179
14:1	176, 186

1 Corinthians

4:15	140
7:1	176
7:25	176
7:30	98
8:1	176
12:17	110
12:19	110
14:5	91

2 Corinthians

8:1–2	175

Galatians

2	191
2:11–21	xxi, 148, 161, 163
2:11–14a	161
2:14b	161
2:15–21	148
2:15–16a	82
2:16	162
2:18–21	162
2:18	162
4:9	91
4:15	110
5:19–23	70

Ephesians

1:1	232
2:5–6	68
2:11–13	69
4:22	140

1 Timothy

4:1	87
5:17	140

2 Timothy

3:2–7	177
3:8	176

Hebrews

2:17	94
3:1	94
5:8	97
7:25	94
8:3	94
9:18	94
11:19	94

1 John

2:18	94

Revelation

6:10	65–67
20:19	87

www.ingramcontent.com/pod-product-compliance
Lightning Source LLC
Chambersburg PA
CBHW050845230426
43667CB00012B/2151